INDEX

VOCABULARY (5859 questions)

PART A: ....
A wide range of vocabulary tests for new learners. Compiled from various resources.
(1657 questions) 1-2

PART B: ....
A rich collection of vocabulary tests for intermediate and upper intermediate levels.
(1988 questions) 2-3

PART C: ....
An assortment of phrasal verbs.
(714 questions) 3

PART D: ....
25 upper level vocabulary tests.
(1000 questions) 3

ANSWER KEY

PART A — ELEMENTARY VOCABULARY — TEST - 1

1. We pick things up with our _____.
   A) arms   B) hands   C) hair   D) heads

2. I lick an ice-cream with my _____.
   A) knee   B) chest   C) lips   D) tongue

3. To eat something I put it in my _____.
   A) mouth   B) elbow   C) nose   D) neck

4. We comb and brush our _____.
   A) fingers   B) shoulder   C) hair   D) sole

5. I brush my _____ regularly, especially after eating.
   A) waist   B) lips   C) teeth   D) thumb

6. I sometimes go to school _____ bus.
   A) in   B) at   C) to   D) by

7. She waited _____ the bus in the bus stop.
   A) for   B) to   C) with   D) of

8. She has got a yellow dress _____.
   A) on   B) in   C) with   D) to

9. Who is the man _____ the red tie?
   A) in   B) with   C) on   D) off

10. I remember her. She was the one _____ green shoes.
    A) on   B) at   C) with   D) by

11. I watch _____ while I am sitting on the sofa.
    A) television   B) picture   C) radio   D) tape

12. I sometimes listen to the _____.
    A) television   B) radio   C) type   D) film

13. I keep my books in a / an _____.
    A) shelter   B) bookcase   C) armchair   D) carpet

14. We stand in a bus _____ to wait for a bus.
    A) station   B) road   C) stop   D) corner

15. The cars wait until the traffic _____ turn green.
    A) railings   B) signs   C) crossing   D) lights

16. You can cross the road at a _____.
    A) cross-road   B) crossing   C) crosser   D) road

17. We should put waste paper in a _____.
    A) box   B) park   C) litter-bin   D) pavement

18. We get wet when it _____.
    A) freezes   B) blows   C) shines   D) rains

19. When it is very cold, everything _____.
    A) rains   B) freezes   C) blows   D) snows

20. Children enjoy playing games when it _____.
    A) snows   B) blows   C) freezes   D) is cold

21. It is cold in England when a north wind _____.
    A) goes   B) blows   C) covers   D) passes

22. It is warm and pleasant when the sun _____.
    A) pours   B) lights   C) shines   D) comes

23. When it rains very heavily, it _____.
    A) waters   B) pours   C) snows   D) freezes

24. My friends say I like to _____ money.
    A) find   B) spend   C) see   D) gain

25. They have everything you _____ for your house.
    A) have   B) like   C) need   D) adore

26. You can _____ everything you need at this supermarket.
    A) lend   B) sell   C) use   D) buy

27. If you cannot _____ your watch, buy a new one.
    A) find   B) do   C) get   D) sell

28. I am _____ my glasses. Where can it be?
    A) using   B) seeing   C) looking for   D) finding

29. My father _____ shoes in a store.
    A) sells   B) makes   C) wears   D) gives

30. I forget to _____ for goods that I buy every time.
    A) sell   B) buy   C) give   D) pay

31. I must buy things _____ my house.
    A) in   B) of   C) for   D) with

32. Can I try this _____ on?
    A) jacket   B) bottle   C) paper   D) shoes

33. Can I have my _____ back?
    A) pay   B) cash   C) money   D) cost

34. I took some biscuits from the _____ in the supermarket?
    A) tin   B) shelf   C) bin   D) bottle

35. We give the money to the _____ in the market?
    A) queue   B) manager   C) cashier   D) customer

36. What is the money you get, usually weekly or hourly?
    A) salary   B) pay   C) wages   D) cash

37. We call abilities you can do as _____.
    A) skills   B) experience   C) job   D) quality

38. Work of the same type you have done before is called _____.
    A) job   B) work   C) experience   D) duty

39. Certificates and exams passed mean _____?
    A) job   B) experience   C) skills   D) qualifications

40. What is a talk with a company about a possible job?
    A) speaking   B) interview   C) experience   D) talk

41. Points in your character are called _____.
    A) ex-skills   B) personal level
    C) ex-hobbies   D) personal qualities

42. My parents decided to send me to a _____ when I was three.
    A) nursery- school   B) private school
    C) primary school   D) secondary school

43. Education is _____ after the age of 7. Every child should be sent to school.
    A) optional   B) compulsory   C) easy   D) strict

44. There are four _____ in an education year in many countries.
    A) terms   B) semesters   C) parts   D) sections

45. Some parents pay to send their children to a _____ school.
    A) private   B) special   C) strict   D) secondary

46. My friend _____ his exams. He is sad.
    A) stayed   B) passed   C) won   D) failed

47. A good education _____ will get you a good job.
    A) work   B) degree   C) history   D) year

48. John receives a _____ from the state to help him pay the university fees.
    A) wages   B) salary   C) grant   D) check

49. He is a _____ of Harward University. He is working in NASA now.
    A) finisher   B) completion   C) graduate   D) pupil

Test 1

50. Students of this class are very _____ on their subjects.
    A) keen   B) enjoy   C) useful   D) good

51. My brother is _____ a book.
    A) riding   B) reading   C) speaking   D) playing

52. Do you want to _____ biscuit?
    A) eat   B) see   C) play   D) read

53. My answer was _____, not wrong.
    A) write   B) ride   C) light   D) right

54. Who are you _____ for?
    A) seeing   B) meeting   C) waiting   D) doing

55. Where do we go to buy things?
    A) bank   B) shop   C) bath   D) shore

56. When I saw him, he was _____ bicycle.
    A) riding   B) driving   C) playing   D) lying

57. What is the antonym of "white"?
    A) wait   B) light   C) lack   D) black

58. Go straight, then turn to right, not _____.
    A) side   B) near   C) left   D) write

59. Continue the logic list.
    Red, green, brown, _____.
    A) poor   B) long   C) good   D) yellow

60. Choose the word which is out of the logic list.
    A) read   B) write   C) speak   D) cry

61. Thieves _____ things.
    A) steal   B) still   C) steel   D) skill

62. I have a curly _____.
    A) here   B) hear   C) heir   D) hair

63. This is a _____ coat, not cotton.
    A) fair   B) fur   C) fare   D) fear

64. Come _____ and sit down!
    A) here   B) her   C) hair   D) heir

65. Large amount of _____ is grown in China.
    A) white   B) weight   C) wheat   D) wait

66. I can't hear the music. Could you turn on the _____?
    A) speakers   B) mouse   C) monitor   D) case

67. We have no money to buy a _____ for the train to London.
    A) price   B) ticket   C) seat   D) place

68. I lost my _____, so I cannot open the door.
    A) key   B) passport   C) wallet   D) money

69. She _____ the class history.
    A) learns   B) shows   C) teaches   D) says

70. He _____ in the war.
    A) bought   B) fought   C) lost   D) taught

71. They always _____ stones at the dog.
    A) give   B) put   C) throw   D) leave

72. The river _____ every winter because of cold weather.
    A) stops   B) flows   C) opens   D) freezes

73. He drinks _____ quickly.
    A) bear   B) beer   C) bare   D) bar

74. She _____ to stay at home.
    A) uses   B) prefers   C) like   D) rathers

75. Choose the word which is out of the logic list.
    A) jacket   B) shirt   C) trousers   D) pocket

76. Choose the word which is out of the logic list.
    A) son   B) aunt   C) daughter   D) child

77. Choose the word which is out of the logic list.
    A) arm   B) leg   C) watch   D) head

78. Choose the word which is out of the logic list.
    A) uncle   B) aunt   C) nephew   D) friend

79. Continue the logic list.
    Sweater, boots, T-shirt, _____.
    A) hair   B) face   C) jeans   D) clothes

80. We hang trousers, jackets, and dresses in the _____.
    A) hanger   B) stool   C) mirror   D) door

81. We keep shirts and underwear in the _____.
    A) bed   B) wash-basin   C) wardrobe   D) tiles

82. I sleep with my head on the _____.
    A) sheets   B) blanket   C) bath   D) pillow

83. I wash my hands in the _____.
    A) bed   B) sink   C) bath   D) toilet

84. I take my _____ off before I go to bed.
    A) blanket   B) clothes   C) watch   D) light

85. I put an extra _____ on my bed.
    A) blanket   B) clothes   C) bed   D) households

86. I go to _____ at midnight.
    A) school   B) breakfast   C) bed   D) sofa

87. He sat on the _____ in the cafe.
    A) bed   B) desk   C) window   D) stool

88. Choose the word which is out of the logic list.
    A) stool   B) armchair   C) sofa   D) vase

89. We always _____ at the hotel when we go abroad.
    A) be   B) leave   C) stay   D) go

90. Bob passes over the _____ on his way to school.
    A) road   B) bridge   C) waterfall   D) farm

91. Continue the logic list.
    Valley, forest, mountain, _____.
    A) lake   B) picture   C) weather   D) man

92. I can see the sunshine behind the _____.
    A) picture   B) wall   C) sofa   D) curtains

93. The picture is on the _____.
    A) vase   B) wall   C) door   D) curtain

94. The _____ is cloudy today.
    A) air   B) world   C) day   D) sky

95. It is always cold in _____.
    A) winter   B) spring   C) fall   D) summer

96. The longest holiday for students is in _____.
    A) winter   B) spring   C) fall   D) summer

97. Do you want to drink _____?
    A) meal   B) ice-cream   C) fruit juice   D) marmalade

98. I haven't got even a _____ on me.
    A) money   B) penny   C) treasure   D) nothing

99. The more you _____, the more you earn.
    A) work   B) read   C) write   D) understand

100. _____ the door, so that no one can enter.
    A) shut   B) close   C) lock   D) hit

Test 1

ELEMENTARY VOCABULARY

TEST - 2

1. Which _____ do you come from?
   A) nation   B) year   C) country   D) date

2. Fiat cars are quite _____. You can afford them easily.
   A) bad   B) expensive   C) easy   D) cheap

3. They often eat _____ for breakfast.
   A) cheese   B) chest   C) cheer   D) chief

4. Would you like to have a _____ soup or fish?
   A) chicken   B) drink   C) breakfast   D) meal

5. If you do not know this word why don't you look up the _____?
   A) newspaper   B) internet   C) computer   D) dictionary

6. It is very _____ today. I would like to go to swimming.
   A) hot   B) cloudy   C) cold   B) good

7. Would you like to drink a _____ of tea?
   A) bottle   B) piece   C) slice   D) cup

8. The question is really _____. You do not even need to think on it.
   A) complete   B) different   C) difficult   D) easy

9. There are four people in my _____, mother, father, sister and me.
   A) group   B) class   C) family   D) side

10. Let's buy something to eat!
    What does the underlined word refer to?
    A) food   B) money   C) drinks   D) souvenirs

11. Choose the word which is out of the logic list.
    A) crossword   B) envelope   C) letter   C) post-office

12. Last _____ the dinner was really awful.
    A) midnight   B) noon   C) evening   D) morning

13. This is the first question and that is the _____.
    A) two   B) second   C) twice   D) later

14. My friend has got a/an _____ in London. It's on the 9th floor.
    A) room   B) apartment   C) flat   D) city

15. Choose the word which is out of the logic list.
    A) hut   B) house   C) flat   D) car

16. _____ companies are growing very fast nowadays. The country doesn't need foreign companies.
    A) local   B) multinational   C) large   D) international

17. What is your _____?
    A) occupation   B) time   C) busy   D) do

18. How many _____ can you speak?
    A) tongues   B) languages   C) nations   D) vocabulary

19. My friend sent me a _____ last week.
    A) writing   B) ladder   C) letter   D) later

20. Choose the word which is out of the logic list.
    A) magazine   B) brochure   C) newspaper   D) news

21. Our geography teacher brings _____ to the lesson.
    A) cap   B) map   C) tap   D) cup

22. All of my friends are _____. Even some of them have children.
    A) single   B) alone   C) lonely   D) married

23. What is the singular form of people?
    A) man   B) single   C) human   D) person

24. Continue the logic list.
    North, south, west, _____.
    A) best   B) rest   C) east   D) test

25. Jane likes _____ stamps. She has got already 75.
    A) collecting   B) taking   C) delivering   D) using

26. Can you help me carry my _____.
    A) body   B) suitcase   C) picture   D) language

27. My mother's sister is my _____.
    A) uncle   B) cousin   C) nephew   D) aunt

28. You are very _____ today. What's up?
    A) sad   B) attractive   C) ugly   D) thin

29. They bought a _____ house in London. It has more than 12 rooms.
    A) small   B) cool   C) large   D) heavy

30. Don't worry, be _____!
    A) happy   B) nice   C) different   D) sorry

31. The film shown in the cinema was _____.
    A) difficult   B) horrified   C) heavy   D) horrible

32. Mary is John's wife and John is her _____.
    A) friend   B) husband   C) relative   D) mate

33. Bob gets up at 7.00 o'clock in the _____.
    A) evening   B) afternoon   C) morning   D) night

34. Choose the antonym of the underlined word.
    I am going to buy a pair of new shoes next week.
    A) cheap   B) old   C) bad   D) small

35. My mother and father are my _____.
    A) owners   B) friends   C) relatives   D) parents

36. What is the synonym of urban?
    A) city   B) village   C) country   D) park

37. My father's brother is my _____.
    A) brother   B) grandfather   C) uncle   D) aunt

38. When Mr. Richard explains the lesson, I can _____ easily.
    A) know   B) memorize   C) understand   D) see

39. The _____ is sunny today.
    A) weather   B) leather   C) whether   D) air

40. Choose the antonym of the underlined word.
    The old man was standing near the bus stop.
    A) new   B) young   C) modest   D) gentle

41. When we got to the airport, he was there.
    What does the underlined word mean here?
    A) went   B) were in   C) saw   D) arrived at

42. The _____ makes bread.
    A) cook   B) shopkeeper   C) baker   D) actor

43. It is time we left. Otherwise, we will miss the train.
    Choose the antonym of the underlined word.
    A) catch   B) keep   C) regret   D) leave

44. How much does it cost?
    Choose the sentence that has a different meaning with the sentence above.
    A) How much is it?
    B) What is its price?
    C) How much do I have to pay for it?
    D) How much money is there in it?

45. Choose the synonym of the underlined word.
    I am planning to go to hairdresser at the weekend.
    A) barber   B) tailor   C) clerk   D) dentist

46. Exactly half of the students were absent.
    Which of the following words is not the antonym of the underlined word.
    A) nearly   B) approximately
    C) obviously   D) about

47. Continue the logic list.
    Hospital, doctor, nurse, _____.
    A) vaccine   B) cock   C) cool   D) officer

48. I am so _____. I want to sleep.
    A) asleep   B) tired   C) easy   D) hard

Test 2

49. He likes mending old radios.
    Choose the synonym of the underlined word.
    A) repairing   B) making   C) using   D) buying

50. Which of the followings is not a transport?
    A) helicopter   B) ship   C) train   D) wheel

51. Continue the logic list.
    Day, week, month, year _____, century.
    A) decade   B) minute   C) time   D) period

52. Which of the followings is not sports?
    A) rugby   B) baseball   C) hockey   D) cards

53. -What is the _____ of your car?
    - Sapphire.
    A) height   B) date   C) color   D) speed

54. The meal is awful! Who is the _____?
    A) cooker   B) cook   C) cock   D) cocky

55. Choose the antonym of the underlined word.
    This game is really exciting.
    A) terrible   B) difficult   C) different   D) boring

56. I _____ play cards. I hate it.
    A) always   B) often   C) never   D) nothing

57. Mars is a/an _____.
    A) place   B) space   C) planet   D) universe

58. Deserts are often _____ regions.
    A) dry   B) wet   C) cold   D) small

59. The pain was _____.
    A) necessary   B) unbearable   C) large   D) incredible

60. Water is _____ for life.
    A) harmful   B) necessary   C) problem   D) matter

61. Gold is a _____.
    A) metal   B) liquid   C) gas   D) mixture

62. The lung is a(an) _____.
    A) part   B) tool   B) instrument   D) organ

63. The machine is out of _____.
    A) work   B) order   C) place   D) condition

64. He was ill last week, but now he is in good _____.
    A) health   B) place   C) area   D) position

65. Hats are out of _____.
    A) modern   B) public   C) fashion   D) mode

66. When children saw him, they were all in deep _____.
    A) horror   B) afraid   C) terror   D) shock

67. The firm is in _____ difficulty.
    A) natural   B) oral   C) financial   D) mental

68. He is on a student grant.
    What does this sentence mean?
    A) He is on duty.
    B) He takes money for his tuition.
    C) He will be a university student.
    D) He is undergraduate student.

69. The heart is about the size of a _____.
    A) head   B) leg   C) arm   D) fist

70. It was a rude _____.
    A) politeness   B) film   C) day   D) joke

71. I am a Beatles _____.
    A) side   B) support   C) lovely   D) fan

72. Bill is a man of _____.
    A) good   B) principle   C) obligatory   D) worth

73. It was not my _____. He broke the window
    A) fault   B) joke   C) rules   D) incorrect

74. The pillow is _____.
    A) boring   B) interesting   C) soft   D) hardly

75. Lora is _____ in Spanish.
    A) good   B) bad   C) fluent   D) middle

76. He was not _____ of my plan.
    A) know   B) course   C) aware   D) wisdom

77. Some of the students of this college stay in the _____.
    A) house   B) dormitory   C) flat   D) country

78. He is _____ Linguistics at the University of Oxford.
    A) working   B) reading   C) knowing   D) studying

79. There won't be a _____ for that film.
    A) queue   B) sequence   C) wait   D) group

80. Each teacher _____ the contract.
    A) wrote   B) agreed   C) pointed   D) signed

81. He has no _____ for music.
    A) face   B) ear   C) eye   D) nose

82. She has got a _____ over her head.
    A) belt   B) tie   C) blanket   D) scarf

83. Their documents are _____.
    A) ready   B) finish   C) absolute   D) modern

84. His mother's illness is _____.
    A) significant   B) serious   C) ignoring   D) impatient

85. I took her _____ and it was 40ºC.
    A) heat   B) body   C) temperature   D) cool

86. Can you _____ a computer.
    A) use   B) work   C) study   D) write

87. Please, take a _____!
    A) sit   B) place   C) down   D) seat

88. I think the job will _____ me very well.
    A) do   B) match   C) suit   D) equalize

89. The boss wasn't there so I left a message to the _____.
    A) deputy   B) secretary   C) assistant   D) helper

90. His father is a/an _____. He works for New York Times.
    A) journalist   B) actor   C) writer   D) scientist

91. English will be very _____ for you in the future.
    A) harmful   B) horrible   C) useful   D) nonsense

92. Between what _____ is education compulsory?
    A) years   B) periods   C) ages   D) times

93. What are the _____ of your exam?
    A) reasons   B) finals   C) results   D) ends

94. I _____ 200$ a week from my job.
    A) take   B) earn   C) pay   D) borrow

95. If you have financial difficulties, I can _____ you some money.
    A) lend   B) borrow   C) rent   D) pay

96. Why don't you _____ a bank account?
    A) make   B) open   C) do   D) pay

97. I don't like to be in _____.
    A) owe   B) borrow   C) lend   D) debt

98. She earns a lot of money. She is very _____.
    A) cruel   B) tolerant   C) well-off   D) large

99. He can't _____ luxuries. He is poor.
    A) stay   B) make   C) owe   D) afford

100. I will have to get a (an) _____ job in the evenings.
    A) plus   B) extra   C) high   D) further

Test 2

ELEMENTARY VOCABULARY

TEST - 3

1. Part of income paid to government is _____.
   A) taxes   B) bills   C) pay   D) account

2. _____ is money for transport.
   A) pension   B) fare   C) interest   D) salary

3. Money parents give children every week is called _____.
   A) part-money   B) pocket money   C) interest   D) rent

4. _____ is money from work, usually hourly or weekly.
   A) wages   B) salary   C) rent   D) interest

5. Money from work, usually monthly, is called _____.
   A) wages   B) salary   C) fee   D) pay

6. I live in the _____, not the town.
   A) area   B) farm   C) apartment   D) country

7. To be a soldier, you join the _____.
   A) force   B) army   C) group   D) government

8. Person who controls a game is _____.
   A) referee   B) score   C) spectator   D) player

9. We're just _____, not professionals.
   A) players   B) crowd   C) team   D) amateurs

10. There are sometimes more players than _____.
    A) spectators   B) referees   C) teams   D) scores

11. She sunbathes at the _____.
    A) sea   B) desert   C) mountain   D) beach

12. They are very _____ on music.
    A) keen   B) fan   C) like   D) respect

13. I _____ a lot of time at the concert.
    A) use   B) waste   C) spend   D) fill

14. We prefer to live _____ to nature.
    A) through   B) close   C) near   D) with

15. I like visiting museums and art _____.
    A) shops   B) stores   C) galleries   D) markets

16. Students get bored with visiting historical _____.
    A) areas   B) fields   C) points   D) places

17. She enjoys swimming and _____ at the beach.
    A) sunbathing   B) speaking   C) eating   D) drinking

18. Helen loves being in the _____.
    A) sky   B) beach   C) countryside   D) work

19. He is a family doctor, he has a _____ to help.
    A) receptionist   B) nurse   C) waiter   D) translator

20. Operator doctor sees his patients in the _____.
    A) house   B) room   C) hall   D) surgery

21. Some patients have _____ throats.
    A) bad   B) low   C) sore   D) down

22. Doctors give patients _____ to take to the chemist.
    A) prescription   B) description   C) check   D) cash

23. Choose the word which is out of the logic list.
    A) cricket   B) target   C) golf   D) rugby

24. We have to send the patients to hospital for _____.
    A) treatment   B) nurse   C) stomach-ache   D) regular

25. If you always feel tired, get more _____.
    A) exercise   B) cure   C) suffer   D) drug

26. Have a good _____, if you want to be healthy.
    A) dinner   B) drug   C) diet   D) ache

27. We saw the doctor in his _____ while operating his patients.
    A) van   B) hut   C) cabinet   D) surgery

28. He listened to my _____.
    A) problems   B) differences   C) life   D) condition

29. I have lost my _____. I don't want to eat anything.
    A) hungry   B) appetite   C) happiness   D) life

30. He always _____ his teeth.
    A) washes   B) waters   C) brushes   D) tidies

31. Policemen wear _____ so everyone knows who they are.
    A) clothes   B) shoes   C) dresses   D) uniforms

32. The man on the phone wanted me to _____ a moment.
    A) stay calm   B) hold on   C) take on   D) put off

33. To make tea, first _____ the water in a kettle.
    A) liquid   B) flow   C) make   D) boil

34. You should _____ tea with a spoon.
    A) stir   B) boil   C) fix   D) clear

35. _____ your hands above your head.
    A) raise   B) rise   C) rice   D) rays

36. Please, do not _____ the sides of the chair.
    A) bend   B) sit   C) lean   D) stand

37. Put a cassette in the machine and _____ the 'start' button.
    A) block   B) tick   C) click   D) press

38. You can _____ the quality of the sound by using the other controls.
    A) adapt   B) adjust   C) adore   D) alarm

39. What a(an) _____ street! Two cars can't pass through together.
    A) easy   B) ugly   C) large   D) narrow

40. I have had a _____ day.
    A) red   B) light   C) complete   D) wonderful

41. The wood was very _____.
    A) tidy   B) sad   C) empty   D) rough

42. The paper is very _____.
    A) thin   B) weak   C) guilty   D) easy

43. She wore _____ clothes at the party.
    A) difficult   B) huge   C) formal   D) sad

44. She felt _____ about her exam.
    A) interested   B) ignorant   C) ugly   D) nervous

45. It was a(an) _____ meal.
    A) powerful   B) tolerant   C) light   D) white

46. The knife was very _____. I cut my finger.
    A) huge   B) dirty   C) ordinary   D) sharp

47. It is a _____ place. Do not come here!
    A) nice   B) dangerous   C) tight   D) dry

48. That is a(an) _____ meeting.
    A) own   B) private   C) strict   D) safe

49. It was _____ news. I couldn't stand.
    A) terrible   B) wonderful   C) clean   D) short

50. The bottle is _____. Throw it away.
    A) necessary   B) flexible   C) tiny   D) empty

51. He was _____. He wasn't set free.
    A) guilty   B) easy   C) cheap   D) weak

Test 3

52. My belt is too _____. I couldn't loose it.
    A) hard B) soft C) useful D) tight

53. The weather was _____. I hated it.
    A) beautiful B) wet C) dry D) nasty

54. He is a _____ man. I do not want to speak to him.
    A) clever B) gently C) stupid D) handsome

55. Mark is a _____ boy. Everyone likes him.
    A) hard B) polite C) rude D) bad

56. The music was too _____.
    A) loud B) small C) wrong D) incorrect

57. She loves meeting people and going to parties. She is a very _____ person.
    A) shy B) ignorant C) learned D) sociable

58. He likes new things and new places, even if they are difficult or dangerous. She is _____.
    A) adventurous B) selfish C) clever D) mean

59. He gets very annoyed if he has to wait for anything. He doesn't like waiting. He is very _____.
    A) sociable B) industrious B) hard D) impatient

60. Peter never gets upset or annoyed when things go wrong. He is a very _____ man.
    A) hard-working B) attractive
    C) easy-going D) mad

61. My friend loves to talk to people and tell them what he thinks. He is _____.
    A) ugly B) talkative C) strong D) sad

62. My brother wants to get an important job in a high position. He is very _____.
    A) stubborn B) learned C) ambitious D) talkative

63. Madison doesn't like work. He is _____.
    A) happy B) poor C) rich D) lazy

64. He is always happy and smiling. He is very _____.
    A) cheerful B) hard-headed C) funny D) intelligent

65. Lora only thinks about herself. She is _____.
    A) naughty B) selfish C) patient D) genius

66. Jake has a lot of common sense. He always knows correct thing to do. He is a _____ boy.
    A) sensitive B) sensual C) sensible D) nonsense

67. He always has good hopes for the future. He thinks everything will be fine. He is very _____.
    A) rude B) pessimist C) optimist D) quiet

68. My sister is very careful about her appearance and how she arranges her desk and her room. She is a/an _____ lady.
    A) tidy B) silly C) unsociable D) cautious

69. His father always remembers to say 'please' and 'thank you'. He is very _____.
    A) impolite B) polite C) rude D) talkative

70. Shoes are usually made of _____.
    A) leather B) wool C) paper D) iron

71. The Sahara is a _____.
    A) river B) continent C) desert D) canal

72. Thank you for the books. They will be very _____ for my studies.
    A) harmful B) useful C) tasteful D) hopeful

73. The government is trying to help _____ families.
    A) rich B) social C) small D) homeless

74. Thanks to modern technology, a visit to dentist is now often quite _____.
    A) harmless B) helpful C) painless D) tasty

75. It was a very _____ football match.
    A) silly B) exciting C) bored D) deep

76. We felt very _____ on holiday.
    A) relaxed B) relaxing C) rest D) unrest

77. It was a(an) _____ film. I nearly fell asleep.
    A) interesting B) boring C) exciting D) relaxing

78. You look rather _____. Why don't you see a doctor?
    A) unhealthy B) tired C) unpleasant D) fair

79. Will you take the job? We must have a quick _____.
    A) mind B) decision C) deciding D) manner

80. I'd like to _____ you on passing your exam.
    A) congratulate B) thank C) excuse D) let

81. We cannot _____ children under 14 to go to movies without their parents.
    A) let B) make C) have D) permit

82. The _____ of train will be 15 minutes late.
    A) coming B) use C) departure D) time

83. I think I will _____ about this bad service.
    A) complain B) think C) consider D) explain

84. They don't get on well. They are having a(an) _____ now.
    A) talking B) war C) fighting D) argument

85. It is very difficult to _____ this machine.
    A) make B) do C) operate D) work

86. It doesn't matter. It is of no _____.
    A) learning B) importance C) significant D) work

87. I don't like the _____ of the furniture in this room.
    A) way B) staying C) compliment D) arrangement

88. He gave the police the _____ of the stolen goods.
    A) shape B) shadow C) description D) explanation

89. My boss needs my _____ on that paper.
    A) mark B) signature C) acceptation D) refuse

90. I do not know which one to _____.
    A) choice B) choose C) chose D) choosy

91. This documentation is not _____. You might be arrested for this.
    A) criminal B) legal C) formal D) incorrect

92. My kitchen is very old. I am going to _____ it.
    A) new B) clean C) paint D) modernize

93. The people demonstrated for more _____.
    A) government B) freedom C) oppression D) life

94. My brother _____ 65 kilos.
    A) weighs B) masses C) makes D) pulls

95. I am worried about the children's _____ on the street.
    A) freedom B) sanction C) safety D) noise

96. You will find all the _____ you want here. It is good place to stay.
    A) law B) peace C) war D) argument

97. There are pictures of _____ in the newspapers everyday. I really don't want to see them.
    A) peace B) freedom C) people D) violence

98. How long is it? The _____ must be very exact.
    A) side B) longing C) area D) measurement

99. The film was a great _____. It made 75 million dollars.
    A) hope B) money C) success D) bank

100. What about six o'clock. Will that time _____ you?
    A) match B) suit C) approve D) agree

Test 3

ELEMENTARY VOCABULARY — TEST - 4

1. Excuse me. Could you _____ me the way to the town hall?
   A) let   B) put   C) talk   D) tell

2. Not more books! There aren't enough _____ to put them on.
   A) leaves   B) cases   C) spaces   D) shelves

3. Don't forget your _____. It's very cold outside.
   A) gloves   B) underwear   C) umbrella   D) scissors

4. There are eleven players in a football _____.
   A) game   B) pitch   C) team   D) group

5. What's wrong with your foot? - One of my _____ hurts.
   A) fingers   B) heels   C) wrists   D) toes

6. Bill's a _____ so he travels all over the world.
   A) baker   B) butcher   C) sailor   D) driver

7. The _____ will help you if you can't find the book you want.
   A) porter   B) agent   C) librarian   D) operator

8. I must book a _____ for our game of tennis tomorrow.
   A) field   B) court   C) green   D) team

9. My car won't start. Could you give me a _____ to town?
   A) bus   B) car   C) hand   D) lift

10. Do you take _____ in your tea?
    A) spoon   B) pepper   C) salt   D) sugar

11. This doll is a present for my _____. I hope she likes it.
    A) husband   B) nephew   C) niece   D) uncle

12. What kind of fruit would you like?
    - A _____ please.
    A) carrot   B) mushroom   C) pear   D) turnip

13. I'll look in my _____ and see if I'm free on Wednesday.
    A) diary   B) dictionary   C) briefcase   D) calendar

14. You don't have to _____! We're not late!
    A) dream   B) laugh   C) rush   D) wait

15. Which do you _____ cream or milk?
    A) rather   B) eat   C) prefer   D) wear

16. You can hang your jacket in the _____.
    A) bedspread   B) chest of drawers
    C) hanger   D) wardrobe

17. The shopping centre is now a pedestrian _____.
    A) arrival   B) palace   C) pavement   D) precinct

18. Could you _____ a photo of me in front of this building?
    A) check   B) make   C) paint   D) take

19. The ice is very _____ so don't walk on it.
    A) high   B) low   C) thick   D) thin

20. Carol speaks so fast that it's _____ to understand her.
    A) difficult   B) easy   C) slow   D) wrong

21. The mechanic hopes to _____ our car by this evening.
    A) make   B) renew   C) repair   D) wander

22. My _____ says I need stronger glasses.
    A) chemist   B) conductor   C) keeper   D) optician

23. Are you ready to go?
    - Not _____. Give me 10 minutes.
    A) for me   B) very much   C) very many   D) yet

24. How much does she earn?
    - That's none of your _____ !
    A) business   B) decision   C) information   D) role

25. The police are looking for the _____ of a red Ford.
    A) detective   B) instructor   C) owner   D) rider

26. I've already got a _____ at a hotel in the town centre.
    A) prescription   B) property   C) reserve   D) reservation

27. The next _____ of the show is at seven thirty.
    A) event   B) performance   C) stall   D) game

28. You can't eat that pear. It isn't _____ yet.
    A) best   B) pale   C) ripe   D) mature

29. Can you _____ the coffee and I'll get the biscuits.
    A) depart   B) disturb   C) feed   D) pour

30. Should I wear my sandals or my _____?
    A) cardigan   B) shorts   C) trainers   D) scarves

31. Shirley tried to stop the car but the _____ didn't work.
    A) brakes   B) crossroads   C) tires   D) controls

32. The referee and the two teams ran out onto the _____.
    A) circus   B) course   C) observatory   D) pitch

33. You need some _____ coffee to wake you up.
    A) awake   B) hard   C) brown   D) strong

34. His suitcase was quite _____ so I could easily carry it.
    A) cheap   B) heavy   C) light   D) short

35. When did you _____ smoking?
    - About two years ago.
    A) cut off   B) give up   C) make up   D) throw away

36. The plane _____ late because of the terrible weather.
    A) blew up   B) grew up   C) went on   D) took off

37. The _____ at the hospital told me not to worry about my leg.
    A) accountant   B) director   C) lodger   D) specialist

38. The President is a very _____ man. Everyone does what he says.
    A) circular   B) direct   C) painful   D) powerful

39. We had to _____ the match because of the bad weather.
    A) call back   B) call off   C) think over   D) find out

40. Pat was surprised when her boss didn't _____ the meal.
    A) buy   B) pay   C) pay for   D) spend

41. All Michael ate was two thin _____ of bread.
    A) rolls   B) loaves   C) slices   D) snacks

42. With this _____ I can get to the windows on the first floor.
    A) index   B) ladder   C) lager   D) step

43. You can _____ a bus just outside the station.
    A) beat   B) catch   C) keep   D) meet

44. Take your overcoat with you _____ it gets cold.
    A) although   B) in case   C) unless   D) until

45. I'd like to _____ this cheque, please.
    A) cash   B) change   C) pay for   D) spend

46. The police put _____ on the robbers to stop them getting away.
    A) handcuffs   B) make-up   C) saddles   D) stretchers

47. Jimmy sent his mother a _____ of flowers for her birthday.
    A) bar   B) bunch   C) pack   D) packet

48. It's raining. _____ take your umbrella with you.
    A) Are you going   B) Let's
    C) You'd better   D) Would you like

49. There's nothing good on television. Let's _____ a video.
    A) carry   B) hire   C) invite   D) phone

Test 4

50. Make sure the knife is really _____ before you cut the meat.
    A) flat   B) sharp   C) sliced   D) thick

51. Thanks very much! I'm very _____ for your help.
    A) generous   B) grateful   C) full   D) sorry

52. I like the color of the jacket but the _____ are too short.
    A) buttons   B) heels   C) collars   D) sleeves

53. Can you just _____ that all the windows are shut?
    A) catch   B) check   C) control   D) reclaim

54. Which _____ does our flight leave from? - Number 12.
    A) carriageway   B) exit   C) gate   D) ground

55. Look at my sweater! It _____ when I washed it.
    A) boiled   B) cut   C) missed   D) stretched

56. Wear a _____ to protect your head in case there's an accident.
    A) brooch   B) crash helmet   C) glove   D) cap

57. Could you _____ your name at the bottom of the letter?
    A) answer   B) cross   C) lay   D) sign

58. James is a terrible cook. He can't even _____ an egg!
    A) blow   B) boil   C) lay   D) smoke

59. Surely they aren't _____ enough to buy such a large car!
    A) cautious   B) well   C) poor   D) wealthy

60. There isn't any water coming out of this _____.
    A) heel   B) lock   C) shelf   D) tap

61. I've put on _____. I eat too many cakes.
    A) gloves   B) mixture   C) waist   D) weight

62. Put your suitcase up on the luggage _____.
    A) lounge   B) park   C) rack   D) store

63. You could hear the crowd shouting in the local football _____.
    A) ground   B) park   C) pool   D) station

64. That'll _____ children! Stop shouting!
    A) do   B) fit   C) help   D) make

65. I can't tell you now. I'll _____ you know later.
    A) get   B) let   C) make   D) tell

66. Give me a _____ some time. You know my phone number.
    A) date   B) line   C) post   D) ring

67. The bus was so _____ that we couldn't all get on.
    A) crowded   B) deep   C) thick   D) various

68. We have a _____ climate so the winters are never very cold.
    A) bright   B) fair   C) high   D) mild

69. It's so _____ in here. Don't you ever clean this room?
    A) cloudy   B) dark   C) dusty   D) misty

70. If you ask a _____ price for your car. I'm sure you'll sell it.
    A) helpful   B) mild   C) reasonable   D) shiny

71. No, don't wear blue. It doesn't _____ you.
    A) fit   B) notice   C) suit   D) take

72. The _____ climbed up the tree and we couldn't see it any more.
    A) deer   B) rabbit   C) squirrel   D) tortoise

73. Can you _____ me the time, please?
    A) say   B) tell   C) speak   D) talk

74. Do you know how _____ it is from Ashgabat to Mary? It's 370 km.
    A) many   B) much   C) far   D) often

75. Can I _____ your phone, please? I must call my parents.
    A) borrow   B) use   C) take   D) lend

76. Don't go. I'm going to _____ some coffee.
    A) make   B) cook   C) boil   D) prepare

77. I am _____ my wife to drive a car.
    A) learning   B) showing   C) practising   D) teaching

78. I had to keep my son home from school today because he had a _____ of 38.
    A) fever   B) headache   C) temperature   D) heat

79. When we were in Spain last year we _____ at a wonderful hotel overlooking the beach.
    A) stayed   B) stopped   C) lived   D) left

80. Is there anything _____ you'd like me to get you?
    A) else   B) more   C) extra   D) much

81. Most banks will _____ people money to buy a house.
    A) lend   B) borrow   C) give   D) take

82. My friend has a _____ job at a chemist's.
    A) half-time   B) spare-time   C) empty-time   D) part-time

83. _____ have you been learning English?
    A) For how long time   B) How long
    C) How long time   D) How many time

84. I hate doing the _____ especially cleaning the windows.
    A) homework   B) housework   C) jobs   D) house-jobs

85. You mustn't be angry with her. It wasn't her _____ that she was late.
    A) blame   B) error   C) mistake   D) fault

86. She _____ to take her neighbor to court if he didn't stop making so much noise.
    A) promised   B) threatened   C) offered   D) suggested

87. You can count _____ me if you ever want any help.
    A) in   B) on   C) up   D) by

88. Each _____ of the family had to take it in turns to do the washing-up.
    A) individual   B) character   C) member   D) person

89. Don't _____ my speech when I am talking.
    A) cut   B) interrupt   C) divide   D) separate

90. You can borrow money this time but don't make _____ of it.
    A) habit   B) feeling   C) help   D) learning

91. I always write my daily activities on my _____.
    A) weekly   B) daily   C) diary   D) minutely

92. James and Jim are twins. They were _____ at birth and they didn't meet until they were both thirty nine.
    A) left   B) deserted   C) separated   D) abandoned

93. What do we call someone whose job is to repair taps and baths?
    A) tailor   B) carpenter   C) bricklayer   D) plumber

94. When I was away on business, my neighbors looked after my home. Which of the followings is the synonym of the underlined word?
    A) pick out   B) give up   C) take care of   D) settle down

95. When you say that you will do something for somebody, you _____.
    A) shout   B) promise   C) ask   D) tell

96. When you say something to someone's ear quietly and secretly, you _____.
    A) say again   B) whisper   C) discuss   D) cry out

97. _____ it was difficult, they managed to find somewhere they all liked.
    A) Although   B) Before   C) Since   D) As soon as

98. Anyone who gets free rides in other people's cars as a way of travelling cheaply is called _____.
    A) passenger   B) traveller   C) goner   D) hitchhiker

99. When you pay no attention to anybody or to act as if you don't see him/her, you _____ him/her.
    A) ignore   B) veiw   C) notice   D) watch

100. He was bitten by mosquito, but he made things worse by _____ the bite all the time.
    A) stoking   B) scratching   C) rubbing   D) scraping

Test 4

CLASSIFIED TOPICS   TEST MASTER

ANIMALS

1. _____ is a white and black striped horse.
   A) zebra   B) donkey   C) horse   D) tiger

2. _____ is a male cow.
   A) sheep   B) bull
   C) hippopotamus   D) cow

3. _____ is a very large grey animal which has big ears and a trunk.
   A) whale   B) giraffe   C) elephant   D) horse

4. _____ is the only mammal which can fly.
   A) eagle   B) butterfly   C) owl   D) bat

5. The best animal friend of human is known to be _____.
   A) dog   B) shark   C) zebra   D) panda

6. The young horse is called _____.
   A) zebra   B) foal   C) donkey   D) calf

7. A _____ has long ears, long teeth, lives in a ground and like to eat carrot.
   A) mouse   B) rabbit   C) dog   D) sheep

8. The young cow is called _____.
   A) lamb   B) foal   C) calf   D) kitten

9. The young sheep is called _____.
   A) kitten   B) calf   C) foal   D) lamb

10. The young dog is called _____.
    A) puppy   B) lamb   C) kitten   D) calf

11. The young cat is called _____.
    A) puppy   B) lamb   C) kitten   D) calf

12. The young of kangaroo grows up in its mother's _____.
    A) sack   B) bag   C) pocket   D) pouch

13. Camel has _____ on his back.
    A) trunk   B) horn   C) pouch   D) lump

14. _____ is a kind of bear which lives in cold places and has a white skin.
    A) deer   B) polar   C) gorilla   D) panda

15. _____ is a very tall animal that has long neck.
    A) giraffe   B) elephant   C) horse   D) cow

BATHROOM

1. _____ is a piece of cloth used for drying something.
   A) tie   B) flannel   C) toilet paper   D) towel

2. _____ is a piece of cloth you use in bathroom to wash yourself.
   A) toilet paper   B) towel   C) flannel   D) scales

3. My friend weighs 120 kilograms, and he has _____ which help him to know how much he weighs.
   A) comb   B) scales   C) razor   D) watch

4. _____ is a substance that you use to wash yourself with.
   A) soap   B) towel   C) flannel   D) tile

5. _____ is a brush for cleaning your teeth.
   A) toothbrush   B) hairbrush   C) paintbrush   D) toothpaste

6. _____ is a sharp instrument for removing hair, especially from a man's face.
   A) scissors   B) razor   C) comb   D) shaving-foam

7. _____ is liquid soap used for washing your hair.
   A) cream   B) shaving-foam
   C) shampoo   D) soap

8. _____ is a thing that you stand under to wash your whole body.
   A) toilet   B) sink   C) bathtub   D) shower

9. _____ is a bar that you use to hang things on.
   A) towel-rail   B) sink
   C) bathtub   D) laundry basket

10. _____ is a piece of plastic or metal that you use to make your hair tidy.
    A) comb   B) razor   C) razor-blade   D) scissors

11. _____ is a long large container that you fill with water to sit in and wash yourself.
    A) laundry basket   B) bathtub
    C) sink   D) toilet

12. _____ is a room where you can have a shower.
    A) dining-room   B) bathroom   C) bedroom   D) kitchen

13. _____ is the thing in a bathroom or kitchen, where you wash you hands, face etc.
    A) refrigerator   B) bathtub   C) sink   D) toilet

14. The floor and walls of bathroom is covered by _____.
    A) papers   B) carpets   C) tiles   D) towels

15. _____ is a brush that is used for cleaning your nails.
    A) hairbrush   B) nail cleaner   C) toothbrush   D) nail brush

CLOTHES

1. _____ is something that you wear to cover your feet.
   A) shoe   B) sweater   C) cap   D) t-shirt

2. _____ is a soft hat with a curved part sticking out at the front.
   A) cap   B) umbrella   C) scarf   D) boot

3. _____ is a cotton shirt with short sleeves and no collar.
   A) blazer   B) shirt   C) jacket   D) t-shirt

4. _____ is a piece of warm woolen clothing for the top half of your body.
   A) glove   B) scarf   C) coat   D) sweater

5. _____ is a piece of clothing worn on your hand, with separate parts for the thumb and each finger.
   A) skirt   B) jeans   C) glove   D) scarf

6. _____ is a narrow piece of cloth that you wear around your neck with a skirt.
   A) blazer   B) tie   C) trousers   D) blouse

7. _____ is a piece of clothing for girls and women that fits around the waist and hangs down like a dress.
   A) skirt   B) trousers   C) blouse   D) jacket

8. _____ is a piece of material that you wear around your neck, head, or shoulders, especially when it is cold.
   A) shirt   B) tie   C) scarf   D) glove

9. _____ is a shirt for women.
   A) skirt   B) t-shirt   C) blouse   D) blazer

10. _____ is a short coat.
    A) blazer   B) jacket   C) suit   D) blouse

11. _____ is a kind of shoe that covers your whole foot and the lower part of your leg, especially worn in winter.
    A) shoe   B) socks
    C) slippers   D) boot

Classified topics

12. _____ is a piece of clothing that you wear on your foot inside your shoe.
    A) socks   B) pants   C) boot   D) sleeve

13. _____ are light trousers and a shirt that you wear in bed.
    A) pajamas   B) swimsuit   C) suit   D) blouse

14. _____ is the part of a piece of clothing that covers your arm.
    A) collar   B) sleeve   C) cuff   D) pocket

15. _____ is a piece of clothing that covers the lower part of your body, with a separate part covering each leg.
    A) trousers   B) skirt   C) blouse   D) boot

DINING ROOM

1. When I looked at the _____ I saw myself in it.
   A) glass   B) mirror   C) window   D) clock

2. Yesterday we didn't have electricity, but we had some _____. We lit them to produce light.
   A) batteries   B) candles   C) papers   D) fires

3. _____ heats the room and consists of hollow metal container that fills up with hot water.
   A) radiator   B) fire place   C) bathtub   D) sink

4. I cut some bread with a _____.
   A) spoon   B) fork   C) knife   D) plate

5. _____ is a small tool used for picking up food, with handle and three or four points.
   A) fork   B) spoon   C) knife   D) plate

6. There were about 0,5 liter coffee in the _____.
   A) spoon   B) vase   C) plate   D) coffee pot

7. The table was covered by table _____.
   A) rug   B) mat   C) carpet   D) cloth

8. He looked at the _____ and realized that it was 3:00 AM.
   A) clock   B) water   C) fire   D) window

9. Famous _____ "Mono Lisa" was painted by Leonardo Da Vinci
   A) picture   B) painting   C) photo   D) plate

10. _____ is a cloth material that is used for cleaning your lips after meal.
    A) napkin   B) table-cloth   C) tie   D) socks

11. We drink soup meals from a _____.
    A) knife   B) fork   C) bowl   D) lampshade

12. _____ is something that is used to take the food from dish to mouth, shaped like a small bowl with a long handle.
    A) fork   B) knife   C) spoon   D) mini-bowl

13. My brother put all flowers in the _____.
    A) bowl   B) pot   C) vase   D) glass

14. There were some money, our documents and phone bills in the _____.
    A) drawer   B) refrigerator   C) air-conditioner   D) sofa

15. I drank orange juice from _____.
    A) glass   B) pot   C) spoon   D) plate

ENVIRONMENT

1. The highest _____ of the mountain Everest is 8860 meters high.
   A) peak   B) island   C) stream   D) boulder

2. After tsunami at the beach there were big _____ with the height of 15 meters.
   A) waves   B) lakes   C) seas   D) sand

3. There weren't any _____ between our gardens and it was very difficult to separate them from each other.
   A) field   B) rock   C) hedge   D) grass

4. Total area of wheat _____ is 19670 km².
   A) sea   B) field   C) lake   D) beach

5. _____ is a large area of salty water.
   A) waterfall   B) lake   C) reservoir   D) sea

6. The water is stored in _____ before it is supplied to people's houses.
   A) reservoir   B) sea   C) lake   D) river

7. _____ is place where water flows down over a rock or from a high place.
   A) lake   B) sea   C) waterfall   D) river

8. _____ is a very high hill.
   A) cliff   B) rock   C) plateau   D) mountain

9. _____ is a large area of flat land that is higher than the land around it.
   A) plateau   B) desert   C) mountain   D) field

10. _____ is a large natural hole in the side of cliff or under the ground.
    A) rock   B) stream   C) cave   D) island

11. _____ is a large rock which is especially found in the mountain.
    A) island   B) stone   C) boulder   D) hill

12. _____ is a large area covered with trees.
    A) sea   B) forest   C) desert   D) field

13. _____ is a large area of hot, dry land where is very much sand.
    A) sea   B) desert   C) forest   D) lake

14. _____ is an area of sand or small stones at the edge of the sea.
    A) beach   B) cliff   C) island   D) desert

15. _____ is an area of high land, like a small mountain.
    A) hill   B) peak   C) valley   D) beach

FAMILY RELATIONSHIPS

1. My mother's or father's mother is my _____.
   A) mother   B) grandfather   C) grandmother   D) father

2. My mother's sister is my _____.
   A) niece   B) uncle   C) nephew   D) aunt

3. My female parent is my _____.
   A) grandmother   B) father   C) daughter   D) mother

4. My wife's mother is my _____.
   A) mother-in-law   B) grandmother   C) daughter   D) granddaughter

5. My uncle's or aunt's child is my _____.
   A) cousin   B) niece   C) nephew   D) brother-in-law

6. My sister's husband is my _____.
   A) brother   B) brother-in-law   C) cousin   D) nephew

7. My children's mother is my _____.
   A) wife   B) mother   C) husband   D) grandmother

8. My wife's sister is my _____.
   A) sister-in-law   B) sister   C) niece   D) cousin

9. My sister's daughter is my _____.
   A) niece   B) nephew   C) cousin   D) sister-in-law

10. My mother's brother is my _____.
    A) uncle   B) father-in-law   C) aunt   D) nephew

Classified topics

11. My child's son is my _____.
    A) daughter B) son-in-law C) son D) grandson

12. My male child is my _____.
    A) grandfather B) daughter C) grandson D) son

13. My sister's son is my _____.
    A) niece B) nephew C) cousin D) sister-in-law

14. My wife's father is my _____.
    A) father-in-law B) grandmother C) daughter D) granddaughter

15. My wife's brother is my _____.
    A) brother-in-law B) brother C) uncle D) grandfather

FOOD

1. _____ is a soft round fruit with yellow and red skin and a large seed inside.
   A) pineapple B) apple C) melon D) peach

2. _____ is a sweet juicy fruit that is round at the bottom and becomes thinner at the top.
   A) peach B) apple C) pear D) cherry

3. _____ is a hard round red or green fruit that is white inside.
   A) watermelon B) apple C) cherry D) grapes

4. _____ is a small round soft red fruit with a large seed.
   A) cherry B) watermelon C) apple D) banana

5. _____ is a long curved yellow fruit.
   A) banana B) apple C) pear D) melon

6. _____ is a large round fruit with a hard yellow, orange, or green skin and a lot of flat seeds.
   A) apple B) melon C) cucumber D) banana

7. _____ is a round white vegetable with a brown or pale yellow skin, that grows under the ground.
   A) tomato B) potato C) cucumber D) cabbage

8. _____ is a long thick orange vegetable.
   A) tomato B) cucumber C) onion D) carrot

9. _____ is a round white vegetable, usually with brown skin, which has a strong smell and taste.
   A) onion B) cabbage C) leek D) pumpkin

10. _____ is a long thin rounded vegetable with a dark green skin, usually eaten row.
    A) cucumber B) carrot C) onion D) beans

11. _____ is a soft round red vegetable, eaten especially in salads.
    A) peas B) pepper C) tomato D) beans

12. _____ is a large round green vegetable with thick leaves that is usually cooked.
    A) cucumber B) onion C) cabbage D) pumpkin

13. He filled my glass with orange _____.
    A) coffee B) alcohol C) juice D) water

14. _____ is a brown powder that is made by crushing the beans of its tree.
    A) coffee B) coca-cola C) alcohol D) flour

15. _____ is a drink made by pouring boiling onto dried leaves, or the leaves that are used to make this drink.
    A) tea B) coffee C) whisky D) juice

HEALTH

1. _____ is a substance for treating an illness, especially that you drink.
   A) ointment B) bandage C) medicine D) plaster

2. _____ is a piece of cloth that you wrap around an injury.
   A) bandage B) ointment C) cast D) injection

3. He broke his leg, so doctor made a _____ around his broken leg.
   A) cast B) ointment C) medicine D) plaster

4. _____ is a special material used for sticking on your skin to cover small wounds.
   A) cast B) medicine C) ointment D) plaster

5. _____ is a hard cover fitted over your arm, leg etc to support a broken leg.
   A) injection B) cast C) tablet D) capsule

6. He had had a big hole in his tooth before the dentist made _____ in the hole.
   A) injection B) cast C) filling D) medicine

7. Doctors use _____ for cleaning patient's skin before injection.
   A) plaster B) bandage C) cotton wool D) cast

8. _____ is a kind of chair used by people who cannot walk.
   A) wheel chair B) stool C) rocking chair D) armchair

9. Doctor gave the patient a _____ on which the medicine the patient should take was written.
   A) prescription B) medicine C) capsule D) cast

10. After the eye test, the optician told me that I should wear a pair of _____.
    A) fillings B) glasses C) casts D) masks

11. During the operation, doctors were wearing _____ which were covering all face except eyes.
    A) casts B) masks C) bandage D) sling

12. _____ is a substance that you rub into your skin as a medical treatment.
    A) tablet B) cotton wool C) medicine D) ointment

13. When the lesson ended, I put my glasses into the _____.
    A) glasses case B) pen case C) bookcase D) briefcase

14. _____ is an equipment that doctors use to listen to someone's heart or breathing.
    A) stethoscope B) heart controller C) blood pressure D) headphones

15. The doctor who does operations in the hospital is called _____.
    A) surgeon B) dentist C) nurse D) optician

JOBS

1. Someone who plays piano is a/an _____.
   A) pianist B) architect C) singer D) painter

2. Someone whose job is to make bread, cakes is a/an _____.
   A) baker B) butcher C) barber D) dentist

3. Someone who works in a shop that sell meat is a/an _____.
   A) baker B) butcher C) fireman D) teacher

4. Someone whose job is to cut men's hair is a/an _____.
   A) singer B) doctor C) pharmacist D) barber

5. Someone whose job is to treat people's teeth is a/an _____.
   A) grocer B) doctor C) dentist D) singer

6. Someone whose job is to treat people who are ill is a/an _____.
   A) dentist B) doctor C) singer D) painter

Classified topics

7. Someone whose job is to stop fires is a/an _____.
   A) repairman   B) electrician   C) fireman   D) architect

8. Someone whose job is to deliver letters and packages to people's houses is a/an_____.
   A) butcher   B) pharmacist   C) house painter   D) mailman

9. Someone whose job is to fix things is a/an_____.
   A) repairman   B) fireman
   C) house painter   D) pianist

10. Someone whose job is to prepare drugs and medicines is a/an_____.
    A) pharmacist   B) doctor   C) dentist   D) scientist

11. The_____ painted the house into blue color.
    A) house   B) painter
    C) baker   D) architect

12. Someone whose job is to design buildings is _____.
    A) teacher   B) architect   C) singer   D) mailman

13. Math _____ gave us a lot of homework.
    A) singer   B) doctor   C) teacher   D) student

14. Historical paintings of famous _____ will be sold for million dollars.
    A) painters   B) singers   C) architects   D) people

15. Someone who sells food, cleaning products in a small shop is a/an_____.
    A) grocer   B) baker   C) butcher   D) barber

LIVING ROOM

1. When the weather became colder, we put some _____ on fire to heat the living room.
   A) log   B) blanket   C) toys   D) sofa

2. _____ is a small pillow that is put on the sofa.
   A) armchair   B) cushion   C) carpet   D) chair

3. In the 20th century its available to control the TV or other electronics with _____ on your hand.
   A) button   B) headphones
   C) remote control   D) screen

4. We stir tea using a _____.
   A) knife   B) teacup   C) fork   D) teaspoon

5. _____ is used for carrying plates, dishes and food
   A) tray   B) pot   C) carpet   D) rug

6. _____ is a hanging cloth that can be pulled across a window.
   A) table cloth   B) curtain   C) rug   D) carpet

7. In our century there is _____ with multicolored screen.
   A) clock   B) cassette recorder
   C) TV   D) mirror

8. The _____ looks like armchair, but wide enough for 2 or 3 people.
   A) deck chair   B) chair   C) stool   D) sofa

9. The _____ is the top part of a room from inside surface.
   A) roof   B) floor   C) wall   D) ceiling

10. We use _____ for drinking tea, coffee, etc.
    A) pots   B) pans   C) cups   D) spoons

11. _____ is an open place in the wall of a room where you can burn wood or coal to heat the room.
    A) radiator   B) fire place   C) refrigerator   D) ceiling

12. _____ is a piece of thick cloth or wool that is put on the floor as a decoration.
    A) curtain   B) rug   C) towel   D) flannel

13. _____ is the room where you relax, watch television.
    A) living room   B) bathroom   C) kitchen   D) laundry room

14. _____ is used to control something like television from a distance.
    A) remote control   B) camera
    C) telescope   D) microphone

15. _____ is a container used for making and serving tea, which has a handle and a spout.
    A) teapot   B) teacup   C) teaspoon   D) jug

MUSIC AND THEATRE

1. _____ is a large group of musicians who play classical music together.
   A) singer   B) actor   C) orchestra   D) film star

2. _____ is someone who shows people to their seats in a theatre, cinema etc.
   A) servant   B) actor   C) usher   D) waiter

3. _____ is the side part of a stage where actors are hidden from people watching the pay.
   A) screen   B) curtain   C) scenery   D) wing

4. _____ is someone who conducts a group of musicians or singers.
   A) orchestra   B) maestro   C) composer   D) singer

5. _____ is a stick used to direct a group of musicians, usually used by conductor.
   A) baton   B) wood   C) stick   D) drum

6. _____ is someone who writes music.
   A) composer   B) producer   C) singer   D) painter

7. _____ is someone who controls the making of a play, film etc.
   A) producer   B) conductor   C) film star   D) star

8. _____ is a round musical instrument which you play by hitting it with your hand or a special stick.
   A) drum   B) guitar   C) violin   D) saxophone

9. _____ is the things on the stage of a theatre that make it look like a real place.
   A) scenery   B) screen   C) pit   D) audience

10. You walk along the _____ to get to your seat in a cinema or a theatre.
    A) stage   B) corridor   C) aisle   D) scenery

11. _____ is the raised floor in a theatre where actors perform a play.
    A) screen   B) stage   C) audience   D) balcony

12. _____ is a woman who performs in a play or film.
    A) actor   B) actress   C) conductor   D) producer

13. _____ is the place where the movies are shot.
    A) cinema   B) studio   C) stage   D) scenery

14. _____ is the people who watch film, play etc.
    A) audience   B) spectators   C) orchestra   D) drummer

15. _____ is a building with a stage where plays are performed.
    A) theatre   B) cinema   C) school   D) house

SPORTS

1. The game similar to tennis, played by hitting a small object with feathers on it over a net is _____.
   A) table-tennis   B) badminton   C) basketball   D) volleyball

2. The game in which two or four people use rackets to hit a ball to each other over a net is _____.
   A) badminton   B) tennis   C) football   D) cricket

3. _____ is a game in which two teams try to kick a ball between two posts at either end of a field.
   A) volleyball   B) swimming   C) football   D) basketball

4. The game played on a table with a green cover and holes round the edge, in which you use cue to hit balls into holes is _____.
   A) snooker   B) bowling   C) boxing   D) darts

5. Hakan _____ the earliest goal in the World Cup history.
   A) scored   B) served   C) threw   D) hit

6. In baseball the man who tries to hit the ball is the _____.
   A) bitter   B) catcher   C) goal keeper   D) server

7. In football the player who can touch the ball with his hands is the _____.
   A) referee   B) catcher   C) defender   D) goalkeeper

8. In horse-racing the man who rides the horse is the _____.
   A) race driver   B) racehorse   C) race course   D) jockey

9. It was his first fight on the _____.
   A) ring   B) lane   C) pitch   D) field

10. The game which is played by rocket is _____.
    A) table-tennis   B) basketball   C) volleyball   D) football

11. _____ showed red card to the player.
    A) goalkeeper   B) referee   C) coach   D) spectators

12. _____ is a kind of race where cars compete among each other.
    A) auto-racing   B) horse-racing   C) biathlon   D) cycling

13. The seat which is put on the horse's back is the _____.
    A) saddle   B) stirrup   C) reins   D) jockey

14. The person who gives directions during a match is a _____.
    A) coach   B) player   C) referee   D) stadium

15. The sport which is done in the sea is _____.
    A) squash   B) skiing   C) baseball   D) swimming

TRANSPORT

1. Volvo will make a new _____ which will be able to carry 25 cars.
   A) transporter   B) van   C) pick-up truck   D) bus

2. As they like traveling a lot, instead of buying a house, they bought a _____.
   A) caravan   B) building   C) car   D) truck

3. _____ is a vehicle bigger than a normal car and smaller than a bus, which can carry 8-12 people.
   A) van   B) train   C) minibus   D) truck

4. The _____ is filled with oil.
   A) truck   B) jeep   C) tanker   D) bus

5. Our Construction Company has more than 100 _____ for transportation of doors and windows from one city to another.
   A) vans   B) buses   C) trucks   D) jeeps

6. He has been waiting at the _____ stop for 20 minutes, but there weren't any.
   A) train   B) truck   C) airplane   D) bus

7. They are moving from their old apartment to a new house. They are taking all their furniture with a _____.
   A) car   B) lorry   C) tanker   D) train

8. A _____ is similar to bicycle, but it has engine which help itself to move more quickly than bicycle.
   A) horse   B) motor-cycle   C) car   D) bus

9. The _____ will arrive at Amsterdam railway station at 3:00 PM.
   A) train   B) plane   C) bus   D) truck

10. Fifty students and four teachers were traveling in a _____.
    A) bus   B) van   C) truck   D) taxi

11. Bill Gates is very rich. He flies from the roof of her office to her house by a _____.
    A) helicopter   B) plane   C) ship   D) boat

12. The _____ arrived at the harbor today with 500 people on its board.
    A) yacht   B) speedboat   C) rowboat   D) ferry

13. The vehicle which is made to travel through rough road is a _____.
    A) bus   B) sports car   C) jeep   D) convertible

14. The vehicle whose roof can fold back or removed is a _____.
    A) bus   B) tanker   C) van   D) convertible

15. _____ is a small fast boat with a powerful engine.
    A) speedboat   B) ferry   C) ship   D) sailboat

WEATHER

1. The sun is shining. It is _____.
   A) foggy   B) sunny   C) dull   D) misty

2. Small drops of water fall from clouds in the sky. It is _____.
   A) snowing   B) raining   C) cloudy   D) stormy

3. The storm with lightning is _____ storm.
   A) thunder   B) rainbow   C) snow   D) wind

4. _____ is a large curve of different colors in the sky that is caused by the sun shining through rain.
   A) rainbow   B) thunderstorm   C) lightning   D) storm

5. It is shining strongly and full of light. It is _____.
   A) bright   B) dull   C) cloudy   D) foggy

6. The season which includes December, January, February is _____.
   A) summer   B) spring   C) winter   D) autumn

7. The season which includes March, April, May is _____.
   A) autumn   B) summer   C) spring   D) winter

8. The season which includes June, July, August is _____.
   A) spring   B) autumn   C) winter   D) summer

9. The season which includes September, October, November is _____.
   A) summer   B) winter   C) spring   D) autumn

10. There is a thick cloudy air near ground, which is difficult to see through. It is _____.
    A) bright   B) foggy   C) sunny   D) stormy

11. _____ weather is dark or grey because the sky is full of clouds.
    A) sunny   B) rainy   C) windy   D) bright

12. There is a layer of cloud close to ground that makes it difficult to see very far. It is _____.
    A) misty   B) sunny   C) dull   D) stormy

13. _____ is soft white pieces of frozen water that fall like rain in cold weather.
    A) rainbow   B) lightning   C) snow   D) rain

14. When it is _____, it is not bright or shiny.
    A) sunny   B) windy   C) dull   D) clear

15. In _____, it snows a lot.
    A) summer   B) winter   C) autumn   D) spring

Classified topics

SYNONYMS

Find the **synonym** of the following words written in capitals.

1. He LOOKS at himself in the glass.
   A) puts   B) likes   C) sees
   D) stares   E) stands

2. Ships and AIRCRAFTS are often equipped with radio telephones.
   A) planes   B) trains   C) railroads
   D) highways   E) boats

3. Hemingway is a FAMOUS writer.
   A) well-known   B) unknown   C) good
   D) interesting   E) loved

4. The children know that the sun RISES in the east.
   A) wakes up   B) reaches   C) appears
   D) sets   E) watches

5. The teacher ASKED why he had missed so many classes.
   A) replied   B) informed   C) wondered
   D) answered   E) said

6. I don't want to know what they are TALKING about.
   A) taking   B) speaking   C) coming
   D) leaving   E) saying

7. The game they LIKED best was writing short stories of their own.
   A) found   B) did   C) enjoyed
   D) wanted   E) wished

8. My friend was sorry as his father was DEAD.
   A) killed   B) living   C) came
   D) was ill   E) was alive

9. My friends can use my notes when they are ILL.
   A) sick   B) hard   C) fresh
   D) fine   E) fear

10. Our classes usually ARE OVER at 7 in the evening.
    A) go on   B) continue   C) finish
    D) begin   E) succeed

11. She said that she WAS GOING to live in London.
    A) intended   B) came   C) planned
    D) went   E) left

12. He thought that he was very SILLY.
    A) clever   B) foolish   C) bright
    D) wise   E) strong

13. They had a big house and AT THE BACK OF it there was a small lake.
    A) behind   B) in front of   C) between
    D) over   E) near

14. TWO HUNDRED YEARS ago the square yard was very clean.
    A) many years   B) two week   C) two centuries
    D) a fortnight E) two months

15. I am not going to write any more NOW.
    A) then   B) at the moment C) after that
    D) early   E) before

16. We shall be REACHING the station in 15 minutes.
    A) moving to   B) leaving for   C) staying at
    D) getting to   E) taking from

17. She saw at once that something terrible had HAPPENED.
    A) solved   B) decided   C) understood
    D) heard   E) taken place

18. She became angry and BEGAN to shout at them.
    A) finished   B) stopped   C) started
    D) set   E) was over

19. They BEGAN to work together twenty years ago.
    A) finished   B) stayed   C) continued
    D) started   E) gave up

20. We took the book last week and now we must GIVE it back.
    A) take   B) return   C) revise
    D) copy   E) hold

21. Switzerland helps developing countries to TRAIN their skilled personnel.
    A) inform   B) prepare   C) learn
    D) give   E) study

22. The girl was so ATTRACTIVE that I constantly looked at her.
    A) simple   B) plain   C) ugly
    D) pretty   E) quick

23. My parents WENT TO Moscow in May and they will come back in June.
    A) started   B) set out   C) visited
    D) left for   E) left

24. If your friend is seriously ill you should GO TO SEE him.
    A) ask about   B) leave   C) see
    D) visit   E) approach

25. I would like to speak to you IMMEDIATELY.
    A) right now   B) just once   C) once
    D) later   E) in 2 days

26. That wasn't pronounced CORRECTLY.
    A) wrongly   B) exactly   C) badly
    D) good   E) well

27. "Will you GO ON, Ashley?" said the teacher.
    A) start   B) finish   C) stop
    D) continue   E) begin

28. What HAPPENED to you?
    A) was result of   B) came
    C) was the matter with D) made
    E) was glad

29. I ENJOYED the trip very much.
    A) was happy   B) interested in C) liked
    D) was surprised E) was glad

30. She is a doctor and ALSO a student.
    A) else   B) too   C) either
    D) neither   E) so

31. His HOLIDAY by the sea was like a dream.
    A) rest   B) rested   C) walk
    D) stay   E) life

32. The housewife TASTED the soup and said it was delicious.
    A) cooked   B) tried   C) tried on
    D) took   E) gave

33. The child couldn't find his ball because he had PUT it under the bed.
    A) take   B) took   C) carried
    D) place   E) placed

34. The streets of Tashkent are WIDE and straight.
    A) broad   B) beautiful   C) narrow
    D) long   E) plain

35. The school he goes to is NEAR his house.
    A) closed   B) far   C) not far from
    D) about   E) by

36. There was an old man in a barge, whose nose was exceedingly LARGE.
    A) tiny   B) huge   C) minute
    D) wide   E) small

Synonyms

37. At the age of 17 he LEFT school and went to work at the factory.
    A) graduated   B) went out   C) entered
    D) stopped   E) quitted

38. I'll LEND you my book if you return it to me.
    A) take   B) show   C) give
    D) send   E) get

39. The festival STARTED in Berlin.
    A) began   B) go on   C) went on
    D) was held E) opened

40. I like to CLEAN my room.
    A) wash   B) white - wash   C) paint
    D) tidy up   E) sweep

41. This film IS ON at the "Friendship" cinema.
    A) is shown   B) performs   C) runs
    D) goes   E) does

42. Mr. Brown was very happy as he HAD RETURNED from his hometown.
    A) had come back   B) had seen   C) had received
    D) had asked   E) had gone

43. He ENTERED the shop and wanted to buy a shirt, but it was too expensive.
    A) wanted   B) arrived   C) came into
    D) got   E) reached

44. I WISH I hadn't gone to the pictures.
    A) take   B) stay   C) desire
    D) argue   E) spend

45. Why don't they ANSWER my question?
    A) say   B) ask   C) reply
    D) reform E) report

46. Mark Twain VISITED the Crimea in 1867.
    A) went to   B) returned   C) ran
    D) started   E) left

47. I have been to Tashkent A NUMBER OF TIMES.
    A) several times   B) some time   C) the same time
    D) any time   E) in no time

48. Soon I FOUND OUT that she had left for Italy.
    A) saw   B) learned   C) heard
    D) knew   E) recognized

49. Argentina is LARGER than Great Britain.
    A) wider   B) older   C) better
    D) bigger   E) richer

50. Pete promised to take our PICTURE but didn't keep his word.
    A) give   B) bring   C) photograph
    D) paint   E) draw

51. Every spring the school leavers HAVE their diplomas.
    A) fail   B) carry   C) bring
    D) organize E) take

52. If you can type 100 words a minute and you would like more responsibility, please CALL 01-722.
    A) shout   B) explain   C) cry
    D) utter   E) phone

53. Samuel told me that they were PLANNING to see the gallery in a few days.
    A) staying   B) playing   C) going
    D) starting   E) coming

54. I liked to read books about TRAVELS in my holiday.
    A) rests   B) walks   C) plays
    D) journeys   E) balls

55. He WENT ON sleeping while we took him into our house.
    A) continued   B) spoke   C) stopped
    D) went   E) finished

56. How are you? I am FINE thanks.
    A) so-so   B) not well   C) O.K.
    D) sick   E) in low spirits

57. There is a SMALL boat with a man in it.
    A) stout   B) large   C) little
    D) tidy   E) thin

Find the **synonym** of the following words:

58. Investigation
    A) option   B) question   C) expression   D) search

59. Explain
    A) Mix   B) define   C) protest   D) train

60. Fine
    A) poor   B) excellent   C) inferior   D) bad

61. Private
    A) general   B) personal   C) community   D) public

62. Large
    A) thin   B) great   C) long   D) soft

63. Crazy
    A) cruel   B) chubby   C) wild   D) mad

64. Fundamental
    A) awful   B) absurd   C) vain   D) basic

65. Famous
    A) well off   B) needy   C) rich   D) well-known

66. Take off
    A) put on   B) dress   C) wear   D) remove

67. Annual
    A) yearly   B) daily   C) monthly   D) weekly

68. Region
    A) farm   B) area   C) beach   D) source

69. Way
    A) bridge   B) road   C) railway   D) field

70. Estimate
    A) guess   B) inform   C) miss   D) confuse

71. Error
    A) mistake   B) correct   C) result   D) right

72. Actually
    A) shortly   B) timely   C) briefly   D) really

73. Define
    A) explain   B) protest   C) train   D) mix

74. Want
    A) hesitate   B) detest   C) refuse   D) wish

75. Fresh
    A) moldy   B) new   C) rotten   D) stale

76. Start
    A) finish   B) come   C) begin   D) leave

77. Mature
    A) infant   B) child   C) young   D) adult

78. Remember
    A) offer   B) forget   C) advice   D) recollect

Synonyms

79. Empty
    A) filled   B) vacant   C) full   D) deep

80. Gift
    A) present   B) punishment   C) penalty   D) fine

81. Area
    A) source   B) farm   C) beach   D) region

82. Fortune
    A) luck   B) belief   C) religion   D) faith

83. Personal
    A) public   B) community   C) general   D) private

84. Watch
    A) look at   B) seek   C) think   D) read

85. Far
    A) nearby   B) near   C) distant   D) close

86. Quantity
    A) month   B) sound   C) discount   D) amount

87. Below
    A) near   B) under   C) above   D) next to

88. Kind
    A) rude   B) gentle   C) intelligent   D) brainy

89. Narrow
    A) soft   B) long   C) thin   D) brief

90. Pardon
    A) forgive   B) forbid   C) allow   D) promise

91. Shout
    A) whisper   B) whistle   C) blow   D) yell

92. Enter
    A) get in   B) desert   C) abandon   D) quit

93. Pleased
    A) sad   B) happy   C) unhappy   D) angry

94. Beautiful
    A) ugly   B) sorrowful   C) plain   D) pretty

95. Little
    A) large   B) huge   C) small   D) big

96. Active
    A) slow   B) idle   C) poor   D) energetic

97. Border
    A) density   B) altitude   C) edge   D) surface

98. End
    A) compare   B) start   C) finish   D) move

99. Old
    A) elderly   B) raw   C) immature   D) young

100. Ask
    A) response   B) reply   C) question   D) call

Synonyms

ANTONYMS

TEST MASTER

Find the **antonym** of the following words written in capitals.

1. I'll have to take the PUPILS into the hills.
   A) teachers B) schoolchildren C) kids D) students E) boys

2. She is the WORST student in our group.
   A) good B) bad C) badly D) best E) nice

3. Breakfast is the FIRST meal of the day.
   A) important B) main C) last but one D) last E) next

4. He is an enemy, REMEMBER.
   A) keep in mind B) remind C) recall D) forget E) believe

5. Her luggage was so HEAVY that she asked the young man to help her.
   A) easy B) large C) least D) light E) vast

6. Her English is POOR.
   A) excellently B) unsatisfactory C) bad D) good E) not good

7. February is the SHORTEST month in the year.
   A) largest B) farthest C) longest D) highest E) biggest

8. TAKING a piece of chalk the pupil on duty began writing on the board.
   A) giving B) sending C) bringing D) spending E) belonging

9. I liked the END of the story most of all.
   A) beginning B) middle C) starting D) meaning E) part

10. Our farm is in the COUNTRY.
    A) street B) valley C) forest D) town E) park

11. I WAS RIGHT last night, wasn't I?
    A) was over B) were ill C) correct D) was wrong E) was busy

12. I don't REMEMBER where I left my umbrella.
    A) know B) forget C) give D) notice E) support

13. What is it then, my SON?
    A) girl B) boy C) daughter D) dear E) friend

14. Some of them BEGAN to talk to me.
    A) started B) finished C) was over D) ended E) founded

15. The hall was FULL with spectators.
    A) easy B) empty C) vacant D) ready E) late

16. There are many other BIG cities in Great Britain with more than a million inhabitants.
    A) large B) short C) small D) great E) low

17. I can't understand why you are so BUSY at home.
    A) engaged B) sleepy C) afraid D) free E) angry

18. I think your FAT cat is ill.
    A) thin B) stout C) big D) thick E) small

19. The prince ran after her and saw the pretty shoe which the girl HAD LOST.
    A) had found B) had left C) had forgotten D) had forgiven E) didn't find

20. It was MIDNIGHT and Cinderella ran away from the palace.
    A) early in the morning B) late night C) midday D) early night E) night

21. They OFTEN stay at the college after classes.
    A) always B) seldom C) usually D) ever E) early

22. Long ago the streets of this town were DIRTY.
    A) clean B) narrow C) wide D) broad E) long

23. He STARTED painting at a very early age and became famous at 27.
    A) began B) gave up C) get up D) continued E) went on

24. The travelers came to the hotel, LEFT their luggage there and went for a walk in the town.
    A) kept B) raised C) caught D) took E) picked out

25. He began TO EARN money very early.
    A) to change B) to touch C) to spend D) to sweep E) to tear

26. It was not EASY for him to find a job in such a long time.
    A) difficult B) pleasant C) necessary D) heavy E) dark

27. The weather was nice and children didn't want to stay INSIDE.
    A) at home B) in the country C) out D) outside E) garden

28. Let's open the window. It's very HOT here.
    A) dark B) cold C) stuffy D) foggy E) easy

29. You speak so FAST that it is nearly impossible to follow what you say.
    A) weak B) low C) slow D) quick E) quite

30. GO OUT OF the room, please, it's very stuffy here.
    A) come out B) leave C) leave for D) stay in E) useful

31. A DARK cloud having appeared in the sky, we decided to stay at home.
    A) bright B) heavy C) white D) cloudless E) merry

32. He says they will go to the TOP of the hill next
    A) near B) above C) bottom D) under E) downstairs

33. They have the SHORT road and it will take them twenty minutes to get to the village.
    A) big B) large C) not strong D) long E) rising

34. That will do. Your answer is quite RIGHT. Your mark is good.
    A) correct B) good C) bad D) wrong E) exact

35. Suddenly we heard a HIGH thin voice.
    A) tall B) small C) short D) low E) long

36. His best KNOWN paintings give a light to today's Europe.
    A) well-known B) famous C) unknown D) bad E) worst

Antonyms

37. We must never FORGET our heroes.
    A) recognize   B) recite   C) remember
    D) forgive   E) thank

38. You are a GOOD swimmer.
    A) hot   B) bad   C) low
    D) normal   E) not well

39. I stood there admiring that BEAUTIFUL picture.
    A) bad   B) nice   C) ugly
    D) terrible   E) plain

40. You can tell him the TRUTH. He will help you.
    A) a form   B) a tale   C) a secret
    D) a lie   E) a fable

41. Adriano is a TALL man.
    A) big   B) little   C) small
    D) short   E) large

42. It's much QUIETER there than here - very beautiful, but no tourists.
    A) more peaceful   B) noisier   C) more essential
    D) more uncertain   E) easier

43. They are good boys, don't LAUGH at them!
    A) smile   B) shout   C) cry
    D) look   E) speak

44. I don't think he will work hard. He is very LAZY.
    A) absent-minded   B) good looking   C) good-natured
    D) delighted   E) hard-working

45. The mountains in Great Britain are not very HIGH.
    A) low   B) long   C) short
    D) tall   E) big

46. He worked MUCH and got a good mark at his
    A) a lot   B) many   C) few
    D) little   E) a few

47. He thinks his son has a GOOD future.
    A) nice   B) fine   C) kind
    D) bad   E) wrong

48. You've got WET through.
    A) warm   B) dry   C) hot
    D) sweet   E) cold

49. Did you come by SEA?
    A) land   B) bed   C) desk
    D) shop   E) tree

50. Don't speak so FAST!
    A) loudly   B) slowly   C) well
    D) proudly   E) quickly

51. I'm LEAVING FOR Rio tomorrow and I'll be back in a week's time.
    A) going to   B) coming from   C) living in
    D) reaching   E) approaching

52. My friend Cyril isn't TALL enough to dance with Natalie.
    A) good   B) nice   C) happy
    D) long   E) short

53. When I WOKE UP it was dark in the room.
    A) got up   B) awoke   C) fell asleep
    D) stayed   E) left

54. I'm glad the interest rate is not very HIGH.
    A) short   B) tall   C) long
    D) low   E) huge

55. We are in a hurry. PUSH the car to one side.
    A) bring   B) move   C) pull
    D) park   E) break

56. The old man had MORE money than sixty thousand pounds.
    A) much   B) larger   C) over
    D) fewer   E) less

57. We heard a LOT OF interesting things over the radio yesterday evening.
    A) little   B) many   C) tremendous
    D) few   E) a great deal

58. I'll BE IN tomorrow morning.
    A) stay   B) be out   C) be over
    D) come   E) give

59. When the Browns paint their living-room and the paint is DRY they will hang a modern picture on the wall.
    A) cold   B) white   C) wet
    D) blue   E) clean

60. Though the watch was very EXPENSIVE, he decided to buy it for her.
    A) dear   B) calm   C) cheap
    D) quiet   E) rich

61. The Thames is a short river but it is WIDE.
    A) long   B) shallow   C) narrow
    D) nice   E) big

62. He GAVE his friend a book last week.
    A) brought   B) took   C) bought
    D) had   E) sold

63. John's parents want him to study law and become President one day. They have HIGH hopes on him.
    A) tall   B) respectful   C) wise
    D) unpleasant   E) small

64. The MORE you read, the more you know.
    A) much   B) many   C) little
    D) least   E) less

65. BEFORE death he decided to leave his money to a hospital.
    A) earlier   B) after   C) above
    D) below   E) over

66. Nina was a small girl and not at all STRONG.
    A) seldom   B) forceful   C) weak
    D) frozen   E) clever

67. She runs FAST.
    A) quickly   B) slowly   C) easily
    D) badly   E) well

68. Tom was a TALL boy of 16.
    A) low   B) short   C) long
    D) little   E) small

69. I must change my jeans. They are really DIRTY.
    A) clear   B) short   C) bright
    D) clean   E) yellow

70. It's EASY to understand this text.
    A) hard   B) difficult   C) simple
    D) longest   E) clear

71. David was POOR and had TO FIND his aunt.
    A) rich / to lose   B) tall / to win
    C) short / to gather   D) clever / to hide
    E) rich / to look for

72. He SAT thinking near the window.
    A) stood   B) saw   C) cried
    D) flew   E) died

73. I have been UNHAPPY since my mother died.
    A) happy   B) busy   C) tired
    D) excited   E) ill

74. - How are you?
    - I am WELL, thank you.
    A) ill   B) greedy   C) fine
    D) O.K.   E) ready

Antonyms

75. This box is very light. The man can EASILY lift it.
    A) hardly   B) hurriedly   C) slowly
    D) earnestly   E) badly

76. My watch is RIGHT.
    A) wrong   B) left   C) heavy
    D) slow   E) fast

77. It happened long after THE NIGHT that I fell down into a pit.
    A) dark   B) evening   C) day
    D) dawn   E) moonlight

78. There's too MUCH crime and violence in the streets of cities nowadays.
    A) sad   B) few   C) glad
    D) little   E) many

79. My RIGHT hand is stronger than yours.
    A) left   B) wrong   C) dirty
    D) pretty   E) crushed

80. Scotland is the land of mountains, NARROW valleys and plains.
    A) wide   B) long   C) fat
    D) thick   E) large

Find the **antonym** of the following words:

81. Leave
    A) arrive   B) desert   C) separate   D) abandon

82. Hide
    A) show   B) cover   C) spend   D) save

83. High
    A) low   B) tall   C) important   D) powerful

84. Brave
    A) heroic   B) bold   C) keen   D) cowardly

85. Behind
    A) near   B) far   C) in front of   D) on

86. Pull
    A) divide   B) hit   C) kick   D) push

87. Horizontal
    A) flat   B) level   C) vertical   D) even

88. Absent
    A) present   B) off   C) away   D) missing

89. Public
    A) different   B) private   C) usual   D) common

90. Bitter
    A) sweet   B) stale   C) rotten   D) moldy

91. Cry
    A) blow   B) speak   C) chat   D) laugh

92. Reduce
    A) limit   B) lessen   C) increase   D) decrease

93. Ill
    A) sick   B) healthy   C) poor   D) painful

94. Adult
    A) disabled   B) aged   C) immature   D) old

95. Dry
    A) barren   B) wet   C) sterile   D) arid

96. Win
    A) earn   B) lose   C) get   D) gain

97. Past
    A) next   B) future   C) present   D) before

98. Sick
    A) ill   B) patient   C) sorry   D) well

99. Cautious
    A) fussy   B) reckless   C) nervous   D) careful

100. Clever
    A) Stupid   B) chubby   C) kind   D) smart

101. Dangerous
    A) stormy   B) risky   C) safe   D) hazardous

102. Increase
    A) carry off   B) go up   C) decrease   D) rise

103. Begin
    A) continue   B) ban   C) urge   D) stop

104. Narrow
    A) thin   B) tight   C) wide   D) sharp

105. Great
    A) huge   B) big   C) small   D) heavy

106. Outside
    A) above   B) on   C) inside   D) under

107. Ill
    A) sick   B) painful   C) poor   D) healthy

108. Noisy
    A) muddy   B) misty   C) moldy   D) silent

109. Finish
    A) conclude   B) end   C) terminate   D) begin

110. Light
    A) rainy   B) misty   C) dark   D) bright

111. Hate
    A) praise   B) commend   C) love   D) detest

112. Cheap
    A) expensive   B) inexpensive   C) free   D) low-cost

113. Finish
    A) terminate   B) conclude   C) end   D) begin

114. Fresh
    A) stale   B) new   C) clean   D) pure

115. Find
    A) lose   B) seek   C) locate   D) look

116. Pull
    A) push   B) kick   C) hit   D) divide

117. Cold
    A) misty   B) icy   C) hot   D) warm

118. Begin
    A) ban   B) urge   C) continue   D) stop

119. Cautious
    A) reckless   B) fussy   C) nervous   D) careful

120. Early
    A) now   B) quickly   C) before   D) late

121. Child
    A) girl   B) infant   C) boy   D) adult

122. Minority
    A) majority   B) population   C) mankind   D) people

123. Better
    A) clear   B) calm   C) worse   D) well

124. Enemy
    A) rival   B) opponent   C) friend   D) client

Antonyms

THE LOGIC LIST

TEST MASTER

Find the words which are out of the logic list:

1. A) correct   B) accurate   C) right   D) wrong
2. A) tongue   B) mouth   C) head   D) lip
3. A) neck   B) eye   C) ear   D) nose
4. A) article   B) booklet   C) headline   D) column
5. A) strike   B) rap   C) pat   D) tap
6. A) book   B) magazine   C) newspaper   D) prescription
7. A) huge   B) large   C) serious   D) big
8. A) north   B) east   C) west   D) earth
9. A) bell   B) key   C) door   D) tenant
10. A) horse   B) lion   C) donkey   D) sheep
11. A) month   B) autumn   C) summer   D) winter
12. A) forest   B) moon   C) river   D) mountain
13. A) body   B) chest   C) shoulder   D) head
14. A) dinner   B) soup   C) supper   D) lunch
15. A) detergent   B) tap   C) shower   D) wash-basin
16. A) pencil case   B) ruler   C) class   D) eraser
17. A) wall   B) ceiling   C) garden   D) room
18. A) tiger   B) monkey   C) bear   D) chicken
19. A) star   B) moon   C) sun   D) sand
20. A) day   B) month   C) year   D) dawn
21. A) number   B) slash   C) comma   D) dot
22. A) rucksack   B) briefcase   C) purse   D) luggage
23. A) player   B) pitch   C) fan   D) referee
24. A) salad   B) tray   C) steak   D) soup
25. A) blanket   B) quilt   C) pillow   D) sofa
26. A) delicious   B) bitter   C) sour   D) spicy
27. A) singer   B) composer   C) leaflet   D) audience
28. A) heat wave   B) ice   C) winter   D) snow
29. A) trousers   B) shirt   C) jacket   D) handkerchief
30. A) fear   B) fright   C) calm   D) alarm
31. A) driver   B) bus   C) pedestrian   D) ticket
32. A) grocer   B) driver   C) baker   D) greengrocer
33. A) sun   B) sand   C) star   D) sky
34. A) ankle   B) kidney   C) liver   D) lung
35. A) apple   B) orange   C) garlic   D) peach
36. A) lake   B) meadow   C) sea   D) stream
37. A) wrong   B) true   C) right   D) correct
38. A) onion   B) potato   C) apricot   D) carrot
39. A) kettle   B) tray   C) teapot   D) curtain
40. A) minute   B) clock   C) hour   D) second
41. A) row   B) run   C) fish   D) swim
42. A) niece   B) sister   C) sister in law   D) brother
43. A) rain   B) star   C) cloud   D) thunder
44. A) bathroom   B) chimney   C) kitchen   D) bedroom
45. A) cook   B) steward   C) chef   D) waiter
46. A) harbor   B) station   C) bridge   D) airport
47. A) knife   B) pin   C) scissors   D) saw
48. A) garden   B) library   C) bank   D) shop
49. A) duck   B) hen   C) tiger   D) goose
50. A) traffic   B) ball   C) lamp   D) crossing   E) vehicle
51. A) England   B) Scotland   C) New Zealand   D) Northern Ireland   E) Wales
52. A) know   B) understand   C) break   D) think   E) remember
53. A) canteen   B) dining-hall   C) warehouse   D) kitchen   E) buffet
54. A) pane   B) window sill   C) window   D) pain   E) frame
55. A) raincoat   B) ticket   C) suit   D) tie   E) hat
56. A) beautiful   B) attractive   C) handsome   D) pretty   E) sensitive
57. A) voyage   B) trip   C) traveling   D) travel   E) athlete
58. A) to dig   B) to grow   C) to plant   D) to water   E) to tidy up
59. A) bridge   B) chair   C) table   D) bench   E) desk
60. A) performance   B) concert   C) flight   D) film   E) play
61. A) spoon   B) soup   C) fork   D) knife   E) plate
62. A) rain   B) umbrella   C) snow   D) storm   E) wind
63. A) dress   B) suit   C) shirt   D) tailor   E) skirt
64. A) carrot   B) potato   C) pigeon   D) cabbage   E) pea
65. A) cucumber   B) plum   C) orange   D) cherry   E) grapes

The Logic List

66. A) stone B) glass C) ink
    D) wood E) iron
67. A) Moscow B) Rome C) London
    D) Washington E) New York
68. A) gymnastics B) photography C) cricket
    D) judo E) football
69. A) kitchen B) bedroom C) garage
    D) dining-room E) hall
70. A) once B) soon C) past
    D) ago E) last time
71. A) beer B) lemonade C) gin
    D) vodka E) whiskey
72. A) duck B) pheasant C) chicken
    D) goose E) berry
73. A) a cat B) a cake C) a dog
    D) a cow E) a sheep
74. A) train B) ship C) boat
    D) captain E) plane
75. A) a spoon B) a fork C) a knife
    D) a plate E) a cupboard
76. A) beef B) lamb C) chop
    D) lettuce E) steak
77. A) above B) that C) under
    D) into E) within
78. A) go B) return C) mile
    D) stay E) change
79. A) fruit B) grass C) flower
    D) plant E) egg
80. A) cotton B) butter C) cheese
    D) bread E) milk
81. A) cousin B) niece C) aunt
    D) nurse E) uncle
82. A) a spoon B) a fork C) a plate
    D) a cup E) a cap
83. A) a room B) a flat C) a street
    D) a house E) a parlor
84. A) applicant B) worker C) painter
    D) interpreter E) builder
85. A) underground B) box-office C) bank
    D) ministry E) school
86. A) scientist B) writer C) bakery
    D) interpreter E) economist
87. A) go B) start C) arrive
    D) come E) congratulate
88. A) goldfish B) horse C) fox
    D) tree E) mouse
89. A) youth B) farmer C) adult
    D) child E) teenager
90. A) speak B) say C) punish
    D) talk E) tell
91. A) postman B) farmer C) field
    D) reporter E) surgeon
92. A) tree B) flower C) bush
    D) leave E) plant
93. A) field B) meadow C) forest
    D) wood E) wardrobe
94. A) table B) bookcase C) tram
    D) sofa E) furniture
95. A) feel B) see C) hear
    D) lay E) want
96. A) suit B) shoe C) hat
    D) pot E) shirt

The Logic List

VOCABULARY A-Z

TEST MASTER

AAAA

1. People fly in _____
2. Kevin Costner, Brad Pitt and Sean Connery are all _____
3. When you grow up you are _____
4. A country that has many kangaroos is _____
5. A machine which keeps you cool in summer is _____
6. It wakes you up in the morning. It's _____
7. The opposite of dead is _____
8. Somewhere to stub your cigar out in is called _____
9. A word that means "good looking or pretty" _____
10. A person who goes to the moon or into outer space is called _____

BBBB

1. A man who isn't married is a _____
2. Another word meaning "luggage" is _____
3. Someone whose job is to cut hair is called a _____
4. Someone without socks or shoes on is _____
5. The red liquid in your body is called _____
6. If you come from Wales, Scotland, or England you are _____
7. Someone who breaks into houses is a _____
8. Something that is fired from a gun is called a _____
9. A small word that means "next to" is _____
10. Something that is used to fasten shirts and cuffs is called a _____

CCCC

1. What chocolate drink came from Mexico? It's _____
2. Where is the longest wall in the world? It's in _____
3. We drink tea and coffee from it and it sits on a saucer. It's a _____
4. Kings and queens live in this building. It's a _____
5. The person in charge of a ship is a _____
6. Another word for a taxi is a _____
7. Barred enclosure for birds _____
8. The capital city of Egypt is _____
9. Something you sit on with four legs, a back and a seat is a _____
10. The opposite of expensive is _____

DDDD

1. What has four legs, barks and wags it's tail?
2. This is a precious stone often found in expensive rings.
3. If you have twelve eggs or twelve loaves of bread, then you have a _____
4. When someone has too much alcohol to drink, they are _____
5. Somebody who can't hear is said to be _____
6. If you have a toothache you might want to visit a _____
7. This kind of book is used to find the spelling of words.
8. Ice cream, pudding, apple pie and cake are all kinds of _____
9. Someone who wants to lose weight or has a health problem goes on a _____
10. Ten years equals a _____

EEEE

1. An arm bends at the _____
2. The opposite of full is _____
3. A bigger copy of a photograph is called an _____
4. "The way out" is also known as the _____
5. The opposite of cheap is _____
6. The machine that makes a car move is it's _____
7. What "E word" means all places?
8. The imaginary line that runs around the middle of the earth is called the _____
9. Tokyo, Kobe and San Francisco are all cities which have been damaged by _____
10. When everything is finished it is the _____

FFFF

1. Someone who works on the land, growing things is called a _____
2. Something you like the most is your _____
3. To apply for a driving license you have to fill out an application _____
4. A thick kind of mist for which London is famous is _____
5. Someone who acts silly or is a bit stupid is called a _____
6. Two weeks is also called a _____
7. Something which is easily broken or damaged is _____
8. Light brown marks on the skin are called _____
9. Something given away for no money is _____
10. Cooking in hot fat is called _____

GGGG

1. What "G word" is an area by a house where people grow flowers?
2. What European country used to be divided into East and West?
3. This "G word" is used to protect the hands or to keep them warm. It's a _____
4. This was first played in Scotland and involves hitting a little white ball into a hole.
5. This is used to stick paper together.
6. Your mother's parents and your father's parents are your _____
7. The color you get when you mix white and black paint together.
8. Dark green or red fruit which grows on vines and are used to make wine are called _____
9. The musical instrument that John Lennon played right-handed and Paul McCartney plays left-handed is a _____
10. This is good to chew and chew and chew. It's _____

HHHH

1. What "H word" is a tool used to knock nails in with?
2. Another word to describe a good-looking man is _____
3. It's worn on your head for either fashion or warmth. It's a _____
4. This "H word" means you really, really don't like something or someone.
5. The joints where the legs join the body are called the _____
6. A holiday newly-weds have after their wedding is called a _____

Vocabulary A-Z

7. If you are ill or have an accident, you would go to a _____
8. How many years are there in a Century?
9. A typhoon that originates in the Atlantic is called a _____?
10. The opposite of heaven is _____

IIII

1. Water at zero degrees centigrade starts to form _____
2. If something is against the law, it is _____
3. A little word which means the opposite of out is _____
4. The colored liquid inside of a pen is called _____
5. A small moving thing which has six legs and either crawls, jumps, walks or flies is called an _____
6. Something used in a band that makes sound is called an _____
7. A word which means 'between countries' and is often used in an Airport name.
8. Someone or something that comes from Ireland is _____
9. A piece of land which is completely surrounded by water is an _____
10. The opposite of outside is _____

JJJJ

1. What is a short, long sleeved coat called?
2. A green stone found in China and Korea and is often carved is called _____
3. Fruit boiled with sugar and spread on toast is called _____
4. A puzzle made up of different shaped pieces which are fitted together again is called a _____
5. Another word for work or employment is _____
6. A person who decides in a competition, contest, or in a law case is called a _____
7. A story which is funny is called a _____
8. The largest planet in the solar system is called _____
9. To travel to a distant place is to go on a _____
10. The sound made by keys, coins and especially small bells is called a _____

KKKK

1. What in Australia jumps along on its two hind legs and carries it's baby in a pouch?
2. A metal container with a handle, lid and spout which is used for boiling water is called a _____
3. A specially shaped piece of metal used to open locks is called a _____
4. What prefix means one thousand?
5. This "K word" means to touch with the lips.
6. What room in the house is all the cooking and washing of dishes done in?
7. What "K word" is the joint which is half way down the leg?
8. Which piece of silverware has a handle and a blade and is used for cutting?
9. What "K word" is a baby goat, but is also slang for 'a child'?
10. To bang on someone's door with your knuckles is to _____

LLLL

1. The meal we eat in the middle of the day is called _____
2. A special room or building where books are kept is called a _____
3. Treated animal skin that is often made into shoes, sneakers, and jackets is called _____
4. When you can't find someplace you are _____
5. In autumn the parts of a tree which turns into reds, golds, and browns are the _____
6. If you borrow money from the bank it's called a _____
7. Another name for an elevator is a _____
8. The opposite of dead is _____
9. What fruit is yellow, oval shaped and sour?
10. To drive legally you need to get a _____

MMMM

1. A word that means crazy or angry is _____
2. S. M. and L. are all sizes of clothes. What does the "M" stand for?
3. Gold, steel and nickel are all different kinds of _____
4. The hair above the upper lip is called a _____
5. What special name is given to hotels built for motorists to use?
6. Someone who plays music is called a _____
7. Something that is slightly wet is said to be _____
8. When ice turns to water it _____
9. A looking glass where you can see your own reflection is more commonly called a _____
10. If you go to the doctor, he will give you pills and potions which are a type of _____

NNNN

1. The opposite of broad is _____
2. The part of the body which joins the head to the torso is called the _____
3. An acupuncturist and a seamstress both use this thin piece of metal to work with.
4. Twelve o'clock or mid-day is also known as _____
5. Almond, cashews and Brazil are all types of _____
6. A person who lives next door to you is your _____
7. A photographic print is made from a _____
8. The "N" on a gear shift stands for _____
9. A quick, short sleep is called a _____
10. Women's stocking and tights and many other things are made from _____

OOOO

1. The shellfish from which we get pearls is called an _____
2. A thick liquid that come from the ground called 'Black Gold' is more commonly know as _____
3. The adjective which means of the mouth is _____
4. The numbers 1,3,5,7,and 9 aren't even. They are _____
5. Which sea-living animal has eight legs and squirts ink when it is frightened?
6. What vegetable often makes your eyes water or cry when you cut it?

Vocabulary A-Z

7. Another word for chance is _____
8. This word means the same as to work at or run a machine.
9. If something is done one time it is done _____
10. When something belongs to you, you are its _____

PPPP

1. A person who takes care of, or brings up another is called a _____.
2. The opposite of rich is _____.
3. Legal or official authority is called _____.
4. Something that is of great value or of high price is _____.
5. A _____ is a humorous use of a word.
6. To be on time is to be _____.
7. A word of politeness used when requesting something. e.g. _____ help me.
8. Tailors often use _____ when preparing clothes.
9. A _____ is something that is produced, usually in a factory.
10. Two things of the same kind to be used together are called a _____.

QQQQ

1. When the earth shakes we call it a _____
2. The amount of a number of something is the _____
3. The female ruler of a country is a _____
4. One fourth of something is a _____
5. A line of people waiting for something is called a _____
6. Something that takes a short time is _____
7. When there is little or no movement or sound, then all is _____
8. What "Q word" is to ask questions as a test of knowledge?
9. To repeat or write words someone else has said or written is to _____
10. To give up something like a job or school is to _____
11. To have an angry argument is to _____

RRRR

1. A dried sweet grape is called a _____
2. Something in its natural state or uncooked is _____
3. Something that isn't imagined or made up is _____
4. The back part of something is the _____
5. To accept, take or get something is to _____
6. A wild dance party with thousands of people is called a _____
7. The thing used for shaving hair from the skin is called a _____
8. A person who is impolite or doesn't show respect is _____
9. A tough elastic material which is used to make tires and erasers is called _____
10. What word is the opposite of urban and means the countryside _____

SSSS

1. A small word that means unhappy is _____
2. A leather seat used for riding on horses or bicycle is called a _____
3. The money you get, usually monthly, for working is your _____
4. To look carefully to find someone or something is to _____

5. Someone who thinks about their own needs all the time is said to be _____
6. What word means "like" or "of the same sort"?
7. To show happiness or amusement by turning the corners of your mouth up is to _____
8. A creature which has eight legs and spins a web to catch food is a _____
9. A small usually round mark on something which is a different color is called a _____
10. A comfortable long piece of furniture used for sitting or lounging is a _____

TTTT

1. The four round, black things covering the metal wheels are known as _____
2. Two babies born at the same time to the same mother are _____
3. The usually white, thick stuff with a minty taste which is used to brush teeth with is called _____
4. Something you aim at is called a _____
5. The noise that follows lightning is _____
6. The traditional bird which is eaten for Thanksgiving in the U.S. and at Christmas in England is a _____
7. A person whose job is to cut and sew cloth into clothes is a _____
8. An instrument used to tell the temperature of things is called a _____
9. Trains, planes, ships, cars, and bikes are all forms of _____
10. A very strong and violent storm that is found in the Pacific is called a _____

UUUU

1. The brother of your mother or father is your _____
2. If something or someone is one of a kind we say they are _____
3. What "U" word' means "dirty"?
4. If it's normal or customary, then it's _____
5. When the top is where the bottom should be then it's _____
6. Something that isn't new but has had previous owners is _____
7. The subway system or tube in London is know as the _____
8. The top part of a shoe or things that are higher are _____
9. The opposite of rural and meaning of the town is _____
10. Something that needs quick action or a prompt decision is _____

VVVV

1. A holiday is also called a _____
2. What "V word" is created when all the air has been pumped out?
3. Someone who for various reasons doesn't eat any animal products at all is a _____
4. The opposite of horizontal is _____
5. What game involves getting a ball over a high net without it hitting the floor and within three touches?
6. One type of rich, soft, plush cloth is _____
7. When something or someone disappears you could say they have _____
8. The land which is between two mountains or hills is called a _____
9. A place which is smaller than a town, but which usually has shops is a _____
10. To offer to do something without payment is to _____

Vocabulary A-Z

WWWW

1. The joint between your hand and your arm is your _____
2. The biggest mammal is a _____
3. The instrument most people wear to tell the time is a _____
4. To close and open one eye quickly is to _____
5. How heavy something is its _____
6. Guns and knives are both kinds of _____
7. To move your hand or arm from side to side especially to say goodbye or attract attention is to _____
8. A building where goods are stored is called a _____
9. A hole dug into the ground to get water or a word which means good is _____
10. The material candles are made of is _____

XXXX

1. What trade name now means to photocopy?
2. This musical instrument is made up of different lengths of wood and struck by small hammers. It's a _____
3. A common abbreviation for Christmas is _____
4. A photograph taken using special short wave rays to see through or into things is an _____
5. Someone who has no real reason to, but hates all foreigners or strangers is _____

YYYY

1. A round toy which moves up and down on a string by the flick of the wrist is a _____
2. The yellow part of an egg is the _____
3. A thick white food made from milk and often flavored with fruit is _____
4. Something which isn't very old is _____
5. A short positive agreement in English is _____
6. A shout caused by excitement or pain is a _____
7. It takes this long for the earth to revolve around the sun. It's a _____
8. The American English word for garden is _____
9. The money used in Japan is _____
10. The day before today was _____

ZZZZ

1. A pattern or path that turns right then left alternately is called a _____
2. A metal fastener which joins two sides together with interlocking teeth is a _____
3. The striped horse-like animal or in British English a pedestrian crossing is a _____
4. One minus one equals _____
5. The lens used on a camera which can change it's focal length is called a _____
6. An area with particular uses or features is termed a _____
7. The American English name for courgette. It's a green or yellow cucumber shaped vegetable.
8. A kind of meditation practiced by monks is _____
9. The park where animals are kept for people to see is a _____
10. The last letter of the English alphabet is _____

Vocabulary A-Z

MISCELLANEOUS

TEST MASTER

A "Pair of" Quiz

1. What pair do we wear on our hands?
2. What pair do we wear on our face to see better?
3. What pair do we wear inside our shoes?
4. What pair do we wear on our ears?
5. What pair do we wear on our face when it's bright?
6. What pair do we wear on our legs?
7. What pair do we wear on our feet?
8. What pair do we sleep in?
9. What pair do we put on when we take our shoes off?
10. What pair do we cut things with?

Automobile Vocabulary

1. You see the road through it.
   A) windscreen
   B) carburetor
   C) ignition
   D) spark plugs
   E) timing chain

2. When you want to go faster, you press this.
   A) brake pedal
   B) clutch
   C) gearbox
   D) accelerator
   E) carburetor

3. You turn these on when it is dark so you can see the road.
   A) headphones
   B) headlights
   C) taillights
   D) panel lights
   E) spotlights

4. Whenever you want to shift up or down, you press this down.
   A) gearbox
   B) gas
   C) accelerator
   D) clutch pedal
   E) brake pedal

5. This cools down your engine.
   A) radiator
   B) battery
   C) distributor
   D) taillights
   E) pump

6. This provides your battery with the electricity it needs.
   A) spark plugs
   B) ignition
   C) generator
   D) accumulator
   E) alligator

7. If the road is bumpy, these help to dampen the bumps.
   A) fenders
   B) bumpers
   C) shock absorbers
   D) turn indicators
   E) steering wheel

8. If you want to turn left or right, you put these on.
   A) headlights
   B) turn indicators
   C) horn
   D) steering wheel
   E) rack and pinion

9. You use this when you start a cold engine.
   A) brakes
   B) choke
   C) amp meter
   D) fuel tank
   E) gearbox

10. This lubricates your engine.
    A) grease
    B) fuel
    C) water
    D) oil
    E) cream

Body

1. You see with your ___
2. You hear with your ___
3. You bite with your ___
4. You hold with your ___
5. You smell with your ___
6. You eat with your ___
7. You walk with your ___
8. You stand on your ___
9. You kneel on your ___
10. You carry a backpack on your ___

Clothes 1

1. We wear them to keep our hands warm.
2. We wear it to keep our heads warm.
3. We wrap it around our necks in winter.
4. 'Levis' and 'Wranglers' are ___
5. Men usually wear one around their necks.
6. We wear them on our feet under footwear.
7. We wear it on top of our clothes to keep us warm.
8. It has buttons up the front, a collar, sleeves and is often white.
9. It goes from the waist down, is most often worn by women.
10. Trousers or a skirt with a matching jacket is called a ___

Clothes 2

1. It's worn around the neck or over the shoulders. Women also wear it over the hair.
2. It's a long two-legged garment. It's a synonym for trousers.
3. They are covering for your hands with separated fingers. They are usually made of leather or knitted wool.
4. They cover your feet and are worn inside a shoe.
5. It's a garment with long or short sleeves usually worn under a jacket.
6. It's a short sleeved coat.
7. It's a woman's dress worn on special occasions.
8. It's a piece of clothing that covers the lower part of your body, with a separate part covering each leg.

Colors 1

1. Tomatoes are ___
2. The sky is ___
3. Clouds are ___
4. Grass is ___
5. Butter is ___
6. Eggplants are ___
7. Carrots are ___
8. Strawberry milkshakes are ___
9. Coffee is ___
10. Chocolate is usually ___

Miscellaneous

Colors 2

1. Dark blue is sometimes called ___
2. What color comes after yellow in a rainbow?
3. Vermilion, crimson and scarlet are shades of ___
4. What color stands out the most?
5. The opposite of black is usually ___
6. How many colors are there in a rainbow?
7. Roses are red, violets are ___
8. How many primary colors are there?
9. Hazel eyes are light ___

Colors 3

1. On a good day, the sky is usually ___ .
2. Lemons and bananas are usually ___.
3. Apples, strawberries and cherries are most often ___.
4. Traffic lights are red, yellow and ___.
5. A zebra is black and ___.
6. The American penny (one cent coin) is ___.
7. A wooden floor is usually ___.
8. Men going to funerals most often wear ___ suits.
9. At a wedding, the bride usually wears a ___ dress.
10. Grapes are usually green or ___.

Colors 4

1. Apples, salad, and grass are all usually ___
2. Buses in London, tomatoes and Rudolf's' nose are all ___
3. Taxis in New York, sweet corn and banana skins are all ___
4. The sky, Thomas the tank engine, and the sea are all ___
5. Taxis in London, coal and a starless sky are all ___
6. Cherry blossoms, strawberry ice cream and pigs are all ___
7. Chocolate, coffee and whiskey are all ___
8. Paper, snow and sugar are all ___
9. Eggplants, violets and blueberry ice cream are all ___
10. Carrots, the sunrise and tangerines are all ___

Country - Nationality - Language

1. He's from Brazil. He's _____.
   B) Brazilish   B) Brazilian   C) Brazilese
2. I'm from Colombia. I can speak _____.
   A) Spanish   B) Colombian   C) Colombish
3. She's from Russia. She can speak _____.
   A) Russia   B) Russy   C) Russian
4. We're from Italy. We're _____.
   A) Italien   B) Italian   C) Italiun
5. My friend is from Korea. He can speak _____.
   A) Korish   B) Korean   C) Koreanese
6. Pablo is from Mexico. He's _____.
   A) Spanish   B) Mexican   C) Mexian
7. Martha is from the United States. She's _____.
   A) American   B) United Statian
   C) United Statianese
8. My father is from China. He can speak _____.
   A) Chiny   B) Chinish   C) Chinese
9. Gloria is from Puerto Rico. She's _____.
   A) Puerto Rich   B) Puerto Rican   C) Puerto Riquean
10. Pierre is from France. He can speak _____.
    A) Franchise   B) Francese   C) French

Days

1. What day is before Saturday?
2. What day is after Wednesday?
3. What day is after Sunday?
4. What day is before Tuesday?
5. What day is two days after Thursday?
6. What day is before Monday?
7. What day is after Monday?
8. What day is before Thursday?
9. What is the third day of the week?
10. What day does school begin?

Educational Subjects

1. The subject which covers drawing, painting, and sculpture is called ___
2. The subject which includes equations, fractions, addition and subtraction is ___
3. The study of land forms and population growths are included in ___
4. The study of the periodic table, gasses, liquids, acids and alkalis is called ___
5. The study of motion, mechanics and energy is part of ___
6. The study of composers, concerto's quavers and blue notes is all included in ___
7. The subject of what has happened to the cultures and countries of the world is ___
8. Money, banking, the country's growth patterns and taxation are all studies in ___
9. The natural world and the study of life and plant forms is called ___
10. Running, playing tennis, and other sports are part of ___

Place Names

1. If you want to see monkeys, lions, tigers and bears, you would go to the ___.
2. A place where famous paintings and sculptures are kept and displayed to the public is called an ___
3. The building where you can go and watch the latest blockbuster film is called a ___.
4. A place where you can go to see many different kinds of fish swimming is called an ___.
5. If you want to watch a basketball game or a soccer match, you would go to a ___.
6. A place which serves drinks such as beer and whiskey and where people go to relax and meet friends is called a ___.
7. The place where rock musicians and orchestras play is called a ___.
8. The place to go if you want to ride on a roller coaster or drive bumper cars is called an ___.
9. A place where you can arrange loans, keep your money in an account which receives interest is called a ___.
10. A place where you can buy stamps, post letters and pay some bills is called a ___.
11. A place where you go to book holidays and buy train tickets is called a ___.
12. If you need to arrange a burial, you would go to a ___.
13. Dirty clothes which can't be washed at home are taken to a ___.
14. If you have a burst pipe or a leaking tap, you need to call a ___.
15. If you don't have a job but are looking for one, you might go to an ___.
16. If you want to hire a lawyer or draw up a will, you would go to a ___.
17. If you want to sell your house, buy a new one, or rent a place to live for a while, you would go to a ___.
18. If your clothes need washing, but you don't have a washing machine, you would go to a ___.

Family

1. Your father's sister is your ___
2. Your sister's husband is your ___
3. Your mother's mother is your ___
4. Your sister's daughter is your ___
5. Your son's son is your ___
6. Your sister's brother is your ___
7. Your mother's brother is your ___
8. Your uncle's son is your ___
9. Your brother's son is your ___
10. Your mother's father is your ___

Miscellaneous

Food

1. A lemon or an unripe apple tastes ___
2. After eating a lot or when something can't have more put in it, we say ___
3. What word means not having enough water, liquid, or moisture?
4. This word is most often heard when talking of wealth. When a cake or sauce contains a lot of dairy products such as butter, cream or eggs we say it is ___
5. When a person wants a drink they are ___
6. What word is used favorably about cakes and bread and is the opposite of dry?
7. The real meaning of this word is to die or suffer from hunger, but we use it colloquially to describe being hungry. This word is ___
8. A word used when talking about fruit or meat that means it is juicy and tastes good is ___
9. Something that taste like unsweetened cocoa or pepper is said to be ___
10. The opposite of sour and means that something tastes of sugar or honey is ___

Group Nouns

1. Taxis, trains, and planes are all forms of ___
2. Apples, oranges, and grapes are all types of ___
3. Tables, chairs, and bookcases are all ___
4. Juice, tea, and milk are all ___
5. Suitcases, trunks, rucksacks are all kinds of ___
6. Collie, sheepdog, and terrier are all kinds of ___
7. Christmas, Ramadan, and Independence Day are all ___
8. Fish, meat, and rice are all kinds of ___
9. Carrots, potatoes, and cabbage are all types of ___
10. Yen, dollars and pounds are all types of ___

House Words

1. Where do you usually cook meals?
2. Where do you usually wash clothes?
3. Where do you usually hang your clothes?
4. Where do you usually get washed?
5. Where do you usually grow flowers and cut the grass?
6. Where do you usually eat dinner?
7. Where do you usually sit on the sofa and watch TV?
8. Where do you usually park the car?
9. Where do you usually store food, drinks and other things?
10. Where do you usually sleep?

Household Appliances

1. You wash clothes in it. It's a ___
2. You clean with it. It's a ___
3. You heat things very quickly in it. It's a ___
4. You press clothes with it. It's an ___
5. You watch movies and play computer games on it. It's a ___
6. You ring your friends and talk. It's a ___
7. It cleans your dirty plates, silverware and pans. It's a ___
8. You boil water in it. It's a ___
9. It makes toast. It's a ___
10. It makes food very, very cold. It's a ___
11. It keeps your food cold. It's a ___

Jobs

1. Where does a receptionist work?
   A) post office B) bakery C) office
2. Where does a cashier work?
   A) school B) supermarket C) police station
3. Where does a headmaster work?
   A) school B) office C) butchers
4. Where does a Chief Constable work?
   A) bus station B) hospital C) police station
5. Where does a porter work?
   A) bakery B) hotel C) school
6. Where does a manager work?
   A) police station B) park C) office
7. Where does a pilot work?
   A) airplane B) train station C) restaurant
8. Where does a busboy work?
   A) bus B) restaurant C) airplane
9. Where does an actress work?
   A) cinema B) theatre C) sports centre
10. Where does an artist work?
    A) restaurant B) cinema C) studio

Months

1. What month comes after November?
2. What month comes before August?
3. What month comes after May?
4. What month comes before February?
5. What month comes after March?
6. What month comes before September?
7. What month comes after October?
8. What month comes before June?
9. What month comes after December?
10. What month comes before July?

Nationalities

1. Tom is from Berlin. His nationality is _____.
   A) Germany B) German C) Dutch
2. Anna is from Leningrad. Her nationality is _____.
   A) France B) French C) Russian
3. David is from New York. His nationality is _____.
   A) Mexican B) American C) Canadian
4. Sarah is from London. Her nationality is _____.
   A) British B) Irish C) Scottish
5. Nicole is from Paris. Her nationality is _____.
   A) France B) French C) English
6. Carlos is from Madrid. His nationality is _____.
   A) French B) Italian C) Spanish
7. Donald is from Geneva. His nationality is _____.
   A) Switzerland B) Austrian C) Swiss
8. Bruce is from Sydney. His nationality is _____.
   A) British B) Australian C) Austrian
9. Keiko is from Tokyo. Her nationality is _____.
   A) Chinese B) Korean C) Japanese
10. Dewa is from Jakarta. His nationality is _____.
    A) Japanese B) Indonesian C) Indian

Nationalities & Languages

1. People from Canada are called _____.
   A) Canuks B) Canadians C) Canadites
2. People from India are _____.
   A) Indies B) Hindus C) Indians
3. He's from Germany. He is _____.
   A) German B) Germany C) Dutch

Miscellaneous

4. She lives in Argentina. She speaks _____.
   A) Argentinian B) Spanish C) Portuguese

5. She lives in Argentinia. She is _____.
   A) Argentinian B) Argentese C) Argentonian

6. People in Israel are _____.
   A) Jewish B) Israeli C) Hebrew

7. People from Israel speak _____.
   A) Jewish B) Israeli C) Hebrew

8. People in Hong Kong speak English and _____.
   A) Hangul B) Cantonese C) Mandarin

9. People in Turkey speak _____.
   A) Turk B) Turkey C) Turkish

10. People from Ireland are _____.
    A) Irish B) English C) Irelandish

Occupations: What is my job?

1. I work in an office. I type letters and the phone.
2. I go to court and defend people's rights.
3. I work in a hospital and take care of sick people.
4. I work in a school and help people learn.
5. You pay me when you buy something at the store.
6. I take care of sick animals.
7. I put out fires.
8. I wear a uniform and a badge. I help keep your neighborhood safe.
9. I help keep your teeth clean.
10. I deliver letters and packages to your home.

Opposites - Nouns

Match the words on the left with their opposites on the right.

1. day	a. bottom	1. _____
2. friend	b. cause	2. _____
3. loss	c. enemy	3. _____
4. result	d. failure	4. _____
5. sea	e. gain	5. _____
6. sorrow	f. joy	6. _____
7. success	g. land	7. _____
8. sunset	h. night	8. _____
9. top	i. peace	9. _____
10. war	j. sunrise	10. _____

Opposites - Adjectives 1

Match the words on the left with their opposites on the right.

1. boring	a. beautiful	1. _____
2. light	b. big	2. _____
3. little	c. black	3. _____
4. loud	d. happy	4. _____
5. new	e. heavy	5. _____
6. poor	f. interesting	6. _____
7. sad	g. old	7. _____
8. short	h. quiet	8. _____
9. ugly	i. rich	9. _____
10. white	j. tall	10. _____

Opposites - Adjectives 2

Match the words on the left with their opposites on the right.

1. alive	a. absent	1. _____
2. careless	b. careful	2. _____
3. easy	c. cheap	3. _____
4. expensive	d. cool	4. _____
5. light	e. dark	5. _____
6. near	f. dead	6. _____
7. present	g. deep	7. _____
8. shallow	h. difficult	8. _____
9. warm	i. dry	9. _____
10. wet	j. far	10. _____

Opposites - Adjectives 3

Match the words on the left with their opposites on the right.

1. cold	a. fast	1. _____
2. early	b. foolish	2. _____
3. hard	c. high	3. _____
4. low	d. hot	4. _____
5. old	e. late	5. _____
6. slow	f. sick	6. _____
7. thin	g. soft	7. _____
8. weak	h. strong	8. _____
9. well	i. thick	9. _____
10. wise	j. young	10. _____

Opposites - Verbs 1

Match the verbs on the left with its opposite on the right.

1. accept	a. die	1. _____
2. allow	b. destroy	2. _____
3. attack	c. laugh	3. _____
4. be born	d. defend	4. _____
5. cry	e. go	5. _____
6. buy	f. prohibit	6. _____
7. build	g. refuse	7. _____
8. come	h. sell	8. _____

Opposites 1

1. He's short, he isn't very ___
2. It's light, it isn't very ___
3. It's small, it isn't very ___
4. He's ugly, he isn't very ___
5. It's short, it isn't very ___
6. It's cheap, it isn't very ___
7. It's near, it isn't very ___
8. He's poor, he isn't very ___
9. She's nasty, she isn't very ___
10. She's sad, she isn't very ___

Opposites 2

1. The room is dirty, it isn't very ___
2. It's loose, it isn't very ___
3. The knife is dull, it isn't very ___
4. The stereo is quiet, it isn't very ___
5. The water is shallow, it isn't very ___
6. The line curves, it isn't very ___
7. Her hair is fair, it isn't very ___
8. That book is thin, it isn't very ___
9. The water level is low, it isn't very ___
10. The road is narrow, it isn't very ___

Opposites 3

1. Hair can be long or ___
2. People can be short or ___
3. Problems can be big or ___
4. Food can be expensive or ___
5. Legs can be fat or ___
6. A car can be new or ___
7. A train can be fast or ___
8. A face can be beautiful or ___
9. Elevators go up or ___
10. Roads can be narrow or ___

People Who Wear Uniforms

1. People who put out fires are called ___.
2. If someone breaks into your house, you call the ___.
3. People who work with doctors in a hospital taking care of sick people are called ___.
4. They deliver the mail from door to door. They are ___.
5. They fly planes. They are ___.
6. They cook in restaurant kitchens. They are called ___.
7. Members of the military who go to sea are called ___.
8. Someone who works for an airline company and who serves food to passengers is called a ___.
9. Someone who works in a bank counting money is called a ___.
10. A man who works in a restaurant serving food is called a ___.
11. A woman who works in a restaurant serving food is called a ___.

Miscellaneous

Soccer Vocabulary

1. The _____ didn't train the players well, so the team lost the game.
   A) coach   B) couch   C) trainee
2. The team that _____ more goals wins the game.
   A) does   B) keeps   C) scores
3. _____ the ball as far as possible.
   A) Kick   B) Jump   C) Leap
4. The _____ must watch carefully for infractions during the game.
   A) judge   B) eyekeeper   C) referee
5. Whenever a player gets hurt, a _____ takes his place.
   A) placement   B) substitute   C) defender
6. A penalty kick is the right given to a player from the opposing team to a _____ kick.
   A) forced   B) free   C) fresh
7. The _____ must keep the ball out of the goal.
   A) goalholder   B) goalwatcher   C) goalkeeper
8. Eleven players from each team participate in a soccer _____.
   A) match   B) field   C) score
9. The first-line players are called _____.
   A) backs   B) forwards   C) defenders
10. A forward is also called a _____.
    A) trooper   B) goalie   C) striker

Things We Carry

1. Used to keep rain off us ___
2. Used to take photos ___
3. Used to carry school books ___
4. Carried by business men ___
5. Used by men to carry money ___
6. Used by women to carry money ___
7. Used to blow your nose on ___
8. Printed daily and read by millions ___
9. Used to get into a house or a car ___
10. Made of plastic or paper and is given by shops ___

Time Words

1. There are 60 seconds in one ___.
2. There are 60 minutes in one ___.
3. 30 minutes is called ___.
4. There are 24 hours in one ___.
5. There are seven days in one ___.
6. In British English, a period of two weeks is called a ___.
7. There are about four weeks in one ___.
8. A three-month period (spring, summer, fall, or winter) is called a ___.
9. There are twelve months in one ___.
10. A period of ten years is called a ___.
11. There are one hundred years in one ___.
12. A period of one thousand years is called a ___.

Transportation Verbs

1. To get where you are going is to ___.
2. To leave or set off is to ___
3. To get off a boat or an airplane is to ___
4. To go by car is to ___
5. To leave the ground in an airplane is to ___
6. To come back to the ground in an airplane is to ___
7. To go somewhere by boat is to ___
8. To pull another boat or car behind yours is to ___
9. To go by plane or helicopter is to ___
10. To go by bus, train, bike or horse is to ___

What Vegetable?

1. ___ are also known as a love apple, is red and juicy and is strictly speaking a fruit.
2. ___ is made into flakes for breakfast cereals, is yellow on the inside and covered with green leaves.
3. ___ are made into lanterns on Halloween and into pie on Thanksgiving?
4. ___ is famous for giving Popeye his strength?
5. ___ are loved by Bugs Bunny and are good for your eye.
6. ___ are used in Russia and Eastern Europe to make a famous red soup called Borsch?
7. ___ are made into chips in the U.K. and into French fries in the USA?
8. Broad, runner, navy, soy, and lima are all varieties of ___.
9. ___ is said to keep vampires away (and most other people too!).
10. ___ come is many colors and different strengths of hotness?

What's the Category

1. shirt, coat, socks, tie
2. pigeon, parakeet, hawk, sparrow
3. teacher, taxi driver, lawyer, doctor
4. bee, ant, ladybug, dragonfly
5. car, bus, motorcycle, train
6. carnation, tulip, rose, daisy
7. trout, bass, tuna, sardine
8. dog, cat, mouse, bear
9. summer, fall, winter, spring
10. boots, slippers, thongs, sandals
11. tomato, eggplant, pepper, corn
12. maple, oak, palm, orange
13. bread, potatoes, apples, pie
14. orange, banana, peach, lemon
15. water, cola, gasoline, beer
16. rye, oats, barley, wheat
17. uncle, aunt, cousin, grandmother
18. one, ten, twenty, twelve
19. baseball, basketball, tennis, soccer
20. rain, snow, hail, sunshine
21. Tokyo, New York, London, Paris
22. Peru, South Africa, Korea, Canada

Which Word is Different?

1. elephant, dog, tiger, cow, snake
2. strawberry, raspberry, blueberry, peach
3. soccer, wrestling, baseball, ping pong
4. man, policeman, fireman, teacher, nurse
5. China, England, Rome, Peru, Germany
6. celery, lettuce, pineapple, egg plant, potato
7. Sally, Ruth, Tom, Mary, Susan
8. bread, tea, coffee, milk, juice
9. airplane, bird, rocket, cat, jet
10. shirt, bag, pants, tie, hat

Word Groups 1
What group do the words belong to?

1. 1, 3, 5, 7
2. Shakespeare, John Steinbeck, Charles Dickens, John Grisham
3. Bach, Mozart, Tchaikovsky, Beethoven
4. square, circle, diamond, heart
5. Susan, Mary, Ann, Beth
6. onion, radish, spinach, turnip
7. pitcher, catcher, third baseman, outfielder
8. London, Manchester, Liverpool, Birmingham
9. Washington, Bush, Lincoln, Reagan
10. Alpha, Beta, Gamma, Delta

Miscellaneous

Word Groups 2
What group do the words belong to?

1. 2, 4, 6, 8
2. New York, Alabama, Ohio, New Jersey
3. car, train, bus, airplane
4. Swiss, American, British, French
5. hamburgers, hot dogs, potato chips, pizza
6. Tom, Fred, Bill, Steven
7. ring, necklace, earrings, bracelet
8. Honda, Ford, Rover, Toyota
9. Yesterday, A Hard Day's Night, Let It Be, Michelle
10. heart, liver, brain, kidneys

Word Groups 3
What group do the words belong to?

1. doctor, dentist, teacher, actor
2. Fuji, Everest, Matterhorn, K2
3. Chad, Kenya, Nigeria, Mozambique
4. slippers, sneakers, shoes, sandals
5. lipstick, mascara, foundation, eye shadow
6. franc, dollar, pound, yen
7. Mickey Mouse, Tom and Jerry, Bugs Bunny, Beavis and Butthead
8. Goldfinger, From Russia with Love, The Man with the Golden Gun,
9. Canberra, Melbourne, Cains, Sydney
10. strawberry, chocolate, coffee, rum and raisin

Word Groups 4
What group do the words belong to?

1. V, X, M, C
2. Chanel, Gucci, Dior, Armani
3. Africa, Europe, Asia, America
4. ostrich, seagull, penguin, flamingo
5. math, French, geography, biology
6. husky, labrador, boxer, collie
7. Tokyo, Canberra, Rome, Dublin
8. chick, puppy, kitten, lamb
9. Seoul, Tokyo, Los Angeles, Atlanta

Word Groups 5
What group do the words belong to?

1. rose, daisy, daffodil, lily
2. Pyramids, Sphinx, Nile, Cairo
3. Sean Connery, Roger Moore, Pierces Brosnan
4. diamond, ruby, emerald, jade
5. stop signal, London buses, United Kingdom post boxes, tomato
6. rainy, sunny, cloudy, snowy
7. Yankees, Mets, Giants, Dodgers
8. Mickey Mantle, Carl Lewis, Ed Moses, Linford Cristie
9. happy, sad, angry, scared

Word Relationships

1. arm : hand - leg : ___
2. beautiful : beauty - young : ___
3. swim : swimming - walk : ___
4. baseball : bat - tennis : ___
5. dog : dogs - woman : ___
6. America : American - Japan ___
7. man : boy - woman : ___
8. I : my - you ___
9. stomachache : doctor - toothache : ___
10. drive : drove - eat : ___
11. daughter : aunt - son : ___
12. pencil : write - gun : ___
13. big : bigger - important : ___
14. one : two - first : ___
15. yesterday : the day before yesterday - last month : ___

Miscellaneous

PART B. SYNONYMS — TEST MASTER

Find the synonym of the following words written in capitals.

1. It was the voice of a born ORATOR.
   A) addressee B) speaker C) talker
   D) order E) chatter box

2. Boxing was his PROFESSION, people came and paid money to see the fight.
   A) subject B) wish C) trade
   D) life E) interest

3. There was something CRUEL in his voice.
   A) strange B) severe C) funny
   D) fresh E) worry

4. One of the novels by Jack London was "Martin Eden", in which the writer DESCRIBED his life.
   A) printed B) depicted C) pointed out
   D) noticed E) touched upon

5. The whole excursion took APPROXIMATELY ten hours
   A) exactly B) about C) precisely
   D) apparently E) respectively

6. All the local residents spent that AWFUL night in a school.
   A) awkward B) average C) terrible
   D) insignificant E) authentic

7. The man was staring at him, and the boy began to TREMBLE.
   A) find B) move C) shiver
   D) share E) escape

8. The restaurant was SUPERB, and the prices were very low, we enjoyed our holidays.
   A) superficial B) excellent C) superior
   D) supersonic E) expensive

9. Airline business is INCREASING nowadays.
   A) enlarging B) consuming C) ratifying
   D) consenting E) investing

10. At last things began to IMPROVE.
    A) injure B) get better C) become worse
    D) collect E) change

11. Everybody PROTESTED to be examined again.
    A) were for B) were against C) were after
    D) were before E) were like

12. Small children sometimes FEAR the dark.
    A) are afraid of B) are terrible C) are angry
    D) are in love E) are fond

13. She thought that he was BRAVE.
    A) coward B) courageous C) strong
    D) quiet E) powerful

14. The great Russian poet Pushkin was a REMARKABLE man.
    A) careless B) clever C) hard
    D) kind E) extraordinary

15. The time will come, no doubt, when a man will BE ALLOWED to be very angry only on special days.
    A) be passed B) be settled C) be permitted
    D) be taken E) be given

16. I want you to accept the invitation of your English DOCTOR friend.
    A) boy B) physician C) physicist
    D) girl E) doctrine

17. You've made 2 BAD MISTAKES in your test.
    A) wrong things B) blunders C) an error
    D) misprints E) slips of the tongue

18. When I met my friend she WAS VERY ANXIOUS about something.
    A) took care of B) was troubled C) got angry
    D) looked for E) was glad

19. She was AWFULLY sorry for her.
    A) respectfully B) politely C) terribly
    D) cordially E) correctly

20. Don't paint IN A HURRY.
    A) exactly B) irritably C) hastily
    D) specially E) really

21. An old man was their CONSTANT buyer.
    A) popular B) capable C) clever
    D) permanent E) attentive

22. GRADUALLY that illness had broken me down.
    A) steps B) inch by inch C) now and then
    D) little by little E) time after time

23. The achievements of science and technology of recent years have influenced the CAREERS of many people.
    A) marketing B) trading C) professions
    D) hands E) works

24. Somebody TAPPED ON the door at night.
    A) knocked at B) closed C) looked through
    D) came up E) took care of

25. When the police arrived the thieves TOOK TO FLIGHT leaving all the stolen things behind.
    A) ran away B) take away C) did away
    D) got up E) climbed on

26. Please, you are so nervous, do try to CONTAIN your anger.
    A) hold back B) consume C) contact
    D) consult E) come back

27. It's high time for the child TO GO TO BYE-BYES.
    A) to say good bye B) to play with toys
    C) to go to sleep D) to part with his parents
    E) to see his friends off

28. I wonder how many similar days I should BE FORCED to spend there.
    A) be heard B) be sent C) be made
    D) be continued E) be rich

29. Shakespeare is sometimes called the BARD-of-the middle age.
    A) poet B) writer C) poem
    D) banner E) song

30. After Columbus's first voyage in 1492, the news of his DISCOVERY spread across Europe.
    A) death B) treason C) exploration
    D) recovery E) victory

31. The Endeavour ANCHORED in a wide bay to take water and food.
    A) sailed B) started C) was seen
    D) was on fire E) attached

32. Columbus was CONVINCED that the earth was round.
    A) reluctant B) happy C) hesitant
    D) assured E) told

33. The Greeks and other ancient Mediterranean people thought that the earth was FLAT.
    A) unlimited B) oval C) plane
    D) bumpy E) round

34. Arbuthnot's work is HARDLY ever real today, but, J.Bull, whom he created, is very much alive.
    A) barely B) always C) constantly
    D) happily E) cheerfully

35. John Bull, the nickname for the English nation, was INVENTED by a Scotsman, John Arbuthnot.
    A) made up   B) given up   C) borrowed
    D) shared   E) removed

36. Don't try to BUTTER me. This trick of yours won't work with me.
    A) spread   B) flatter   C) press
    D) ban   E) frighten

37. The company asked for ADDITIONAL information.
    A) emphatic   B) careful   C) certain
    D) further   E) unusual

38. The traffic rules must be OBSERVED by everybody.
    A) seen   B) heard   C) followed
    D) taken   E) learnt

39. Children need some RELAXATION after all those hard exams.
    A) vacation   B) holidays   C) time
    D) period   E) rest

40. -Who's that man you spoke to just now?
    -I don't know, he is completely UNFAMILIAR to me.
    A) foreign   B) strange   C) unknown
    D) new   E) for

41. Grey's going TO GET a splendid job.
    A) to go   B) to put   C) to obtain
    D) to receive E) to win

42. He is a person who understands his OBLIGATIONS and attends to them.
    A) restrictions   B) annoyances   C) observations
    D) hardship   E) duties

43. Mount Cook, THE CROWN of the New Zealand Southern Alps, rises to 3756 meters above the surface.
    A) summit   B) foot   C) beauty
    D) rock   E) earth

44. He was PUT TO DEATH 2 days go.
    A) released   B) left   C) executed
    D) found   E) disappeared

45. What EXCUSE have you got this time?
    A) matter   B) problem   C) factor
    D) reason   E) explanation

46. The professor's INTRODUCTORY remarks concerned the development of culture in that region.
    A) preliminary   B) final   C) next
    D) supplementary E) useful

47. The captain of the ship LEFT his town.
    A) abandoned   B) sought   C) visited
    D) looked for E) left for

48. When I opened the box at home I FOUND that the shoes were not mine.
    A) talked   B) sent   C) recognized
    D) discovered E) called

49. I offered him a cup of coffee, which he REFUSED politely.
    A) rejected   B) took   C) gave
    D) finished   E) obtained

50. It was a lucky CHANCE that he could do it.
    A) business   B) opportunity   C) matter
    D) manager   E) pension

51. I want a set of books for someone who is KEEN ON reading.
    A) severe on   B) quick at   C) fond of
    D) sharp at   E) afraid of

52. In Sydney, William Westwood was turned over to a cruel settler as AN UNPAID laborer.
    A) a paid   B) a free   C) an illegal
    D) an unnoticed E) a permanent

53. Our classmates often take part in different sport COMPETITIONS.
    A) events   B) races   C) meetings
    D) news   E) things

54. A SMOOTHFACED man of forty faced me.
    A) graceful   B) shaven   C) beautiful
    D) famous   E) handsome

55. He carried a BUNCH of flowers in his hands.
    A) bouquet   B) bundle   C) packet
    D) bucket   E) flock

56. Tom is an INDUSTRIOUS boy.
    A) hard working   B) gracious   C) graceful
    D) huge   E) lazy

57. Oh, my dear! I'll be back BEFORE YOU SAY JOHN ROBINSON.
    A) in an hour   B) hardly   C) very soon
    D) at sunset   E) in some time

58. What DIARY PRODUCTS do you like to eat?
    A) creamery   B) meals   C) animal
    D) first course E) desserts

59. Puppies lived in a DOG-HOUSE.
    A) kennel   B) barn   C) cave
    D) box   E) garage

60. The tickets to the theatre will be booked IN ADVANCE.
    A) later   B) soon   C) the next day
    D) earlier E) beforehand

61. I have no idea where the relatives on my father's side live, LET ALONE visiting them.
    A) not a single   B) leave alone   C) only one of
    D) not speaking of E) lonely one

62. Vasco da Gama was a Portuguese EXPLORER born around 1460.
    A) traveler   B) scientist   C) king
    D) ruler   E) conqueror

63. The Vikings liked to make up long tales about their BRAVE deeds.
    A) timid   B) fearless   C) past
    D) strong   E) stupid

64. The daily performance was killingly DULL.
    A) unforgettable   B) dutiful   C) dynamic
    D) boring   E) bright

65. Doctor Manson CURED a lot of miners that's why he won great popularity and respect with them.
    A) treated   B) recovered   C) gave
    D) took   E) rescued

66. Australian aborigines are dark skinned people whose DESCENDANTS came to the continent from Asia about 25,000 years ago.
    A) predecessors   B) relatives   C) offsprings
    D) colonists   E) supporters

67. I LIKE collecting stamps.
    A) am ill   B) am good at   C) am fond of
    D) am afraid of   E) am proud of

68. I am a BIG FISH IN A SMALL COMPANY.
    A) to be important in a big company
    B) to be respected everywhere
    C) to be important in a small company
    D) to be estimated everywhere
    E) not to be important in a small company

69. Nobody believed his VOW because it wasn't for the first time.
    A) belief   B) idea   C) view
    D) oath   E) opinion

70. The first colonists from England made new homes and began TO WIDEN industrial towns.
    A) establish   B) waste   C) broaden
    D) burden   E) steal

Synonyms

71. He STUDIED the document for a long time.
    A) read carefully   B) taught   C) looked at
    D) examined carefully   E) looked through

72. Did you manage to stop the FIGHT between those two boys?
    A) show   B) stage   C) picture
    D) talk   E) struggle

73. The woman adds water to UNITE the flour and the milk.
    A) connect   B) make   C) join
    D) complex   E) combine

74. I can call back the faint ODORS of the wild flowers.
    A) orders   B) ado   C) fits
    D) harmony   E) fragrances

75. If the shops were not so CROWDED, the clerks would not be so tireD)
    A) cold   B) full   C) old
    D) fresh   E) fast

76. Her interest in people and other animals was warm, personal and FRIENDLY.
    A) cordial   B) antagonistic   C) harmful
    D) cool   E) hostile

77. A dolphin asks for HELP.
    A) assistance   B) assistant   C) support
    D) provision   E) sponsor

78. Edison's idea was TO CHECK the mistakes of his son.
    A) to rise   B) to develop   C) to verify
    D) to close   E) to renew

Find the synonym of the following words.

79. Important
    A) complex   B) secondary   C) detailed   D) significant

80. Stubborn
    A) shy   B) obstinate   C) pliable   D) yielding

81. Accustomed
    A) flexible   B) limp   C) stiff   D) used to

82. Stare
    A) peep   B) pry   C) gaze   D) pause

83. Overdue
    A) impending   B) punctual   C) prompt   D) delayed

84. Keen
    A) slow   B) enthusiastic   C) reluctant   D) apathetic

85. Duty
    A) obligation   B) shade   C) period   D) native

86. Shorten
    A) shrink   B) thrust   C) fling   D) shove

87. Firm
    A) soft   B) solid   C) uneven   D) loose

88. Rubbish
    A) scrap   B) crump   C) stone   D) litter

89. Peril
    A) danger   B) secure   C) hole   D) safe

90. Flush
    A) bruise   B) blush   C) rush   D) brush

91. Bring round
    A) persuade   B) bring back   C) bring on   D) bring down

92. Bring forward
    A) bring down   B) bring up   C) bring round   D) suggest

93. Unattended
    A) sluggish   B) heedless   C) alone   D) empty

94. Group
    A) parcel   B) party   C) package   D) present

95. Task
    A) lead   B) donation   C) summit   D) mission

96. Peak
    A) bottom   B) summit   C) rear   D) front

97. Bump
    A) jolt   B) piece   C) lump   D) handle

98. Command
    A) urge   B) force   C) order   D) seize

99. Enterprise
    A) hospitality   B) immunity   C) imagination   D) undertaking

100. Resident
    A) confident   B) hesitant   C) incident   D) inhabitant

101. Identify
    A) bump   B) throw in   C) catch   D) recognize

102. Beg
    A) predict   B) implore   C) guess   D) oblige

103. Spell
    A) native   B) period   C) shade   D) obligation

104. Delight
    A) sadness   B) joy   C) calmness   D) gloom

105. Genuine
    A) fake   B) counterfeit   C) false   D) authentic

106. Damage
    A) mend   B) fix   C) incite   D) ravage

107. Use up
    A) consume   B) stack   C) draw up   D) put by

108. Behavior
    A) business   B) conduct   C) connection   D) container

109. Stationary
    A) stationery   B) portable   C) mobile   D) still

110. Walk over
    A) wash up   B) defeat   C) keep away   D) waver

111. Praise
    A) blame   B) commend   C) censure   D) criticize

112. Mystery
    A) coherent   B) enigma   C) curious   D) reverse

113. Stop
    A) cease   B) eliminate   C) commence   D) commend

114. Respect
    A) esteem   B) belief   C) scorn   D) contempt

115. Splendid
    A) terrible   B) dreadful   C) awful   D) marvelous

116. Exhausted
    A) anxious   B) worn-out   C) cheerful   D) vigorous

117. Sway
    A) river   B) shudder   C) ruin   D) swing

118. Widespread
    A) Infrequent   B) scarce   C) prevalent   D) rare

Synonyms

119. Defect
    A) advantage   B) clash   C) decay   D) drawback
120. Force
    A) oblige   B) eliminate   C) halt   D) liberate
121. Talkative
    A) Know-all   B) scrupulous   C) chatty   D) fastidious
122. Precious
    A) Enormous   B) vigorous   C) gorgeous   D) valuable
123. Profession
    A) celebration   B) restoration   C) attention   D) occupation
124. Contrary
    A) customary   B) conflict   C) common   D) opposite
125. Unpredictable
    A) constant   B) steady   C) dense   D) volatile
126. Row
    A) contest   B) argument   C) chat   D) quiz
127. Hug
    A) embrace   B) push   C) stab   D) poke
128. Ban
    A) prohibit   B) produce   C) create   D) happen
129. Sign
    A) truth   B) trace   C) truce   D) trunk
130. Brag
    A) enrage   B) boast   C) madden   D) infuriate
131. Disagreement
    A) poise   B) conflict   C) harmony   D) stamina
132. Enormous
    A) tidy   B) shoddy   C) mini   D) huge
133. Hang on
    A) rely on   B) hold on   C) keep on   D) count on
134. Take away
    A) spread   B) distribute   C) hand over   D) remove
135. Outcome
    A) arrival   B) exit   C) result   D) commence
136. Sufficient
    A) fake   B) unreal   C) adequate   D) rare
137. Maintenance
    A) heritage   B) racket   C) alimony   D) extortion
138. Material
    A) supervision   B) substance   C) superstition   D) surface
139. Run down
    A) turn over   B) run over   C) find out   D) criticize
140. Fling
    A) let in   B) hold   C) hurl   D) seize
141. Temporary
    A) provisional   B) permanent   C) constant   D) enduring
142. Go off
    A) spoil   B) break   C) clear up   D) rest
143. Remedy
    A) gift   B) argument   C) reward   D) cure
144. Seldom
    A) rarely   B) frequently   C) regularly   D) often
145. Ban
    A) produce   B) prohibit   C) create   D) happen
146. Raw
    A) rotten   B) tough   C) moldy   D) uncooked
147. Lucrative
    A) crucial   B) fragile   C) profitable   D) decisive
148. Discover
    A) carry out   B) sort out   C) find out   D) bring out
149. Simply
    A) merely   B) actually   C) usually   D) frequently
150. Classify
    A) tie up   B) sort out   C) stir up   D) tear up
151. Devious
    A) scornful   B) liberal   C) honest   D) crooked
152. Stress
    A) omit   B) emphasize   C) leave out   D) ignore
153. Contaminate
    A) renovate   B) mend   C) purify   D) pollute
154. Timetable
    A) scheme   B) plot   C) schedule   D) minutes
155. Slowly
    A) briefly   B) gradually   C) deeply   D) mainly
156. Harm
    A) Peril   B) trouble   C) damage   D) rush
157. Incidentally
    A) far away   B) in any case   C) by the way   D) in my opinion
158. Summit
    A) rear   B) bottom   C) peak   D) front
159. Skin
    A) peel   B) pip   C) seed   D) stone
160. Walk out
    A) leave   B) lay out   C) work out   D) burst out
161. Glimmer
    A) darken   B) shimmer   C) slit   D) shelter
162. Goods
    A) legacy   B) heritage   C) possessions   D) patrimony

Synonyms

ANTONYMS TEST MASTER

Find the antonym of the following words written in capitals:

1. He was an HONEST man.
   A) liar   B) good   C) bad
   D) truthful E) wonderful

2. The climate of Great Britain is MILD.
   A) difficult B) strong   C) severe
   D) bad   E) good

3. She was afraid to walk FARTHER as she knew her life was in danger.
   A) mother   B) out near C) near
   D) nearer   E) away

4. If you know one FOREIGN language it will be easier for you to learn the second one.
   A) local   B) modern   C) popular
   D) old   E) native

5. Tom's father was a CRUEL man.
   A) honest   B) kind   C) funny
   D) serious   E) light

6. It seemed to her that he was very DECENT.
   A) dishonest B) be tired of C) fat
   D) handsome E) unhealthy

7. I opened the door and saw a DECEASED man.
   A) weak   B) sick   C) invisible
   D) new born E) old

8. Tom is very LAZY. He doesn't like to do anything.
   A) modest   B) modern   C) clever
   D) energetic E) nervous

9. My sister is very SERIOUS.
   A) energetic B) polite   C) kind
   D) intelligent E) light-minded

10. Mr. Brown decided TO PROTECT that young man.
    A) to help B) to accuse C) to care
    D) to shout E) to criticize

11. He lives A LONG WAY FROM his school.
    A) far   B) near   C) late
    D) behind   E) in front of

12. Such trees grow only in the countries the climate of which is hot and DAMP.
    A) cold   B) cool   C) dry
    D) sunny   E) windy

13. The boy was PUNISHED and he couldn't go to play with his friends.
    A) encouraged B) beaten C) defended
    D) invited   E) overcome

14. In the 18th century England SEIZED many colonies in the old and new word.
    A) captured B) freed   C) occupied
    D) lost   E) gained

15. Father said that he could STAY AT home and work in the garden.
    A) leave   B) live   C) be
    D) leave for E) go into

16. At present all kinds of specialists need FOREIGN languages for their work.
    A) old   B) different C) native
    D) several E) many

17. I wish you PROSPERITY.
    A) success B) good luck C) happiness
    D) poverty E) riches

18. She was quite ALONE among them.
    A) single   B) only   C) adapted
    D) distant E) separate

19. The FOREIGNERS were very amused when they saw this palace.
    A) guests   B) farmers   C) natives
    D) neighbors E) reporters

20. Emily was in BAD temper.
    A) large   B) great   C) excellent
    D) narrow   E) miserable

21. The day before yesterday I WENT TO SEE my sick grandmother.
    A) came in B) visited   C) left
    D) called on E) invited

22. Her character is very MILD.
    A) gentle   B) angry   C) difficult
    D) rude   E) bad

23. The British seem to like their weather as it is ISLAND weather.
    A) isolated B) light   C) mild
    D) difficult E) continental

24. I think it is a LEGAL party as it has been functioning for a long time.
    A) lawful   B) possible C) illegal
    D) illiterate E) important

25. My mother was a KIND person.
    A) cruel   B) good-natured C) nice
    D) bad   E) merry

26. About one million Welshmen still speak NATIVE language.
    A) original B) natural   C) folk
    D) other   E) foreign

27. MODERN factories have sprung up around the city.
    A) small   B) new   C) out of date
    D) fresh   E) bad

28. The Welsh ARE FULL OF idealism and good humor.
    A) complete B) whole   C) weak
    D) lack   E) empty

29. When he was nine, he ENTERED the gymnasium and became an excellent student.
    A) finished B) got   C) went away
    D) came   E) completed

30. She likes GETTING letters but dislikes writing them.
    A) receiving B) taking   C) sending
    D) reading   E) finding

31. There are many ANCIENT cities in Turkey.
    A) big   B) old   C) fashionable
    D) modern   E) beautiful

32. There's a DEEP lake between these two villages.
    A) shallow B) charming C) good-looking
    D) handsome E) unpleasant

33. Our traditions are very ANCIENT and our people are proud of them.
    A) present B) old   C) modern
    D) real   E) young

34. I didn't know she was so LEARNED.
    A) well read B) bookish C) accomplished
    D) plain   E) ignorant

35. One day my brother told the story to one of his FRIENDS.
    A) advisers B) enemies   C) assistants
    D) backers E) patrons

36. Nobody knew he was leaving the country; only Anne knew the TRUTH.
    A) loyalty B) honor   C) belief
    D) lie   E) light

37. Why did they TURN him OUT?
    A) dismiss B) employ   C) refuse
    D) free   E) examine

38. This is a SHARP knife.
    A) new   B) slow   C) blue
    D) dull   E) old

39. The train LEAVES ON TIME.
    A) is late B) is slow   C) is fast
    D) express train E) is before time

40. Tom DUG OUT his money and ran away.
    A) burned   B) broke   C) forgot
    D) carried E) buried

41. I'm sorry to trouble you, but could you LEND me some sugar?
    A) take   B) borrow   C) land
    D) buy   E) show

Antonyms

42. Is service INCLUDED?
    A) involved   B) embraced   C) urged
    D) excluded   E) improved

43. You spoke very RUDELY to him.
    A) slowly   B) politely   C) quickly
    D) warmly   E) sharply

44. I told him about my plan and he at once AGREED.
    A) adored   B) admitted   C) affected
    D) rejected   E) appointed

45. At first he HESITATED but we insisted on his telling the truth.
    A) was in two minds   B) was sure   C) was surprised
    D) was glad   E) was offended

46. The number of champions in Russia is INCREASING from day to day.
    A) improving   B) decreasing   C) raising
    D) brightening   E) widening

47. During his long voyage Darwin studied DIFFERENT plants and animals in all parts of the world.
    A) various   B) all kinds of C) strange
    D) identical   E) other

48. - Mother what is a FATHERLAND; is it the land belonging to my father?
    - Oh, no honey, it is the land of your birth.
    A) powerful state   B) government   C) native country
    D) settlement   E) father's land

49. They ACCEPTED the invitation.
    A) accused   B) admitted   C) refused
    D) invited   E) consented

50. Everything, INCLUDING herself, was black and white.
    A) comprising   B) embracing   C) entering
    D) excluding   E) stimulating

51. I heard him speaking but was too tired to listen to him and CONCENTRATE.
    A) solve   B) relax   C) release
    D) rebuild   E) resign

52. He was rather RUDE to me last night.
    A) savage   B) brutal   C) violent
    D) polite   E) ruthless

53. They always go to school TOGETHER.
    A) with each other   B) separately   C) altogether
    D) common   E) themselves

54. "Get me out of this", was the FEEBLE reply.
    A) wise   B) polite   C) strong
    D) weak   E) useful

55. Mr. Mott LANDED at Harwich an hour ahead of the expedition ship in the ship's helicopter.
    A) grounded   B) took off   C) put down
    D) speeded   E) lacked

56. My friend stopped his car and asked me to HOP IN.
    A) jump in   B) get out   C) give in
    D) take from   E) keep out

57. It is said that a large army of young Canadians LONGS FOR knowledge, but it is not easy to obtain it with the heavy cost of education.
    A) dislikes   B) desires   C) craves
    D) looks for   E) achieves

58. Many believed that Marlborough, the English commander, was simply PROLONGING the war for his own profit and glory.
    A) shortening   B) continuing   C) extending
    D) supporting   E) denying

59. John Bull was described as a man of the gentleman farmer type, good natured, but easily OFFENDED.
    A) hurt   B) insulted   C) sick
    D) understood   E) pleased

60. Rescue workers PULLED a man, and two children FROM this cold, rushing water.
    A) saved from   B) took out   C) pushed into
    D) removed from E) lifted up

61. I hope we get home before SUNSET.
    A) sunshine   B) sunrise   C) sunshade
    D) sunburst   E) sunbeam

62. I spent all my money on a new pair of boots. I understand it was FOOLISH but I couldn't stop myself from doing it.
    A) nice   B) pleasant   C) realistic
    D) clever   E) easy

63. The milk is delivered about 6 A.M so we have FRESH milk for breakfast.
    A) old   B) sound   C) specific
    D) dirty   E) sour

64. His work was NOT INTERESTING.
    A) dull   B) bright   C) troublesome
    D) full   E) difficult

65. "Yes, yes!", she CRIED. "I understand you don't love me"
    A) shouted   B) asked   C) wondered
    D) whispered   E) answered

66. Can you tell me how to get to the PUBLIC Library?
    A) national   B) wide   C) common
    D) mutual   E) private

67. All of the foreign members are OUTSTANDING people.
    A) prominent   B) exceptional   C) ordinary
    D) proud   E) educated

68. His brother was a BRAVE soldier.
    A) courageous   B) coward   C) heartless
    D) clever   E) noble

69. The INVISIBLE Man tells Dr. Camps about his adventures.
    A) Blind   B) Noisy   C) Strange
    D) Visible   E) Famous

70. He WENT ON smoking, though I asked him.
    A) stopped   B) started   C) liked
    D) kept on   E) continued

71. A great many people participated in the OPENING of the conference.
    A) closure   B) beginning   C) failure
    D) discussion   E) permission

72. The Thames is a short river but it is wide and DEEP.
    A) small   B) shallow   C) long
    D) great   E) big

73. Having PASSED his exams he began to look for a job.
    A) taken   B) failed in   C) sun burnt
    D) fought   E) proved

74. She was ACCEPTED as secretary for an American Company.
    A) accused   B) accomplished C) acquired
    D) announced   E) rejected

75. Percy Dixon's face turned RED with anger.
    A) mad   B) black   C) ashamed
    D) tortured   E) pale

76. All the students INCLUDING Duncan will take part in coming football match.
    A) from   B) besides   C) except
    D) within   E) with

77. Money which is spent on education and health now is an investment for the FUTURE.
    A) tuition   B) present   C) delight
    D) past   E) world

78. His parents were DIVORCED before his birth.
    A) engaged   B) married   C) accused
    D) accustomed   E) used

79. His parents were very RELIGIOUS and the boy had to sing at church services.
    A) devoted   B) faithful   C) reluctant
    D) atheistic   E) competent

80. The airport is A LONG WAY FROM the centre of the city.
    A) far from   B) not far from C) in the distance
    D) remote   E) distant

Antonyms

Find the antonym of the following words:

81. Blunt
    A) dismal   B) sharp   C) sullen   D) dull
82. Prohibit
    A) permit   B) forbid   C) ban   D) prevent
83. Shove
    A) press   B) drag   C) move   D) thrust
84. Compulsory
    A) optional   B) essential   C) obligatory   D) necessary
85. Profit
    A) toss   B) benefit   C) gain   D) loss
86. Liberate
    A) rescue   B) confine   C) deliver   D) divorce
87. Stiff
    A) hard   B) rigid   C) limp   D) firm
88. Barren
    A) fertile   B) dry   C) arid   D) fruitless
89. Tough
    A) hard   B) tender   C) cruel   D) violent
90. Rebel
    A) mutiny   B) suppress   C) fight   D) rise up
91. Kick off
    A) steer   B) conclude   C) commence   D) start
92. Innocent
    A) criminal   B) patient   C) naive   D) persistent
93. Fine
    A) lank   B) skinny   C) thick   D) slim
94. Tug
    A) drag   B) draw   C) jerk   D) thrust
95. Agitate
    A) sooth   B) stir up   C) poke   D) provoke
96. On purpose
    A) permanently   B) crucially   C) intentionally   D) inadvertently
97. Trivial
    A) everyday   B) significant   C) worthless   D) minor
98. Sparse
    A) rough   B) scanty   C) rare   D) dense
99. Dismiss
    A) sack   B) discharge   C) appoint   D) fire
100. Do up
    A) tie   B) bind   C) loosen   D) fasten
101. Immense
    A) tight   B) tiny   C) enormous   D) huge
102. Wholesale
    A) mortgage   B) pawn   C) retail   D) barter
103. Overcast
    A) muddy   B) misty   C) level   D) clear
104. Take on
    A) sack   B) convey   C) release   D) shift
105. Thorough
    A) crooked   B) careless   C) dejected   D) cheerful
106. Oppose
    A) combat   B) resist   C) support   D) fight
107. Neglect
    A) care   B) reflect   C) overlook   D) dare
108. Rise up
    A) run down   B) shut down   C) break down   D) put down
109. Absurd
    A) silly   B) foolish   C) ridiculous   D) sensible
110. Flimsy
    A) strong   B) evil   C) weak   D) minute
111. Abbreviate
    A) lengthen   B) shorten   C) reduce   D) cut
112. Consume
    A) hoard   B) use up   C) sell   D) exhaust
113. Marvelous
    A) splendid   B) awful   C) wonderful   D) magnificent
114. Smooth
    A) reckless   B) savage   C) solid   D) rough
115. Certain
    A) doubtful   B) generous   C) hazardous   D) tedious
116. Conceal
    A) hide   B) dream   C) ban   D) exhibit
117. Retain
    A) engage   B) block   C) hinder   D) release
118. Poverty
    A) wealth   B) lack   C) need   D) destitution
119. Deliberate
    A) accidental   B) planned   C) calculated   D) intentional
120. Sadness
    A) sorrow   B) glee   C) depression   D) bleakness
121. Sober
    A) drunk   B) cheeky   C) solemn   D) moderate
122. Vacant
    A) obscure   B) occupied   C) worthless   D) bright
123. Modest
    A) humble   B) big-headed   C) passionate   D) fussy
124. Vague
    A) indefinite   B) distinct   C) uncertain   D) obscure
125. Miserable
    A) Gloomy   B) competitive   C) sorrowful   D) joyful
126. Ally
    A) adversary   B) partner   C) friend   D) associate
127. Stingy
    A) rude   B) generous   C) gaunt   D) ignorant
128. Adjacent
    A) apart   B) void   C) bleak   D) blank
129. Flat
    A) icy   B) even   C) bumpy   D) slippery
130. Impartial
    A) fair   B) dishonest   C) wicked   D) biased
131. Put down
    A) patronize   B) celebrate   C) commend   D) refuse
132. Tame
    A) docile   B) mild   C) wild   D) primitive
133. Curious
    A) furious   B) indifferent   C) decisive   D) determined
134. Offensive
    A) boring   B) pleasing   C) disgusting   D) revolting
135. Generous
    A) eager   B) clumsy   C) clever   D) mean
136. Arrogant
    A) modest   B) ignorant   C) rude   D) illiterate
137. Chubby
    A) stout   B) fat   C) skinny   D) gross

Antonyms

THE LOGIC LIST — TEST MASTER

Find the word which is out of the logic list:

1. A) scour B) voyage C) trip D) journey
2. A) resign B) step down C) quit D) swap
3. A) scatter B) squash C) crush D) squeeze
4. A) thick B) enormous C) immense D) huge
5. A) drought B) harvest C) mow D) crop
6. A) rescue B) slaughter C) kill D) murder
7. A) suggest B) reiterate C) advice D) recommend
8. A) soup B) chop C) mince D) steak
9. A) choice B) prediction C) decision D) preference
10. A) hold over B) slate C) run down D) slag off
11. A) nude B) bare C) bashful D) unclothed
12. A) proficient B) clumsy C) skilful D) expert
13. A) shortage B) riches C) wealth D) affluence
14. A) battle B) fight C) settlement D) combat
15. A) wealthy B) penniless C) broke D) needy
16. A) conclude B) question C) ask D) inquire
17. A) entirely B) partly C) quite D) completely
18. A) expect B) await C) disappoint D) wait for
19. A) crease B) wrinkle C) crumple D) smooth
20. A) entire B) accurate C) true D) exact
21. A) imitation B) fake C) genuine D) counterfeit
22. A) screw B) jug C) pliers D) hammer
23. A) success B) feat C) effort D) victory
24. A) laborer B) executive C) administrator D) manager
25. A) enthusiastic B) eager C) reluctant D) zealous
26. A) boycott B) ban C) embargo D) complaint
27. A) shout B) cheer C) clap D) chant
28. A) indifferent B) solemn C) serious D) grave
29. A) touchy B) irritable C) nervous D) weary
30. A) obscurity B) interval C) gap D) space
31. A) in spite of B) owing to C) because of D) caused by
32. A) follow B) track C) interrogate D) purse
33. A) perform B) fail C) achieve D) accomplish
34. A) hail B) sleet C) pond D) drizzle
35. A) question B) conclude C) inquire D) interrogate
36. A) innocent B) lawbreaker C) criminal D) culprit
37. A) acquittal B) accusation C) allegation D) charge
38. A) tired B) injured C) run down D) exhausted
39. A) austere B) moderate C) severe D) harsh
40. A) teapot B) cup C) tap D) kettle
41. A) difficulty B) ease C) impediment D) obstacle
42. A) rob B) smuggle C) strike D) hijack
43. A) hazard B) security C) danger D) jeopardy
44. A) apparent B) obscure C) obvious D) clear
45. A) terminate B) end C) stop D) initiate
46. A) unimportant B) trivial C) vital D) insignificant
47. A) pinch B) swindle C) steal D) whim
48. A) skip B) bounce C) bound D) kneel
49. A) compress B) squeeze C) scatter D) crush
50. A) interest B) profit C) advantage D) confidence
51. A) perfume B) fragrance C) flavor D) odor
52. A) slap B) wave C) point D) wink
53. A) book B) leaflet C) reality show D) journal
54. A) solely B) pack C) heap D) flock
55. A) simply B) only C) regularly D) merely
56. A) thief B) spy C) robber D) burglar
57. A) leave B) join C) quit D) abandon
58. A) kick off B) begin C) reveal D) commence
59. A) skin B) seed C) rind D) shell
60. A) principal B) secondary C) chief D) main
61. A) halt B) hold C) maintain D) retain
62. A) task B) duration C) interval D) term
63. A) brief B) extensive C) short D) summary
64. A) vote B) coalition C) issue D) party
65. A) fair B) unbiased C) impartial D) bigoted
66. A) impress B) astonish C) stun D) astound
67. A) inquire B) question C) conclude D) ask
68. A) entire B) exact C) right D) accurate
69. A) outset B) phase C) step D) period
70. A) open B) candid C) sincere D) arrogant
71. A) plainly B) evidently C) rapidly D) obviously
72. A) shrimp B) lobster C) mussel D) pigeon
73. A) snowy B) minty C) sunny D) cloudy
74. A) beautiful B) shabby C) dainty D) exquisite
75. A) ownership B) place C) position D) locality
76. A) speedy B) rapid C) delayed D) hasty
77. A) forbid B) prohibit C) bewilder D) hinder
78. A) neat B) untidy C) disorderly D) sloppy
79. A) content B) satisfied C) gloomy D) pleased
80. A) chum B) ally C) opponent D) friend
81. A) extreme B) excessive C) rare D) exorbitant
82. A) settlement B) combat C) war D) battle
83. A) chant B) yell C) clap D) shout
84. A) outcome B) consequence C) gap D) result
85. A) hurt B) injure C) damage D) split
86. A) placard B) brochure C) leaflet D) catalogue
87. A) shock B) bewilder C) astonish D) enlighten
88. A) tremble B) quake C) squat D) quiver
89. A) face B) crouch C) come across D) encounter
90. A) hazard B) security C) danger D) peril
91. A) alert B) heedless C) imprudent D) reckless
92. A) stick B) cuddle C) attach D) adhere
93. A) silent B) clamor C) racket D) noise
94. A) decisive B) intelligent C) clever D) bright
95. A) adoration B) report C) explanation D) description
96. A) little B) wide C) tiny D) minute
97. A) sluggish B) watchful C) attentive D) vigilant
98. A) indebted B) fickle C) thankful D) grateful
99. A) parade B) battle C) demonstration D) meeting
100. A) tomb B) cradle C) grave D) cemetery

The Logic List

MISCELLANEOUS

TEST MASTER

Analogies 1 - Find the Appropriate Match

1. Tooth-Dentist, Hair-_____?
2. Pure-Purify, Short-_____?
3. Soccer-Ball, Badminton-_____?
4. Loose-Tight, Deep-_____?
5. Wise-Wisdom, Rough-_____?
6. Big-Bigger, Bad-_____?
7. Polite-Impolite, Responsible-_____?
8. Soccer-Field, Basketball-_____?
9. Help-Helper, Sail-_____?
10. Give-Given, Swell-_____?
11. Actor-Actress, Widower-_____?
12. Dog-Bites, Bee-_____?
13. Feet-Socks, Hands-_____?
14. Cats-Meow, Cows-_____?
15. Doctors-Patients, Teachers-_____?
16. Roof-Roofs, Wolf-_____?
17. Careful-Carefully, Fast-_____?
18. Circle-Round, Triangle-_____?
19. Cat-Kitten, Pig-_____?
20. Hyena-Mammal, Crocodile-_____?

Analogies II - Find the Appropriate Match

1. Sheep-Mutton, Pig-_____?
2. Cow-Calf, Cat-_____?
3. Xing-Crossing, Xmas-_____?
4. Meat-Protein, Cake-_____?
5. Fish-A school of, Hens-_____?
6. Chicory-Bitter, Chocolate-_____?
7. Deprive-Of, Attentive-_____?
8. Hens-Eggs, Cow-_____?
9. Oven-Kitchen, End table-_____?
10. Elbow-Arm, Knee-_____?
11. Pure-Purify, Soft-_____?
12. Decide-Decision, Depart-_____?
13. Datum-Data, Phenomenon-_____?
14. Suitcases-Few, Luggage-_____?
15. Dime-Ten cents, Nickel-_____?
16. Addition-Plus, Subtraction-_____?
17. Wise-Wisely, Hard-_____?
18. Form-Fill out, Tank-_____?
19. 365 days-Year, 366 days-_____?
20. Soap-Bar of, Cigarettes-_____?

Beverages

1. What bitter black drink was invented by the Aztecs, but is now usually served made with milk and sugar?
2. What soft drink is made of water, flavoring and sometimes ice cream and which was traditionally sold at a bar known as a fountain?
3. What drink is usually made from grapes and is classified as red, white or rose?
4. When the wine is distilled and matured it becomes ___
5. What alcoholic drink was originally made in Scotland or Ireland from grain?
6. What drink is served with milk or lemon and is made by pouring boiling water over the leaves?
7. A brown colored, carbonated alcoholic drink.
8. What word is the collective term for any or all alcoholic drinks?
9. What drink is made from the ground beans of a shrub?
10. What drink is made of yoghurt and water?

Business Expressions 1

1. I thought this time things were going to be better. Losing the contract was ___ to swallow.
   A) bottom line   B) blue collar
   C) a bitter pill   D) back to the drawing board
   E) blow-by-blow

2. We've lost the contract thanks to your incompetence. You really ___, didn't you?
   A) back to the drawing board   B) bottlenecks
   C) bottom line   D) blue collar
   E) blew it

3. I'd be better off stopping my legal job and doing jobs for cash. The _____ is the only way to make money these days.
   A) blow-by-blow   B) back to the drawing board
   C) bottlenecks   D) black economy
   E) bottom line

4. The product didn't work in the States. As they say there, it really _____.
   A) back to the drawing board   B) bottlenecks
   C) bombed   D) blow-by-blow
   E) bottom line

5. However, the same product sold really well in England. As they say there, it _____.
   A) back to the drawing board   B) bottlenecks
   C) bottom line   D) blue collar
   E) went like a bomb

6. He used to work on the factory floor. Yes, he really started out as a _____ worker.
   A) blue collar   B) back to the drawing board
   C) bottlenecks   D) bottom line
   E) blow-by-blow

7. There are many reasons why this should be a success. However, the _____ is that it has been a big flop.
   A) bottom line   B) back to the drawing board
   C) bottlenecks   D) blow-by-blow
   E) a bitter pill

8. Production has been unable to keep pace with demand. We are doing our best to eliminate the _____.
   A) blow-by-blow   B) back to the drawing board
   C) blew it   D) a bitter pill
   E) bottlenecks

9. We'll have to start again on this one. It's time to go _____.
   A) blow-by-blow   B) blew it
   C) black economy   D) bombed
   E) back to the drawing board

10. Don't leave out any details. I want a full _____ account of what happened in the meeting.
    A) blow-by-blow   B) blew it
    C) black economy   D) bombed
    E) went like a bomb

Miscellaneous

Business Expressions 2

1. At the start of the meeting everybody was very quiet and reserved but he told a few jokes to _____.
   A) across the board   B) break the ice
   C) broke the news   D) back to the drawing board
   E) take on board

2. He's not very quick on the uptake, it takes him quite a while to _____ new ideas.
   A) on to a good thing   B) take on board
   C) bullish   D) breathing down
   E) brief

3. We're going to have to reduce budgets in every single department. There will be _____ cuts.
   A) back to the drawing board   B) brief
   C) on to a good thing   D) brainstorm
   E) across the board

4. My boss never gives me any freedom. She's always _____ my neck.
   A) broke the news   B) brief
   C) breathing down   D) back to the drawing board
   E) bullish

5. We need a name for our new brand. The best thing is to get a few people together and try to _____ a name.
   A) brief   B) on to a good thing
   C) broke the news   D) bullish
   E) brainstorm

6. I'm very happy with our sales prospects for the next year. I'm feeling really _____.
   A) bullish   B) back to the drawing board
   C) broke the news   D) on to a good thing
   E) brief

7. We would have liked to have looked at that but that wasn't part of the _____ you set us.
   A) brief   B) on to a good thing
   C) back to the drawing board   D) breathing down
   E) broke the news

8. I've heard all about it. Sally _____ to me.
   A) brainstorm   B) on to a good thing
   C) back to the drawing board   D) breathing down
   E) broke the news

9. I'm well aware that this is potentially a good new product and that we are probably _____ with it.
   A) on to a good thing   B) back to the drawing board
   C) brainstorm   D) breathing down
   E) across the board

10. I guess this market study shows that nobody wants to buy our product. It's _____ for us.
    A) back to the drawing board   B) brainstorm
    C) breathing down   D) across the board
    E) take on board

Business Expressions 3

1. I reckon we owe you about the same as you owe us. Why don't we just _____?
   A) call his bluff   B) called it a day
   C) calls the shots   D) chicken
   E) call it quits

2. We've been working on this for fourteen hours now. Isn't it time we _____?
   A) called it a day   B) call it quits
   C) calls the shots   D) chicken
   E) call his bluff

3. Let's face it, he decides. He's the boss so he's the one that _____.
   A) called it a day   B) calls the shots
   C) call it quits   D) chicken
   E) call his bluff

4. He says he will go elsewhere if we don't lower our price but I don't think he will. I think we should _____.
   A) call his bluff   B) call it quits
   C) called it a day   D) calls the shots
   E) chicken

5. I'm sure that there is a lot of corruption in that country. If we order an internal audit we may be opening _____.
   A) carry the can   B) chicken
   C) can't win   D) chicken and egg
   E) a can of worms

6. Someone is going to have to take responsibility for this disaster. Who is going to _____.
   A) can't win   B) carry the can
   C) chicken   D) a can of worms
   E) chicken and egg

7. Whatever we do, we are going to come out badly. It's a _____ situation.
   A) a can of worms   B) carry the can
   C) chicken   D) can't win
   E) chicken and egg

8. She always likes to think things through very carefully. She likes to _____.
   A) chicken and egg   B) chicken
   C) chew things over   D) call his bluff
   E) call it quits

9. We need a loan to start the company and we need a company to get the loan. It's a _____ situation.
   A) calls the shots   B) chew things over
   C) chicken   D) call his bluff
   E) chicken and egg

10. We wanted to expand into Asia but we were a bit frightened. We were soon sorry for being so _____.
    A) chicken and egg   B) chicken
    C) calls the shots   D) chew things over
    E) call it quits

Change the Words
Change the underlined word(s) to a one-word equivalent.

1. In place of a job, he's looking for a course to take.
2. Please go on. This story is very interesting.
3. I'm getting accustomed to coming here all by myself.
4. Last night a train ran into a bank of snow.
5. Don't forget to bring a pail of milk when you come home.
6. It's extremely cold outside; in the open air.
7. The champion fought better than his opponent.
8. From my hotel window I have a view of the bay.
9. She did not forgive him for his rudeness.

Count / Non-Count Food Partitives

1. Please go to the store and pick up a _____ of milk.
   A) bag   B) half gallon   C) dozen   D) pound

2. This recipe calls for a _____ of butter.
   A) dozen   B) tube   C) stick   D) can

3. My cat eats a _____ of tuna every day.
   A) can   B) loaf   C) bottle   D) bag

4. I like to drink a _____ of mineral water after I exercise.
   A) pound   B) stick   C) teaspoon   D) bottle

5. I want to make a peanut butter and jelly sandwich. But the _____ of peanut butter is empty.
   A) six-pack B) jar   C) head   D) box

6. I need three _____ of yogurt from the dairy section.
   A) tubes   B) pounds   C) containers D) dozens

Miscellaneous

7. If you want coffee with breakfast, you should buy a _____ of coffee tonight.
   A) gallon B) pound C) cup D) quart

8. I would like a large, green _____ of lettuce for tonight's salad.
   A) head B) jar C) can D) half a cup

9. Would you like a _____ of chocolate or vanilla ice cream?
   A) half dozen B) pint C) bag D) can

10. Pick up _____ of whole wheat bread at the bakery.
    A) half a pound B) a box C) a twelve-pack D) a loaf

11. I need _____ eggs for the Easter egg hunt.
    A) a gallon B) a quart of C) half a dozen D) a teaspoon of

12. I need a _____ of ground beef to make hamburgers for the picnic.
    A) pint B) box C) head D) pound and a half

13. We need a _____ of rice to make our special chicken and rice dish.
    A) box B) gallon C) loaf D) teaspoon

14. The _____ of toothpaste are located in the health and beauty section of the supermarket.
    A) quarts B) tubes C) pints D) sticks

15. Pick up a _____ of soda for the party tonight.
    A) head B) jar C) bag D) six-pack

16. Order _____ Swiss cheese at the deli counter.
    A) a pint B) half a pound C) a quart D) a jar

17. This recipe needs a _____ of salt.
    A) teaspoon B) loaf C) six-pack D) stick

18. Go get a _____ of bananas in the produce section at the front of the store.
    A) head B) dozen C) bunch D) pint

19. We need a _____ of orange juice for tomorrow morning.
    A) pound B) quart C) bag D) stick

20. Buy a _____ of chocolate chip cookies for dessert.
    A) bag B) half a gallon C) teaspoon D) loaf

Gender-Free Language
What are the gender-free words for the following?

1. stewardess - _____?
2. policeman - _____?
3. mailman - _____?
4. chairman - _____?
5. spokesman - _____?
6. anchorman - _____?
7. poetess - _____?
8. actress - _____?
9. housewife - _____?
10. manpower - _____?
11. wife or husband - _____?
12. mothering - _____?
13. foreman - _____?
14. salesmanship - _____?
15. man, mankind - _____?

Finish the Sentence

1. She usually is a careful driver but yesterday she had a(an) _____.
   A) accident B) happening C) incident

2. She was fishing from the river _____.
   A) cliff B) valley C) bank

3. It took him three times to pass his driving _____.
   A) competition B) match C) test

4. He took a map with him in case he got _____.
   A) lost B) found C) discovered

5. She was fired from her last _____.
   A) business B) job C) house

6. If my toothache doesn't stop, I'll go to the _____.
   A) doctor B) dentist C) hospital

7. Water expands when it _____.
   A) freezes B) thaws C) flows

8. The teacher was angry because Tom kept asking lots of stupid _____.
   A) questions B) mistakes C) answers

9. He said he was going to sail around the world in his _____.
   A) car B) parachute C) yacht

10. Wait while I rewind the _____.
    A) television B) tape C) book

Food and Nutrition Quiz

1. One of the following does not belong to this food group:
   A) banana B) beef C) peach
   D) nectarine E) prune

2. The food group in question 1 is:
   A) Meat, Poultry, Fish, Beans, Eggs, and Nuts Group
   B) Fats, Oils and Sweets Group
   C) Fruit Group
   D) Bread, Cereal, Rice and Pasta Group
   E) Milk, Yogurt, and Cheese Group

3. What food doesn't belong to this food group?
   A) chicken B) steak C) lamb
   D) crab E) kiwi

4. The food group in question #3 is:
   A) Bread, Cereal, Rice and Pasta Group
   B) Meat, Poultry, Fish, Beans, Eggs, and Nuts Group
   C) Vegetable Group
   D) Milk, Yogurt, and Cheese Group
   E) Fats, Oils and Sweets Group

5. What food doesn't belong to this food group?
   A) apricot B) squash C) zucchini
   D) potato E) broccoli

6. The food group in question 5 is:
   A) Meat, Poultry, Fish, Beans, Eggs, and Nuts Group
   B) Fruit Group
   C) Vegetable Group
   D) Fats, Oils and Sweets Group
   E) Bread, Cereal, Rice and Pasta Group

7. What food doesn't belong to this food group?
   A) chocolate milk B) cream cheese C) ice cream
   D) salad dressing E) yogurt

8. The food group in question 7 is:
   A) Fruit Group
   B) Dairy Group
   C) Vegetable Group
   D) Meat, Poultry, Fish, Beans, Eggs, and Nuts Group
   E) Fats, Oils and Sweets Group

9. What food doesn't belong to this food group?
   A) cookies B) candy C) salad dressing
   D) cherries E) butter

10. The food group in question 9 is:
    A) Dairy Group
    B) Vegetable Group
    C) Meat, Poultry, Fish, Beans, Eggs, and Nuts Group
    D) Bread, Cereal, Rice and Pasta Group
    E) Fats, Oils and Sweets Group

Miscellaneous

11. What food doesn't belong to this food group?
    A) noodles   B) crackers   C) scallion
    D) macaroni   E) cous cous

12. The food group in question 11 is:
    A) Bread, Cereal, Rice and Pasta Group
    B) Meat, Poultry, Fish, Beans, Eggs, and Nuts Group
    C) Vegetable Group
    D) Fats, Oils and Sweets Group
    E) Fruit Group

13. Which of the following beverages has no fat, sugar, or oils?
    A) milk   B) root beer
    C) coffee with cream   D) iced tea unsweetened
    E) lemonade

What Fruit...?

1. What fruit gave Sir Isaac Newton a headache and is famous in the stories of Adam and Eve?
2. What fruit was traditionally stepped on by foot to make wine?
3. What fruit is needed to make a 'Pina Colada' cocktail?
4. What fruit comes in 'bunches' and has an easy to peel yellow skin?
5. What fruit is 'Seville' famous and is used to make marmalade?
6. What red fruit is sour and used to make marmalade and juice?
7. What fruit are 'water', 'cantaloupe', and 'honeydew' all types of?
8. What fruit are people likened to if they have an excess of body fat around the hips and bottom?
9. What fruit when dried becomes a prune?
10. What fruit is used to make jam and is served with a shortcake base?

House Words

1. Where do you find a toaster and a kettle?
2. Where do you find pillows, blankets, and an alarm clock?
3. Where do you find shampoo, soap, and a shower?
4. Where do you find a T.V., a sofa and a coffee table?
5. Where do you find coat hangers and clean clothes?
6. Where do you find bicycles, the car and various odds and ends?
7. Where do you find spades, a hose, bulbs and gardening gloves?
8. Where do you find a cot, nappies or diapers, and a romper suit?
9. Where do you find a washing machine, soap powder and dirty socks?
10. Where do you find lavatory paper, air freshener and a seat cover?

Interjections

1. Paraphrase the interjection used in the following dialogue.
   A: I've forgotten to tell John about the party.
   B: Eh?
   A) What did you say?   B) Really?   C) How come?

2. Which of the following interjections is NOT an expression of surprise or wonder?
   A) Gee!   B) Gosh!   C) Boo!

3. You are vegetarian and you are offered a dish of raw meat. What do you think?
   A) Ugh!   B) Hurrah!   C) Yippee!

4. Somebody has just stepped on your toe. Which interjection would best fit the situation?
   A) Yoo-hoo! B) Ouch!   C) Eh!

5. You are most likely to hear or use the interjection boo _____.
   A) at a theatrical performance
   B) while listening to a political speech
   C) on both of the above mentioned occasions

6. _____, Mary! Come here! I want to talk to you.
   A) Oops   B) Mmm   C) Hey

7. 'Ta' is synonymous of _____.
   A) take it easy   B) thank you   C) tra-la-la

8. A: I scored 660 points at the TOEFL test!
   B: ___! That's amazing!
   A) Wow   B) Aha   C) Woe

9. Your children are making a lot of noise and you want to hear the news on the radio. How do you urge silence?
   A) Shh!   B) Tut-tut   C) Ow!

10. _____! The spinach soup is out of this world!
    A) Mmm   B) Yuk   C) Uh

Meat

1. When the flesh of a cow or bull is used as meat it's called _____.
2. This meat is sliced and served fried with eggs, sausages and bread for breakfast.
3. What word is used for the meat of a pig when it's used as meat?
4. Young sheep's meat is called _____.
5. The flesh of a fully grown sheep is called _____.
6. The flesh of a deer used for eating is known as _____.
7. The collective word for the flesh of animals such as rabbits, pigeons and deer hunted for sport or food is _____.
8. Roe and Caviar are the eggs of _____.
9. Roosters, hens, ducks, and turkeys when bred for food or for their eggs are collectively known as _____.
10. The bits considered less valuable of an animal such as the heart, wings, and liver that are used for food are known as _____.

The logic list
Complete the logic list of words.

1. Shark, carp, catfish, trout _____.
   A) salamander   B) toad   C) frog
   D) herring   E) turtle

2. Piano, organ, bagpipe, violin _____.
   A) kettle   B) kettledrum   C) violet
   D) pinochle   E) organic

3. Sea, ocean, river, lake, _____.
   A) seaman   B) riverside   C) beach
   D) pond   E) shelf

4. Arm-chair, coffee-table, settee, scatter-cushion, _____.
   A) wall-unit   B) walking stick C) hall-mirror
   D) coat hanger   E) umbrella stand

5. Oak, silver-birch, poplar, willow, _____.
   A) ashtray   B) ash   C) seed
   D) cork   E) rubber

6. Tree, trunk, root, leaf, _____.
   A) paper   B) branch   C) fruit
   D) roof   E) mushroom

7. Bread, butter, sugar, cream, _____.
   A) shark   B) scholar   C) kids
   D) cheese   E) steam

8. A hat, a cap, a scarf, a shirt, _____.
   A) an umbrella   B) a shade   C) trousers
   D) a bag   E) a stick

9. Speak, talk, tell, say, _____.
   A) run   B) swim   C) utter
   D) laugh   E) go

10. Teacher, headmaster, form mistress, principal _____.
    A) child   B) pupil   C) woman
    D) teenager   E) man

11. Worker, teacher, businessman, doctor, _____.
    A) letter carrier B) classroom C) park
    D) weather   E) girl

Miscellaneous

12. Wood, metal, brick, glass, _____.
    A) ink   B) clay   C) sugar
    D) pepper   E) fruit

13. Tree, plant, flower, bush, _____.
    A) field   B) bird   C) animal
    D) grass   E) insect

14. Farm, village, town, city, _____.
    A) park   B) harbor   C) garden
    D) corner   E) settlement

The most general meaning
Find the word with the most general meaning.

1. A) clever   B) honest   C) kind
   D) polite   E) good

2. A) stories   B) novels   C) poems
   D) books   E) tales

3. A) apple   B) fruit   C) pear
   D) apricot   E) cherry

4. A) a cow   B) a horse   C) a mule
   D) an animal   E) a dog

5. A) men   B) women   C) girls
   D) boys   E) people

6. A) cabin   B) palace   C) house
   D) hut   E) building

7. A) brick   B) stone
   C) construction materials   D) wood
   E) clay

8. A) dollars   B) money   C) franks
   D) sums   E) pounds

9. A) dancing   B) drawing   C) acting
   D) art   E) singing

10. A) man   B) woman   C) person
    D) boy   E) girl

Types of Hats

1. Panama, top and felt are all types of _____
2. Baseball players wear them and now it is fashionable to wear them backwards.
3. Worn by motorcycle riders on their heads.
4. A flat hat made of felt worn by school girls and French men.
5. It is usually white and lacy when worn by brides. It begins with the letter "V".
6. A square cloth folded in half and tied under the chin which begins with the letter "H".
7. A long piece of material wrapped around the heads of some Indian men.
8. The headgear worn by kings and queens.
9. The headgear that is attached to a coat or jacket and can be pulled up. It begins with a "H".
10. This hat is mainly worn by babies, but was originally made to keep the sun off women's faces.

Word definition

1. Someone who carries a message is _____.
   A) worker   B) messenger   C) peace maker
   D) foreigner   E) stranger

2. A writer of verses of any kind is _____.
   A) an author   B) a novelist   C) a dramatist
   D) a poet   E) a writer

3. A food made from milk is _____.
   A) ham   B) cheese   C) stew
   D) pepper   E) roll

4. The part of a room you walk on is _____.
   A) ceiling   B) carpet   C) rug
   D) floor   E) wall

5. A bulb like vegetable with a strong smell and flavor and unpleasant taste is _____.
   A) onion   B) potato   C) tomato
   D) carrot   E) cabbage

6. The first letter of a word or a name means _____.
   A) signature   B) alphabet   C) voice
   D) initial   E) injury

7. Someone you do not know is _____.
   A) inhabitant   B) man   C) woman
   D) native   E) stranger

8. A sea voyage for pleasure is _____.
   A) by sea   B) ship   C) seashore
   D) cruise   E) sea steamer

9. Someone who makes or looks after machines is _____.
   A) economist   B) worker   C) teacher
   D) engineer   E) member

10. UFO stands for _____.
    A) Unknown Flying Object
    B) Unmanned Flying Object
    C) Unidentified Flying Object
    D) Unreal Flying Object
    E) Unrecognizable Flying Object

11. A public sale where things are sold to the people who offer the most money for them is _____.
    A) audience   B) attic   C) auction
    D) atlas   E) astrologer

12. A very large pool of water with land all around is _____.
    A) garden   B) object   C) oath
    D) nut   E) lake

13. Two stored buses are called _____.
    A) liners   B) the underground   C) street-cars
    D) double-deckers   E) coaches

USE OF ENGLISH — TEST MASTER

TEST A

What teenagers do with their money

Thirteen-year-olds do not spend as much money as their parents suspect - at least not according to the findings of a __(1)__ survey, *Money and Change*. The survey __(2)__ three hundred teenagers, 13-17 years old, from __(3)__ Britain.

By the time they __(4)__ their teens, most children see their weekly allowance rise dramatically to an amazing national average of £5.14. Two thirds think they get __(5)__ money, but most expect to have to do something to get it.

Although they have more cash, worry about debt is __(6)__ among teenagers. Therefore, the __(7)__ of children __(8)__ an effort to save for the future.

Greater access to cash __(9)__ teenagers does not, however, mean that they are more irresponsible __(10)__ a result. The economic recession seems to have encouraged __(11)__ attitudes to money, even in the case of children at these ages. Instead of wasting what pocket __(12)__ they have on sweets or magazines, the 13-year-olds who took __(13)__ in the survey seem to __(14)__ to the situation by saving more than half __(15)__ their cash.

1. A) late   B) recent   C) latest   D) fresh
2. A) included   B) contained   C) counted   D) enclosed
3. A) entire   B) all over   C) complete   D) the whole
4. A) reach   B) get   C) make   D) arrive
5. A) acceptable B) adequate   C) satisfactory D) enough
6. A) gaining   B) heightening C) increasing   D) building
7. A) most   B) maximum   C) many   D) majority
8. A) make   B) do   C) have   D) try
9. A) among   B) through   C) between   D) along
10. A) like   B) as   C) for   D) in
11. A) aware   B) knowing   C) helpful   D) cautious
12. A) cash   B) money   C) change   D) savings
13. A) part   B) place   C) share   D) piece
14. A) reply   B) answer   C) respond   D) return
15. A) from   B) as   C) of   D) for

TEST B

Becoming a nurse: the interview

The reality of an interview is never as bad as your fears. For some __(1)__ people imagine the interviewer is going to jump on every tiny mistake they __(2)__. In truth, the interviewer is as __(3)__ for the meeting to go well as you are. It is what __(4)__ his or her job enjoyable.

The secret of a good interview is preparing for it. What you wear is always important as it creates the first impression. So __(5)__ neatly, but comfortably. Make __(6)__ that you can deal with anything you are __(7)__. Prepare for questions that are certain to come up, for example: Why do you want to become a nurse? What is the most important __(8)__ a good nurse should have? Apart from nursing, what other careers have you __(9)__? What are your interests and hobbies?

Answer the questions fully and precisely. __(10)__, if one of your interests is reading, be prepared to __(11)__ about the sort of books you like. __(12)__, do not learn all your answers off __(13)__ heart. The interviewer wants to meet a human __(14)__, not a robot. Remember, the interviewer is genuinely interested in you, so the more you relax and are yourself, the more __(15)__ you are to succeed.

1. A) reason   B) idea   C) explanation   D) excuse
2. A) perform   B) do   C) make   D) have
3. A) keen   B) wanting   C) interested   D) delighted
4. A) does   B) causes   C) happens   D) makes
5. A) dress   B) wear   C) put on   D) have on
6. A) evident   B) sure   C) definite   D) clear
7. A) requested   B) questioned   C) enquired   D) asked
8. A) character   B) quality   C) nature   D) point
9. A) thought   B) regarded   C) considered   D) wondered
10. A) For instance B) That is   C) Such as   D) Let's say
11. A) say   B) talk   C) discuss   D) chat
12. A) However   B) Although   C) Despite   D) Therefore
13. A) at   B) in   C) on   D) by
14. A) character B) being   C) somebody   D) nature
15. A) easy   B) possible   C) likely   D) probable

TEST C

The four-minute mile

It is the nature of athletic records that they are broken and their place is taken by new ones. Yet in many sports __(1)__, there is a mark which is not __(2)__ in itself, but which becomes a legend as athletes __(3)__ to break it. The most __(4)__ of these is the attempt to run the mile in __(5)__ than four minutes.

In 1945, the mile record was __(6)__ to 4 minutes, 1.5 seconds. And there, for nine years, it stuck. Then, in 1954, a medical student __(7)__ Roger Bannister decided to try and break the record. He had been __(8)__ for this day since running the mile in 4 minutes, 2 seconds the __(9)__ year.

Two other runners set the pace for him, and __(10)__ 250 yards to go he burst ahead for the finish. He wrote __(11)__: 'My body had exhausted all its energy, but it __(12)__ on running just the same. Those __(13)__ few seconds seemed never-ending. I could see the line of the finishing tape. I jumped like a man making a desperate attempt to save himself from danger.' Bannister's time was 3 minutes, 59.4 seconds. __(14)__ this record has been broken on many __(15)__ since, Bannister's achievement will never be forgotten.

1. A) happenings B) events   C) games   D) matches
2. A) central   B) major   C) significant   D) considerable
3. A) try   B) try on   C) try out   D) try for
4. A) known   B) public   C) noticeable   D) famous
5. A) smaller   B) less   C) lower   D) under
6. A) broken down   B) lessened
    C) decreased   D) brought down
7. A) entitled   B) called   C) nicknamed   D) known
8. A) trying   B) studying   C) running   D) training
9. A) early   B) previous   C) past   D) former
10. A) on   B) in   C) with   D) by
11. A) afterwards B) then   C) next   D) after
12. A) went   B) continued   C) ran   D) got
13. A) last   B) late   C) latest   D) later
14. A) But   B) In spite of C) However   D) Although
15. A) times   B) times   C) occasions   D) incidents

Use of English

TEST D
Traffic Lights

The first traffic signal was invented by a railway signaling engineer. It was installed __(1)__ the Houses of Parliament in 1868. It __(2)__ like any railway signal of the time, and was operated by gas. __(3)__, it exploded and killed a policeman, and the accident __(4)__ further development until cars became common.

__(5)__ traffic lights are an American invention. Red-green __(6)__ were installed in Cleveland in 1914. Three-color signals, operated __(7)__ hand from a tower in the __(8)__ of the street, were installed in New York in 1918. The __(9)__ lights of this type to __(10)__ in Britain were in London, on the junction between St. James's Street and Piccadilly, in 1925. Automatic signals were installed __(11)__ year later.

In the past, traffic lights were __(12)__. In New York, some lights had a statue on top. In Los Angeles the lights did not just __(13)__ silently, but would ring bells to __(14)__ the sleeping motorists of the 1930s. These are gone and have been __(15)__ by standard models which are universally adopted.

1. A) outside B) out C) out of D) outdoors
2. A) resembled B) looked C) showed D) seemed
3. A) However B) Therefore C) Although D) Despite
4. A) forbade B) disappointed C) avoided D) discouraged
5. A) New B) Recent C) Modern D) Late
6. A) methods B) ways C) systems D) means
7. A) by B) with C) through D) in
8. A) middle B) heart C) focus D) halfway
9. A) original B) primary C) first D) early
10. A) show B) appear C) happen D) become
11. A) a B) in the C) in a D) the
12. A) various B) particular C) rare D) special
13. A) change B) alter C) vary D) move
14. A) rise B) raise C) wake D) get up
15. A) reproduced B) replaced C) removed D) remained

TEST E
The best stone in the world

In 1769 George and Eleanor Coade bought a factory manufacturing artificial stone in southeast London on a __(1)__ at Pedlar's Acre, south __(2)__ the river. The family were __(3)__ running a successful factory in the south-west of England. Within a year of moving __(4)__ the capital, George Coade died, leaving his wife and daughter to __(5)__ on the business. The Coade Stone they perfected __(6)__ to become the most permanent stone ever made. The product developed by the factory's former __(7)__, Richard Holt, was a kind of baked clay. The two women __(8)__ with his recipe, and __(9)__ in creating a new kind of stone which was almost a hundred percent weather-proof.

The advantage of Coade Stone is that while natural stone slowly breaks down and erodes away, Coade Stone seems to be __(10)__ to survive in all weather conditions for many years. The National Gallery, the Royal Opera House and Buckingham Palace __(11)__ display their original ornaments made of Coade Stone. __(12)__ mother and daughter were clever businesswomen. They __(13)__ only the top artists of the day to model their stone into statues and other ornaments.

After the deaths of Eleanor Coade and her daughter the factory survived for twenty years, but in 1840 it __(14)__ closed. With it went the Coade Stone recipe which was __(15)__, and has never been rediscovered.

1. A) territory B) place C) ground D) plot
2. A) to B) of C) from D) than
3. A) already B) just C) yet D) however
4. A) at B) in C) to D) on
5. A) go B) carry C) get D) run
6. A) claimed B) had C) was D) would
7. A) landlord B) possessor C) owner D) tenant
8. A) experimented B) tried C) experienced D) tested
9. A) managed B) succeeded C) achieved D) completed
10. A) capable B) possible C) able D) good
11. A) still B) only C) just D) yet
12. A) Either B) Also C) Each D) Both
13. A) employed B) worked C) staffed D) teamed
14. A) lastly B) at last C) in the end D) finally
15. A) missing B) disappeared C) lost D) left

TEST F
On your bike!

If you are getting fed up wasting time looking for parking space, my __(1)__ to you is to consider the bicycle as an alternative __(2)__ of transport. Cycling is probably the cheapest and healthiest way of getting __(3)__ in our congested city centers. __(4)__ it is convenient and environmentally desirable, it can be an unattractive __(5)__ on a cold wintry morning. It is much easier to __(6)__ onto a nice warm bus or jump into your car, __(7)__ the sight of cyclists as they weave their way in and out of the traffic may fill you with __(8)__ as you sit waiting in yet __(9)__ traffic jam. In spite of the __(10)__ that worsening pollution is getting many people __(11)__, causing more and more health problems, and __(12)__ it is fashionable to express one's __(13)__ of the environmentally safe bicycle, it is hard to __(14)__ the danger cyclists face in sharing the road with cars. __(15)__ cycling is not as risky as it looks at first sight, there are more and more accidents involving cyclists.

1. A) advice B) warning C) plan D) solution
2. A) method B) way C) means D) instrument
3. A) on B) through C) over D) about
4. A) Despite B) In spite C) Although D) Even as
5. A) choice B) advice C) propose D) transport
6. A) enter B) be C) travel D) get
7. A) even B) however C) though D) and
8. A) approval B) envy C) angry D) criticism
9. A) other B) more C) another D) longer
10. A) truth B) reality C) fact D) event
11. A) round B) down C) over D) together
12. A) while B) despite C) as D) in spite of
13. A) favor B) agreement C) belief D) approval
14. A) refuse B) criticize C) deny D) think
15. A) Even though B) However C) Whereas D) Although

Use of English

TEST G

Picture this

Getting friends and family to pose for photos is hard enough, but how would you cope with a rabbit, an owl or a butterfly that simply __(1)__ to keep still?

Simon King, wildlife film-maker and photographer, says you don't need any formal __(2)__ to get started. The whole __(3)__ is that photographing wildlife should be fun. Simon offers the following __(4)__:

Specialize from the start. You're more likely to get good __(5)__ sooner if you __(6)__ on one type of wildlife - insects for instance - __(7)__ than just going off to the woods or park with your camera and snapping whatever you see.

__(8)__ something that isn't hard to photograph. Choosing an animal that's hard to __(9)__, or will run away if it sees you __(10)__ unnecessary problems. How about flowers, or a group of birds?

__(11)__ second-hand camera shops and local papers for quality __(12)__. You don't need to __(13)__ a fortune - Simon started with just a second-hand camera that cost around £30. But you will need a single lens reflex camera.

Remember it's the __(14)__ photograph that counts, not just the subject. __(15)__ you're composing a picture and try to be as artistic as possible.

1. A) disobeys   B) dislikes   C) refuses   D) avoids
2. A) training   B) education   C) exercise   D) lecture
3. A) thought   B) idea   C) dream   D) plan
4. A) lessons   B) facts   C) warnings   D) tips
5. A) progress   B) luck   C) results   D) events
6. A) think   B) concentrate   C) limit   D) depend
7. A) more   B) other   C) better   D) rather
8. A) Decide   B) Pick   C) Prefer   D) Collect
9. A) spot   B) notice   C) meet   D) glance
10. A) creates   B) starts   C) puts   D) leads
11. A) Visit   B) Look   C) Find   D) Search
12. A) instruments B) equipment   C) material   D) tools
13. A) cost   B) make   C) spend   D) lose
14. A) big   B) all   C) whole   D) full
15. A) Think   B) Guess   C) Invent   D) Imagine

TEST H

Shopping in Japan

Unlike millions of Britons, who will not know how much the Christmas turkey, child's bicycle and the January sales have __(1)__ them until the credit card bill arrives, the Japanese __(2)__ to settle up before they've even __(3)__ their shopping list.

The Japanese like to improve on every idea, even if the idea is cash. So they have been __(4)__ about the pre-paid card. It __(5)__ the bother of banknotes and it saves the Japanese __(6)__ the fear of being in __(7)__ to someone else.

It __(8)__ with the convenient pre-paid telephone card and has __(9)__ through train ticket cards, taxi cards, and supermarket cards all the way to McDonald's hamburgers cards.

Few Westerners can understand why anyone __(10)__ want to give money to a supermarket or a department store __(11)__ by buying a pre-paid card. But credit companies are held in some suspicion in Japan. People have traditionally preferred cash and will happily stroll the streets with quite large __(12)__ of money in their pockets. The fact that street crime is fairly __(13)__ helps.

Pre-paid cards are now as __(14)__ as chopsticks and twice as convenient. About 500 million cards were sold in the first five years after they became __(15)__.

1. A) lost   B) cost   C) charged   D) priced
2. A) prefer   B) desire   C) enjoy   D) select
3. A) written about B) written off
   C) written out   D) written up
4. A) keen   B) enthusiastic C) exciting   D) eager
5. A) does away with B) does out of
   C) does without   D) does out
6. A) of   B) from   C) for   D) by
7. A) payment   B) bill   C) debt   D) interest
8. A) opened   B) invented   C) introduced D) started
9. A) followed   B) developed   C) changed   D) turned
10. A) would   B) will   C) may   D) must
11. A) in time   B) in front   C) in future   D) in advance
12. A) savings   B) sums   C) deposits   D) masses
13. A) seldom   B) slight   C) rare   D) slow
14. A) common   B) usual   C) regular   D) often
15. A) prepared   B) possible   C) ready   D) available

TEST I

The personal trainer

What does a personal trainer do?

I meet each client to discuss what he or she is looking for. It could be __(1)__ from improving general fitness to losing - or, in a few cases, - __(2)__ weight. I then devise a training program for them which I think will __(3)__ them to achieve their __(4)__. If they've had anything __(5)__ with them, say a back __(6)__, I speak to their doctor who will __(7)__ me what not to do. If someone eats and drinks too much, it's easy to suggest they __(8)__, but if that doesn't __(9)__, I look at their diet. I prefer to train on a one-to-one __(10)__, though I do sometimes work with __(11)__ if they are friends and want to train together.

Who needs a personal trainer?

I think most people do. A trainer will __(12)__ you to try __(13)__. You achieve 20 per cent more than you could training alone, no __(14)__ how dedicated you are. I've got a lot of Americans on my books, and I actually prefer them. __(15)__ most Brits, who still haven't really got the idea, Americans know how to work out.

1. A) nothing   B) everything   C) anything   D) something
2. A) adding   B) gaining   C) putting   D) finding
3. A) help   B) ensure   C) let   D) organize
4. A) hope   B) intention   C) aim   D) wish
5. A) ill   B) bad   C) off   D) wrong
6. A) wound   B) hurt   C) injury   D) accident
7. A) persuade   B) advise   C) suggest   D) order
8. A) cut out   B) cut off   C) cut back   D) cut down
9. A) work   B) function   C) manage   D) advance
10. A) way   B) method   C) basis   D) style
11. A) crowds   B) couples   C) twins   D) doubles
12. A) move   B) push   C) make   D) insist
13. A) stronger   B) better   C) more   D) harder
14. A) matter   B) point   C) way   D) doubt
15. A) Compared   B) Contrary   C) Different   D) Unlike

Use of English

TEST J

The fall guy

Nick Gillard earns a living working as a stuntman on films and TV shows but his first __(1)__ of show business was trick-riding circus horses when he was just 12 years old. Four years later he got the chance to __(2)__ in his first film. 'I really enjoyed working on the film,' Nick remembers, 'so I started asking how I'd __(3)__ becoming a stuntman.' Nick couldn't just __(4)__ as a stuntman straight away. First he had to get __(5)__ by the British Stunt Register, which represents stunt professionals in Britain. To do this he had to reach instructor __(6)__ in six sports including skiing, riding and gymnastics. Since qualifying __(7)__ the age of 19, Nick has worked on many movies and he has doubled for some of the biggest stars in Hollywood.

Safety and timing are all-important for stunt professionals - they plan everything down to the __(8)__ detail. 'We take the utmost __(9)__. It's not like being an actor where you can __(10)__ the shot again if it goes wrong. It's got to work first time.' Nick has __(11)__ some terrifyingly dangerous stunts. For one film he jumped across a bridge in a speed boat, and in Alien 3 he was __(12)__ on fire, without air, for more than two minutes. Filming on location __(13)__ him all __(14)__ the world, often for months __(15)__ a time.

1. A) lesson   B) experiment   C) attempt   D) taste
2. A) play   B) practice   C) perform   D) show
3. A) go on   B) go about   C) go by   D) go for
4. A) put up   B) establish   C) set up   D) introduce
5. A) applied   B) allowed   C) agreed   D) accepted
6. A) line   B) level   C) measure   D) mark
7. A) in   B) on   C) at   D) by
8. A) tiniest   B) lowest   C) least   D) lightest
9. A) caution   B) care   C) attention   D) guard
10. A) have   B) make   C) give   D) take
11. A) made   B) done   C) led   D) given
12. A) put   B) caught   C) set   D) lit
13. A) takes   B) brings   C) flies   D) fetches
14. A) about   B) through   C) across   D) over
15. A) at   B) on   C) for   D) in

TEST K

Yachtswoman

Lisa Clayton's dream was to become the first woman in history to sail single-handed, non-stop and unassisted around the world. On 17 September 1994, she set sail in Spirit of Birmingham on what could have been the final __(1)__ of her life. Here are some of her notes on the journey.

Day 182

The loneliness got worse __(2)__ the day. When you haven't __(3)__ a ship or land for four months, __(4)__ talked to anyone, it really gets you __(5)__. The sense of isolation is frightening.

Day 217

I __(6)__ a lot of my trip feeling frustrated and frightened, __(7)__ it was because of the __(8)__ winds, a broken heater or the sharks. I remember thinking, 'This is crazy!' The sun was out, the sea was __(9)__ and here I was __(10)__ tears! Then I saw the most wonderful __(11)__ - a 12m whale which swam __(12)__ the boat for hours.

Day 286

Two days before I crossed the __(13)__ line a helicopter came out scanning the seas for me. That's when I finally thought, 'I'm going to do it.' About 50 boats escorted me into the harbor where thousands of people were waiting, __(14)__ me on. And, as I docked, fireworks and cannons __(15)__. It was just mad!

1. A) excursion   B) travel   C) journey   D) tour
2. A) from   B) by   C) since   D) at
3. A) crossed   B) discovered   C) passed   D) joined
4. A) let alone   B) not only   C) without even   D) not counting
5. A) back   B) out   C) off   D) down
6. A) took   B) spent   C) had   D) stayed
7. A) whether   B) unless   C) either   D) if
8. A) low   B) weak   C) mild   D) light
9. A) sparkling   B) glowing   C) flickering   D) flashing
10. A) full of   B) in   C) down with   D) on
11. A) scenery   B) view   C) sight   D) outlook
12. A) alongside   B) close   C) besides   D) ahead
13. A) ending   B) final   C) finishing   D) last
14. A) crying   B) cheering   C) shouting   D) screaming
15. A) broke out   B) let out   C) set off   D) went off

TEST L

Night visitor

She put the key in the keyhole as quietly as she could but she found it __(1)__ as the door was old and rusty. As she __(2)__ opened the door, it squeaked __(3)__ on its old hinges. 'I wish they'd oil the thing a bit more __(4)__,' she muttered to herself __(5)__. She closed the door __(6)__ behind her and then tiptoed __(7)__ across the room. Unfortunately, this time it was the floorboards that betrayed her as they creaked __(8)__ with every step she took. It had been so __(9)__ since the old house had been built - it had __(10)__ been about two hundred years before and for all Helen knew they had __(11)__ replaced the original floorboards. Helen's heart began to beat __(12)__. It was one o'clock. Helen's parents must have gone to bed __(13)__. This was most unusual. Rarely __(14)__ to bed before she got home. No sooner had she put her foot on the first stair __(15)__ she heard a muffled voice call out, 'Who's there? Is that you, Helen?

1. A) hardly   B) easy   C) hard   D) easily
2. A) slowly   B) loudly   C) careful   D) noisy
3. A) lightly   B) noisily   C) softly   D) gently
4. A) frequent   B) oftener   C) sooner   D) frequently
5. A) with angry   B) angry   C) angrily   D) from anger
6. A) shyly   B) efficiently   C) carefully   D) fast
7. A) softly   B) gentle   C) finely   D) shortly
8. A) aloud   B) loud   C) loudly   D) allowed
9. A) along   B) long time   C) long   D) a long time
10. A) probably   B) certainly   C) definitely   D) may not
11. A) rarely   B) scarcely   C) never   D) occasionally
12. A) fastly   B) more faster   C) more fast   D) faster
13. A) early   B) more earlier   C) the earliest   D) more early
14. A) they went   B) they did go   C) they have gone   D) did they go
15. A) then   B) than   C) that   D) there

Use of English

TEST M

A hectic time

Dear Trevor,

I know it's been ages since I wrote to you but I've been very busy __(1)__ we decided to move into the country. The house in the village is not quite ready __(2)__ but as you can imagine __(3)__ the last few weeks we've had to chase up builders and plumbers and we've __(4)__ got a long way to go.

It's been such a long time since we __(5)__ to work on it. I've almost forgotten how long it's been exactly. We must have started it about seven years __(6)__ and we've __(7)__ spent a small fortune on it. We are __(8)__ living in our rather cramped flat where you __(9)__ us a few years ago but it __(10)__ to get unbearable and we __(11)__ to moving out. We are still __(12)__ around from morning __(13)__ night and it's been particularly hectic __(14)__ the last week. Anyway, __(15)__ all this was going on Karen fell and sprained her ankle which was the last thing we needed!

1. A) every time   B) ever since   C) while   D) before
2. A) still   B) already   C) yet   D) soon
3. A) for   B) as   C) while   D) since
4. A) yet   B) already   C) nearly   D) still
5. A) have started   B) start   C) did start   D) started
6. A) before   B) ago   C) previous   D) since
7. A) still   B) not   C) already   D) yet
8. A) already   B) still   C) yet   D) longer
9. A) were visiting   B) have visited
   C) had been visited   D) visited
10. A) begun   B) is beginning   C) begins   D) begin
11. A) have looked   B) looked forward
    C) will look forward   D) are looking forward
12. A) rush   B) rushed   C) rushing   D) be rushed
13. A) and   B) into   C) till   D) through
14. A) during   B) from   C) in   D) while
15. A) in   B) during   C) while   D) for

TEST N

The mystery of the Marie Celeste

We spotted the Marie Celeste drifting in mid-Atlantic on December 5, 1872. Since the ship looked damaged, the captain said the three of us __(1)__ board her at once __(2)__ investigate and __(3)__ him back any information we could get hold of. We __(4)__ climb on board without too much difficulty but we couldn't see any sign of life anywhere. The crew of the Marie Celeste __(5)__ have abandoned ship __(6)__ the ship's small lifeboat was missing. Some navigational equipment which a ship of that kind __(7)__ had on board was also missing. The crew __(8)__ had much time to abandon ship because they had not __(9)__ with them many of their personal possessions. Luckily, we __(10)__ to find the ship's log which helped us a great deal in our __(11)__. The last time the captain of the Maria Celeste had __(12)__ an entry in the ship's log was November 21. Something extraordinary must have taken __(13)__ between this date and December 5. The captain of the ship, Benjamin Briggs, had extensive __(14)__ of the high seas so what had made him __(15)__ the decision to abandon ship in the middle of nowhere?

1. A) have   B) had to   C) could   D) ought
2. A) in order that   B) so that   C) in order to   D) for to
3. A) take   B) get   C) carry   D) bring
4. A) couldn't   B) managed   C) unable   D) were able to
5. A) can't   B) must   C) hadn't   D) could
6. A) since   B) on account of
   C) as a result of   D) owing to
7. A) shouldn't   B) should have
   C) shouldn't have   D) should be
8. A) ought not have   B) must not
   C) couldn't have   D) would have
9. A) taken   B) fetched   C) brought   D) had
10. A) could   B) able   C) knew   D) managed
11. A) information   B) solution   C) suggestion   D) investigation
12. A) took   B) passed   C) wrote   D) made
13. A) part   B) care   C) place   D) control
14. A) qualification   B) education   C) experience   D) travel
15. A) bring   B) choose   C) have   D) take

TEST O

The big day

Whatever candidates may think about examiners, they are not in fact __(1)__ monsters, dripping red ink instead of blood, but ordinary people who will do their best to pass candidates as __(2)__ as candidates follow certain basic rules of the game. Many candidates are __(3)__ in the First Certificate not because their English is __(4)__ but because they are __(5)__ about the requirements of the examination. Before you __(6)__ for the examination, make sure you know what is expected of you; you are __(7)__ to do well unless you answer all the questions set, and don't include __(8)__ material. Don't start writing as __(9)__ as you get the paper - think first, write __(10)__! If part of an answer is incorrect, you __(11)__ cross it out and write the preferred answer neatly above it. If your handwriting __(12)__ illegible, it will be difficult for the examiner to give you credit for it, __(13)__ it is right or __(14)__. You will also lose marks if your essay is written in an __(15)__ style for the type of writing and intended audience.

1. A) insensible   B) unsensible   C) unsensitive   D) insensitive
2. A) much   B) far   C) long   D) soon
3. A) unhappy   B) inaccurate   C) incorrect   D) unsuccessful
4. A) inadequate   B) misguided
   C) illegible   D) misunderstood
5. A) ill-informed   B) informed   C) dissinformed   D) mal-informed
6. A) will sit   B) would sit   C) have sat   D) sit
7. A) improbably   B) impossible   C) unlikely   D) unlucky
8. A) irrelevant   B) illiterate   C) indirect   D) illogical
9. A) quickly   B) immediately   C) fast   D) soon
10. A) after   B) afterwards   C) later   D) slower
11. A) will   B) would   C) should   D) have
12. A) was   B) were   C) be   D) is
13. A) however   B) whenever   C) whether   D) if
14. A) no   B) none   C) false   D) not
15. A) unappropriate   B) misappropriate
    C) inappropriate   D) disappropriate

TEST P

Bad news

The mass media nowadays are our main source of information about what's happening in the world and the impression one __(1)__ from them about human __(2)__ is pretty depressing. My blood __(3)__ rises every time I switch the television on. Apart from gossip about __(4)__ personalities, the picture they paint of human __(5)__ is that they are violent and bloodthirsty. They just report crimes, violations of human rights and the way we are destroying our natural __(6)__. They rarely report __(7)__ in science or medicine; it's a bleak picture. Last night, there was a report about a mass __(8)__ from a prison in Chicago during which five prison guards __(9)__ dead as the prisoners were __(10)__ their getaway. Then there was the story of someone who __(11)__ gunned down by police when he went berserk and massacred ten innocent __(12)__ in a shopping centre somewhere - again - in the United States. I see now where Hollywood __(13)__ get their ideas from. They just turn on the news and they've got themselves a __(14)__ scenario. It seems to me that news __(15)__ have become a form of entertainment.

1. A) takes B) collects C) gets D) draws
2. A) nature B) character C) species D) persons
3. A) level B) impression C) pressure D) temperature
4. A) film affairs B) film business C) show star D) show business
5. A) beings B) characters C) personalities D) people
6. A) wealth B) springs C) materials D) resources
7. A) breakaways B) break-ins C) break-ups D) breakthroughs
8. A) break-in B) break-out C) breakthrough D) break-up
9. A) have been shot B) have shot C) were shooting D) were shot
10. A) taking B) making C) trying D) escaping
11. A) had B) has been C) got D) was got
12. A) by-passers B) passers-by C) pedestrians D) onlookers
13. A) screenplayers B) scriptplayers C) scenewriters D) screenwriters
14. A) ready-made B) take-away C) give away D) high class
15. A) bulletins B) broadcasters C) forecasts D) reporters

TEST R

E-mail or snail mail?

Modern technology has brought about enormous improvements in communications and yet many people are still very worried __(1)__ using the latest computer technology. I am often __(2)__ to meet colleagues who still don't know what the 'e' in e-mail stands for and they are too __(3)__ to ask.

They assume you have to be skilled __(4)__ computers to send a message via e-mail but in fact it is __(5)__ thing in the world. It is also __(6)__ to send an e-mail message __(7)__ to send an ordinary letter or a 'snail' message which also takes __(8)__ longer. An e-mail message is only __(9)__ more expensive than a local telephone call to send; on top of the call itself you also have to pay a fee to your 'server'. If you send a letter by __(10)__ mail it will take a couple of days to get there whereas an e-mail will not take __(11)__ than a few seconds. Once you become __(12)__ to using the system you will be __(13)__ at how much more __(14)__ it is than other means of communication. Of course, before you have access to e-mail, you will need a fairly __(15)__ computer, which can be quite expensive.

1. A) for B) about C) at D) with as
2. A) surprising B) irritating C) surprised D) irritated
3. A) embarrassing B) embarrassed C) tired D) tiring
4. A) about B) into C) to D) in
5. A) simplest B) the more simple C) simpler D) the simplest
6. A) cheaper B) more cheaper C) cheapest D) the cheaper
7. A) as B) than C) that D) from
8. A) much B) more C) as D) lot
9. A) little B) slightly C) less D) least
10. A) second-hand B) low-paid C) part-time D) first-class
11. A) more long B) longest C) as long D) longer
12. A) capable B) accustomed C) clever D) good
13. A) amazed B) puzzled C) experienced D) pleased
14. A) confident B) certain C) efficient D) skilful
15. A) strong B) great C) powerful D) large

EVERYDAY VOCABULARY — TEST MASTER

AT THE AIRPORT

When you travel by air you have to get to the airport early in order to __1__ about an hour before your flight. If you have a lot of luggage, you can put it in a __2__ and push it to the __3__ where someone will __4__ your ticket and weigh your luggage. If you have __5__, it can be expensive. Your heavy luggage is put on a __6__ and carried away. A light bag is classed as __7__ and you can take it with you on to the plane. A(an) __8__ looks at your passport and a(an) __9__ checks your hand luggage before you go into the __10__ to wait till your flight is called. If you want to, you can buy some cheap __11__ goods here. Then you see on the __12__ or you hear a(an) __13__ that you must __14__ your plane. You go through the __15__, then there is sometimes a __16__ before you actually enter the plane. When all the __17__ are __18__, and when the captain and his crew are ready in the cockpit, the plane begins to __19__ to the end of the __20__. Finally, permission is received from the control tower and the plane moves faster and faster in order to __21__.

1. A) check   B) check in
   C) board   D) security check
2. A) on board   B) immigration officer
   C) trolley   D) runway
3. A) check-in desk   B) check in
   C) check   D) security check
4. A) check in   B) check
   C) pass   D) depart
5. A) security guard   B) hand luggage
   C) departure lounge D) excess baggage
6. A) conveyor belt   B) take off
   C) security check   D) board
7. A) excess baggage   B) hand luggage
   C) runway   D) departure lounge
8. A) security guard   B) passenger
   C) security check   D) immigration officer
9. A) security guard   B) passenger
   C) security check   D) immigration officer
10. A) departure gate   B) departures board
    C) departure lounge D) board
11. A) announcement   B) security guard
    C) duty free   D) runway
12. A) departure gate   B) departures board
    C) departure lounge D) board
13. A) announcement   B) security guard
    C) duty free   D) runway
14. A) depart   B) guard
    C) lounge   D) board
15. A) departure gate   B) departures board
    C) departure lounge D) board
16. A) security guard   B) luggage
    C) security check   D) immigration officer
17. A) security guard   B) passengers
    C) security check   D) immigration officer
18. A) on board   B) on trolley
    C) on lounge   D) on runway
19. A) trolley   B) taxi   C) run   D) take on
20. A) trolley   B) taxi   C) runway   D) board
21. A) conveyor belt   B) take off
    C) security check   D) board

IN THE AIR

Flying is fun. I like being in a big __1__ with the __2__ (stewards and stewardesses) looking after me. They walk up and down the __3__ bringing meals and drinks; and if the flight is going through some __4__ they warn everybody that it might be bit bumpy and ask us to fasten our __5__. On a long flight I like listening to music through the __6__ available to all passengers, and sometimes I have a sleep. I enjoy it all so much that I never want the plane to __7__.

1. A) airliner   B) airline   C) cabin   D) land
2. A) airliners   B) aisle   C) cabin crew   D) passengers
3. A) airline   B) aisle   C) turbulence   D) land
4. A) seat belts B) aisle   C) turbulence   D) land
5. A) seat belts B) seats   C) belts   D) land
6. A) airliners   B) headphones C) telephones   D) aisles
7. A) take off   B) seat   C) crew   D) land

BANK ACCOUNT

It's very simple to __1__ bank __2__ in Britain. There are very few __3__. Just go to your local __4__, __5__ a few forms, and that's it. You will probably only have to pay __6__ if there is no money in your account or if you borrow money from the bank, in other words if you have a(an) __7__.

1. A) account   B) close   C) open   D) fill in
2. A) account   B) accountant C) open   D) fill in
3. A) overdrafts B) documents   C) formalities D) openings
4. A) overdraft B) branch   C) formalities D) account
5. A) account   B) collect   C) open   D) fill in
6. A) account   B) bank charges
   C) formalities   D) documents
7. A) overdraft B) branch   C) formality   D) open

CURRENT AND DEPOSIT ACCOUNTS

For regular everyday use most people prefer a __1__ account. This normally earns no __2__ but you are given a __3__ book, which makes shopping and paying bills very easy. A(an) __4__ account earns interest but it's not so easy to __5__ your money. You sometimes have to give a week's __6__.

1. A) free   B) current   C) cheque   D) withdraw
2. A) interest   B) deposit   C) notice   D) dollar
3. A) notice   B) note   C) cheque   D) withdraw
4. A) interest   B) deposit   C) finance   D) current
5. A) pay   B) invest   C) cheque   D) withdraw
6. A) notice   B) current   C) work   D) money

Everyday Vocabulary

USING YOUR ACCOUNT

At regular intervals, perhaps monthly, you will receive a __1__ from the bank, giving details of each __2__ (money you put in) and __3__ (money you take out). If you're not sure how much money you have in your account, you can just go to your bank and ask what your __4__ is. If you have to make a regular payment, like rent, you can ask the bank to pay this amount for you automatically. This arrangement is called a __5__.

1. A) balance   B) deposit
   C) standing order   D) statement

2. A) balance   B) deposit
   C) standing order   D) statement

3. A) withdrawal   B) deposit
   C) standing order   D) statement

4. A) balance   B) deposit
   C) standing order   D) statement

5. A) balance   B) deposit
   C) standing order   D) statement

SPENDING

Some people spend more money than they receive. In other words, their __1__ is greater than their __2__. If you take more money out of the bank than you have in your account, you are __3__. To keep a(an) __4__ of your spending, it's a good idea when you write a cheque to fill in the __5__, which stays in the book. Most cheques are __6__ cheques, which means that no one else can __7__ them. They must be paid into someone's account

1. A) expenditure   B) income
   C) cash   D) record

2. A) expenditure   B) income
   C) cash   D) record

3. A) counterfoil   B) underdrawn
   C) overdrawn   D) crossed

4. A) counterfoil   B) record
   C) income   D) expenditure

5. A) counterfoil   B) record
   C) overdrawn   D) expenditure

6. A) counterfoil   B) record
   C) overdrawn   D) crossed

7. A) expenditure   B) income
   C) cash   D) overdraw

BOOKS AND READING 1

Match each kind of book below with the kind of material you would normally find in it.

1. Maps
2. Exercises and diagrams etc. for school study
3. Meanings of words
4. Information about a subject
5. An exciting story of crime or adventure
6. Instructions, e.g. on how to maintain, repair and use a car
7. Tourist information and advice about a place or country
8. A list of important, famous people and details of their lives

A) Guidebook
B) Dictionary
C) Manual
D) Atlas
E) Thriller
F) Textbook
G) Who's Who
H) Encyclopedia

BOOKS AND READING 2

I love books. I love to read. I'm a real __1__, and I love to __2__ in bookshops, just looking briefly at one book after another. I look at the __3__, the photos or drawings. If there *are* foreign or technical words in the book, I look at the __4__ at the back for their meanings (unless they're explained in __5__ at the bottom of the pages) and I look at the __6__ also at the back, which is a list of other books on the same subject. And I use the library a lot. I __7__ two or three books a week, and I have to pay a(an) __8__ if I return them late. Friends often recommend books to me, and I also read book __9__ in the newspapers. I don't always agree with them, but anyway they let me know what new books are being __10__.

1. A) review   B) footnote   C) glossary   D) bookworm

2. A) borrow   B) browse   C) lend   D) publish

3. A) reviews   B) illustrations
   C) dictionaries   D) bibliographies

4. A) reviews   B) footnotes   C) glossary   D) bookworm

5. A) pricelists   B) footnotes   C) glossaries   D) dictionaries

6. A) reviews   B) covers   C) contents   D) bibliography

7. A) borrow   B) browse   C) lend   D) book

8. A) fine   B) attention   C) time   D) bookworm

9. A) reviews   B) illustrations C) pricelists   D) names

10. A) created   B) produced   C) punished   D) published

CARS AND DRIVING

The amount of petrol a car uses is called the __1__ and it is measured in __2__. The petrol goes in the __3__. The way a car behaves (speed, brakes, acceleration etc.) is called the car's __4__. We can talk about the back of a __5__ (car, bus, lorry etc.) but more often we use the word __6__. The speedometer, fuel gauge, and so on are called __7__. To __8__ means to pass another vehicle going in the same direction. If you have to go backwards, you __9__. The outside surface of the car, made of metal or fiberglass, is called the __10__. Make sure you __11__ before turning left or right.

1. A) fuel consumption   B) petrol tank
   C) petrol quality   D) pipe

2. A) rear   B) indicate
   C) mpg (miles per gallon)   D) scales

3. A) fuel consumption   B) petrol tank
   C) pipe   D) tube

4. A) quality   B) price   C) performance D) action

5. A) truck   B) petrol tank C) vehicle   D) overtake

6. A) rear   B) indicate   C) wheel   D) reverse

7. A) vehicles   B) instruments C) performance D) body

8. A) speed up   B) over speed C) overload   D) overtake

9. A) run back   B) look back   C) return   D) reverse

10. A) vehicle   B) instruments C) indicate   D) body

11. A) show   B) indicate   C) slow down   D) reverse

Everyday Vocabulary

A VISIT TO THE CINEMA

Fiona and I went to the __1__ the other day to see 'Devil' at the Odeon. The __2__ by the Daily Express __3__ was good, and we decided to go to the 8 o'clock __4__. When I arrived, Fiona was waiting for me in the __5__, looking at a __6__ for 'Devil' on the wall. We went into the __7__ and sat down. I don't like to be too close to the __8__ and I usually sit in the back __9__ if possible, and I prefer a seat on the __10__ so I can stretch my legs. Before the main film there was a Mickey Mouse __11__ then a __12__ for the following week's film. 'Devil' was a __13__ film and I was quite terrified, but Fiona thought it was funny.

1. A) cinema   B) pub   C) picnic   D) theater
2. A) foyer   B) show   C) repetition   D) review
3. A) yard   B) trailer   C) critic   D) performance
4. A) film   B) action   C) critic   D) performance
5. A) foyer   B) living room C) aisle   D) office
6. A) picture   B) poster   C) screen   D) mirror
7. A) office   B) home   C) auditorium   D) saloon
8. A) foyer   B) screen   C) mirror   D) review
9. A) row   B) sit   C) auditorium   D) yard
10. A) foyer   B) screen   C) aisle   D) review
11. A) cinema   B) cartoon   C) critic   D) film
12. A) trailer   B) repetition   C) show   D) artist
13. A) trailer   B) comedy   C) thriller   D) horror

A FILM REVIEW

Marlon Brando is a superb actor and in 'On the Waterfront' he gave his finest __1__. It is his best-known __2__. The __3__ also included Eva Marie Saint and Karl Maiden and the film's __4__, Elia Kazan, never made a better film. Parts of the film were shot in the __5__ in Hollywood, but a lot was made on __6__ in the streets of New York, which makes it at times like a __7__. The critics loved the film but it was not only a __8__ success. It was a great __9__ success as well, and made an enormous profit. The __10__ is about a young man's attempt to be a boxing champion.

1. A) performance   B) action
    C) critical   D) plot
2. A) comedy   B) role   C) film   D) play
3. A) performance   B) documentary
    C) critics   D) cast
4. A) player   B) actor   C) plot   D) director
5. A) location   B) home office C) studio   D) box office
6. A) location   B) role   C) studio   D) box office
7. A) performance   B) documentary
    C) critical   D) trailer
8. A) perform   B) role   C) critical   D) cast
9. A) location   B) auditorium C) studio   D) box office
10. A) location   B) role   C) plot   D) director

MEDICAL STAFF AND PATIENTS

Match each of these people with the correct definition below.

1. an ordinary doctor
2. someone who looks after sick people in hospital
3. person who helps people with mental problems
4. sick person receiving treatment
5. sick person who has to stay in hospital
6. sick person who has to visit the hospital regularly for treatment
7. someone who operates on sick people
8. person badly injured in an accident, fire, war
9. person who helps at the birth of a baby
10. person who studies to be a doctor
11. person who specializes in one area of medical treatment

A) patient
B) psychiatrist
C) in-patient
D) specialist
E) casualty
F) out-patient
G) surgeon
H) nurse
I) midwife
J) medical student
K) general practitioner

DOCTORS' SURGERIES AND HOSPITALS

When I go to the doctor, I tell the __1__ my name and take a seat in the __2__ room. My doctor is very busy so I have to make a(an) __3__ before I go to see him. He asks me what's wrong with me, I tell him the __4__ of my illness, for example high temperature, difficulty in breathing, or pains, and then he will usually __5__ me. He'll listen to my heart with his __6__, he'll hold my wrist to feel my __7__, he'll take my __8__ with his __9__. The problem is usually something simple and he might give me a __10__ for some medicine, which I take to the __11__. Of course, if I needed more serious __12__, I'd have to go to hospital. There I'd be put in a bed in a(an) __13__ with 10 or 20 other people. If there were something seriously wrong with me, I might need a(an) __14__.

1. A) receptionist   B) chemist
    C) ward   D) appointment
2. A) operation B) ward   C) waiting   D) examine
3. A) agreement   B) attempt
    C) speech   D) appointment
4. A) treatments B) pulse   C) symptoms   D) prescription
5. A) operate   B) bill   C) treat   D) examine
6. A) periscope B) pulse   C) symptom   D) stethoscope
7. A) skin   B) pulse   C) symptoms   D) blood
8. A) pulse   B) temperature C) blood   D) heart
9. A) meter   B) barometer
    C) thermometer   D) kilometer
10. A) prescription   B) bill
    C) receipt   D) medicine
11. A) receptionist   B) chemist
    C) biologist   D) therapist
12. A) treatment B) threat   C) symptom   D) stethoscope
13. A) operation room   B) ward
    C) waiting room   D) dormitory
14. A) operation B) receipt C) prescription D) examining

Everyday Vocabulary

EDUCATION

When children are two or three years old, they sometimes go to a __1__ school, where they learn simple games and songs. Their first real school is called a __2__ school. In Britain children start this school at the age of five. The __3__ year in Britain begins in September and is divided into three __4__. Schools __5__ for the summer holiday in July. __6__ education begins at the age of about eleven, and most schools at this level are __7__ which means boys and girls study together in the same classes. In Britain education is __8__ from five to 16 years of age, but many children choose to remain at school for another two or three years after 16 to take higher exams. Most children go to __9__ schools, which are maintained by the government or local education authorities, but some children go to __10__ schools, which can be very expensive. University courses normally last three years and then students __11__, which means they receive their __12__. At university, teaching is by __13__ (an individual lesson between a teacher and one or two students), __14__ (a class of students discussing a subject with a teacher), __15__ (when a teacher gives a prepared talk to a number of students) and of course private study. Most people who receive a university place are given a __16__ by the government to help pay their __17__ and living expenses.

1. A) primary   B) nursery
   C) boarding   D) co-educational
2. A) primary   B) graduate   C) compulsory   D) secondary
3. A) academic   B) nursery school
   C) graduate   D) co-educational
4. A) fees   B) forms   C) degrees   D) terms
5. A) finish   B) break up   C) over   D) run
6. A) good   B) private   C) secondary   D) higher
7. A) academic   B) nursery school
   C) graduate   D) co-educational
8. A) voluntary B) forbidden   C) compulsory   D) free
9. A) boarding   B) private   C) state   D) secondary
10. A) primary   B) private   C) state   D) boarding
11. A) break up B) practice   C) graduate   D) lecture
12. A) fees   B) tutorial   C) degree   D) certificate
13. A) discussion B) tutorial   C) lesson   D) lecture
14. A) lecture   B) meeting   C) discussion   D) seminar
15. A) lecture   B) meeting   C) discussion   D) seminar
16. A) award   B) grant   C) certificate D) present
17. A) fees   B) expenditures
    C) degree   D) total

ELECTIONS

People sometimes try to __1__ the result of an election weeks before it takes place. Several hundred people are asked which party they prefer, and their answers are used to guess the result of the coming election. This is called a(an) __2__. Meanwhile each party conducts its election __3__ with meetings, speeches, television commercials and party members going from door to door encouraging people to __4__ their party. In Britain everyone over 18 is eligible to __5__. The place where people go to vote in an election is called a __6__ and the day of the election is often known as __7__ day. The voters put their votes in a __8__ box and later they are counted. The __9__ with the most votes is then declared the winner.

1. A) vote   B) elect   C) predict   D) support
2. A) opinion poll B) campaign   C) paradox   D) elector
3. A) campaign   B) ballot   C) commercials   D) summits
4. A) vote   B) improve   C) predict   D) support
5. A) vote   B) elect   C) predict   D) support
6. A) campaign   B) ballot box
   C) polling   D) polling station
7. A) vote   B) election   C) predict   D) polling
8. A) election   B) ballot   C) polling   D) vote
9. A) voter   B) member   C) candidate   D) president

GOVERNMENT

In most countries, except __1__ states there are several different political parties. The one with the __2__ of seats normally forms the government, and the parties which are against the government are called the __3__. Sometimes no single party wins enough seats, and several parties must combine together in a __4__ to form a government. The principal ministers in the government form a group called the __5__. The leader of this group, and of the government, is the __6__. Of course, there *are* many different kinds of parties and governments. A socialist or communist party is often described as __7__. A conservative party on the other hand, is usually said to be __8__. Political situations are always changing. Sometimes in a party or between two parties there is a big argument or deep difference of opinion. This is called a(an) __9__. When, on the other hand, two parties work together, this is sometimes called an __10__.

1. A) cabinet   B) majority   C) coalition   D) one-party
2. A) majority   B) alliance   C) coalition   D) opposition
3. A) majority   B) alliance   C) coalition   D) opposition
4. A) majority   B) alliance   C) coalition   D) opposition
5. A) cabinet   B) majority
   C) left-wing   D) one-party state
6. A) cabinet minister B) majority
   C) prime minister   D) president
7. A) right-wing B) left-wing   C) alliance   D) coalition
8. A) right-wing B) left-wing   C) alliance   D) coalition
9. A) opposition B) coalition   C) alliance   D) split
10. A) opposition B) coalition   C) alliance   D) split

RENTING A FLAT

The first thing I had to do in Belfast was to find somewhere to live, if possible a small, one-bed roomed __1__. I didn't want to share a kitchen or toilet; I wanted to be independent in my own self- __2__ place. I decided I could pay a __3__ of £50 a week. I couldn't find what I wanted in the newspaper __4__ so I went to a(an) __5__. They offered me a nice place. It was in a modern __6__ on the third floor. I had to pay the agency a __7__, and the __8__ wanted a big __9__ and __10__ from my employer and bank manager.

1. A) apartment   B) block   C) flat   D) hotel
2. A) contained   B) rent
   C) fee   D) accommodation
3. A) borrow   B) rent   C) lend   D) get
4. A) advertisements   B) references
   C) pictures   D) headlines
5. A) newspaper agency B) police officer
   C) state agency   D) accommodation agency
6. A) land   B) block   C) flat   D) room
7. A) reference   B) rent   C) fee   D) deposit
8. A) landlord   B) ownership   C) tenant   D) deposit
9. A) advertisement   B) reference
   C) flat   D) deposit
10. A) advertisements B) references
    C) advertisements D) deposit

Everyday Vocabulary

BUYING A HOUSE

Tony and Sheila's first home was a(an) __1__ house, one of a line of houses all connected. But several years later when they had a small child, they found it rather __2__ for three people. They wanted something more __3__ and so decided to move. They went to a(an) __4__ and looked at details of the houses he had to offer. They looked at a __5__ house (one of a pair attached to each other), liked it, and asked a __6__ to inspect it for them. He said that it was in good __7__, and they therefore decided to buy it. Luckily they sold their house quickly and soon a(an) __8__ firm was taking all their furniture and other possessions to their new home. But already, after a couple of years, they are hoping to move again. Tony's business is doing well and they want to get a(an) __9__ to design a modern, __10__ house for them, and a(an) __11__ to build it.

1. A) detached B) semi-detached
   C) cramped D) terraced
2. A) detached B) semi-detached
   C) cramped D) terraced
3. A) cramped B) detached C) spacious D) stuffy
4. A) builder B) estate-agent
   C) architect D) tenant
5. A) detached B) semi-detached
   C) cramped D) terraced
6. A) architect B) surveyor C) tenant D) builder
7. A) condition B) manner C) mood D) case
8. A) builder B) estate-agent
   C) architect D) removals
9. A) builder B) estate-agent
   C) architect D) landlord
10. A) detached B) apartment C) cramped D) villa
11. A) agent B) surveyor C) architect D) builder

EATING OUT

I'm a terrible cook. I've tried hard but it's no use. I've got lots of __1__, I choose a __2__. I want to cook, I read the __3__. I prepare all the necessary __4__ and follow the instructions. But the result is terrible, and I just have a sandwich or some other quick __5__. So I often __6__. I don't like grand restaurants. It's not the expense; it's just that I don't feel at ease in them. First the __7__ gives me a(an) __8__ which I can't understand because it's complicated and has lots of foreign words. At the end of the meal when I pay the __9__. I never know how much to leave as a __10__. I prefer __11__ places, like hamburger shops where you pay at once and sit down and eat straightaway. And I like __12__ places, where you buy a meal in a special container and take it home.

1. A) cookery books B) menus
   C) recipe D) ingredients
2. A) menu B) take-away C) food D) dish
3. A) cookery books B) menu
   C) recipe D) ingredients
4. A) cookery books B) menu
   C) recipe D) ingredients
5. A) eat out B) take away C) snack D) fast food
6. A) eat out B) take away C) snack D) cook
7. A) servant B) waiter C) hostess D) receptionist
8. A) cookery book B) menu
   C) recipe D) ingredient
9. A) bill B) income C) tip D) receipt
10. A) gift B) money C) tip D) dish
11. A) eat out B) cookery C) snack D) fast food
12. A) eat out B) take-away C) fast food D) take-out

ENTERTAINING AT HOME

Maureen often gives dinner parties at home. She loves __1__. She lays the table: puts the __2__ in the right places, sets out the plates and puts a clean white __3__ at each place. For the meal itself, she usually gives her guests some kind of __4__ first, for example soup or melon. Next comes the __5__, which is usually meat (unless some of her guests are __6__ or if they're on a special __7__) with a __8__ of salad. For __9__ it's usually fruit or ice-cream, and then coffee. When everyone has gone home, she must think about doing the __10__, as in the kitchen the __11__ is full of dirty __12__.

1. A) diet B) entertaining C) crockery D) side dish
2. A) dessert B) main course C) cutlery D) side dish
3. A) sink B) paper C) cutlery D) napkin
4. A) main course B) dessert C) starter D) side dish
5. A) main course B) dessert C) main course D) side dish
6. A) vegetarian B) entertaining C) crockery D) cook
7. A) diet B) entertaining C) cutlery D) main course
8. A) diet B) dessert C) cutlery D) side dish
9. A) side dish B) dessert C) starter D) main course
10. A) washing up B) cooking C) diet D) cutlery
11. A) refrigerator B) crockery C) cutlery D) sink
12. A) sink B) crockery C) meal D) napkins

GAMBLING

Some people are __1__ gamblers which means that they simply cannot stop __2__ on horses or playing games of __3__. It can be like a disease. If you're lucky, you can win a __4__ but if you're unlucky it can __5__ your life. And most people are unlucky. The __6__ are always against the gambler. At the race course it is the __7__ who win and the __8__ who lose. From a game of roulette in the __9__, the house makes a profit, the gambler often goes __10__.

1. A) punter B) betting C) broke D) compulsive
2. A) playing B) betting C) cheating D) racing
3. A) lucky B) odds C) fortune D) chance
4. A) wreck B) treasure C) fortune D) money
5. A) wreck B) odd C) fortune D) improve
6. A) wrecks B) odds C) fortunes D) luck
7. A) casinos B) bookmakers C) brokers D) horses
8. A) punters B) bookmakers C) brokers D) horses
9. A) casino B) race C) cafe D) gamble
10. A) breaking B) rich C) broke D) unlucky

SMOKING

To many people smoking is not just a pleasure, it is a(an) __1__. They need it, depend on it, can't stop it. If they haven't smoked for some hours, they feel a(an) __2__ for a cigarette. They often __3__ smoke, which means they light another cigarette immediately they have __4__ the one before. Smoking is often considered __5__ since many people don't like the smell of cigarettes or the sight of the smoker's __6__ fingers or __7__ -trays full of cigarette-ends. Above all, smoking is __8__ to health and in many countries a warning is printed on every __9__ of cigarettes. Scientists have proved that there is a link between smoking and a disease which can be __10__-cancer.

1. A) addiction B) craving
   C) entertainment D) joy
2. A) hatred B) craving C) disgust D) repulsion
3. A) chain B) pain C) repeat D) packet
4. A) put off B) put out C) put in D) put up

Everyday Vocabulary

5. A) harmful   B) joyful   C) stained   D) antisocial
6. A) dirty   B) craving   C) stained   D) broken
7. A) smoke   B) fire   C) ash   D) kitchen
8. A) harmful   B) harmless   C) helpful   D) useful
9. A) carton   B) packet   C) box   D) envelope
10. A) harmful   B) harmless   C) useful   D) fatal

DRINKING

Drinking habits vary. Some people don't drink alcohol at all, just __1__ drinks like fruit juice. They are called __2__. Others like to __3__ a glass of wine slowly, just to be __4__. Others like to drink glass after glass of beer, or possibly __5__ such as whisky, brandy or vodka. Soon they become __6__ and if they continue, they'll get __7__ and wake up the next morning with a bad __8__. Some people are dependent on alcohol. They can't do without it. They are __9__. One thing is certain. If you drive, you shouldn't drink. Stay __10__.

1. A) heavy   B) bitter   C) sweet   D) soft
2. A) alcoholics   B) teetotalers C) sober   D) soft drinkers
3. A) dip   B) tip   C) sip   D) rip
4. A) antisocial   B) sociable   C) socialist   D) spirits
5. A) springs   B) foods   C) juices   D) spirits
6. A) sober   B) sociable   C) tipsy   D) hangover
7. A) sober   B) sociable   C) drunk   D) tipsy
8. A) sober   B) backache   C) tipsy   D) hangover
9. A) alcoholics   B) teetotalers C) hangovers   D) tipsy
10. A) sober   B) sociable   C) tipsy   D) hangover

INDUSTRY

The health of a big, developed country's __1__ depends largely on its industry. Factories have to keep busy. They must __2__ and sell their __3__ in large quantities. __4__ must make and sell ships; car __5__ must make and sell cars. A period of industrial success, when everything goes well and large profits are made, is called a(an) __6__. On the other hand a period when there is not much industrial activity is called a __7__. To maintain a high level of production is not simple. For example Japan, a very successful industrialized country, has very few natural __8__ such as oil or coal, and has to __9__ them from other countries in order to keep its industries going, and thus to supply needs at home and also to __10__ its goods to its overseas __11__.

1. A) imports   B) productions C) economy   D) exports
2. A) import   B) produce   C) create   D) export
3. A) shipyards   B) plants   C) discoveries   D) products
4. A) shipyards   B) ports
    C) factories   D) manufacturers
5. A) yards   B) plants   C) centers   D) resources
6. A) slump   B) increase   C) boom   D) import
7. A) export   B) slump   C) boom   D) decrease
8. A) markets   B) products   C) imports   D) resources
9. A) import   B) produce   C) borrow   D) export
10. A) import   B) produce   C) lend   D) export
11. A) markets   B) bazaars   C) shops   D) trades

AGRICULTURE

A country which wishes to be __1__ in food will encourage its __2__ to produce as much as possible so that it will not be dependent on food imports. If there is not much rain, __3__ must be built on rivers to provide water to __4__ the land. If the land is not naturally rich, chemical __5__ must be used to make it __6__. Then __7__ (of wheat, rice etc.) will grow, the __8__ will be good, and in addition the __9__ (cattle, sheep etc.) will have grass to eat. If this does not happen, the __10__ sector of the country's economy will suffer and the country will have to import food from abroad.

1. A) infertile   B) fertile
    C) self-sufficient   D) agricultural
2. A) farmers   B) crops   C) dams   D) harvest
3. A) farms   B) crops   C) dams   D) bridges
4. A) irrigate   B) fertile   C) dry   D) moisturize
5. A) fertilizers B) agriculturals C) crops   D)) harvest
6. A) unproductive   B) agricultural
    C) irrigated   D) fertile
7. A) corns   B) plants   C) crops   D) flowers
8. A) irrigation   B) agriculture C) crop   D) harvest
9. A) wild animals   B) crops
    C) dams   D) livestock
10. A) fertilizer   B) agricultural C) irrigation   D) livestock

A SUMMIT MEETING

The American President and the Russian __1__ have announced their intention to __2__ a(an) __3__ in Vienna next month. The two countries have already had __4__ talks and decided on a(an) __5__ for the meeting. The main __6__ will be a discussion about the nuclear arms situation. At a __7__ conference held in Washington yesterday a government __8__ told journalists that the unfortunate __9__ of last year's talks between the two countries had been caused by disagreements over arms. He said the Vienna meeting would be a chance for the two nations to __10__ their differences.

1. A) spokesperson   B) leader
    C) citizen   D) people
2. A) settle   B) declare   C) ask   D) hold
3. A) summit meeting   B) breakdown
    C) gathering   D) agenda
4. A) settle   B) preliminary C) gathering   D) prime
5. A) topic   B) subject   C) agenda   D) time
6. A) summit meeting   B) breakdown
    C) item   D) agenda
7. A) spokesperson   B) leader
    C) agenda   D) news
8. A) spokesperson   B) leader
    C) worker   D) prime minister
9. A) breakup   B) breakdown
    C) breakin   D) breaking
10. A) settle   B) lead   C) support   D) hold

DIPLOMATIC RELATIONS

Neighboring countries A and B had always had very good, close relations, but in 1992, owing to a disagreement over the exact location of the border between them, a(an) __1__ began to develop. Finally, in 1994, in __2__ at military activity by country B near the border, country A announced its intention to __3__, __4__ relations with country B. Both countries withdrew their __5__ and the __6__ in the two countries were closed down, It is hoped that a solution will be found and that it will be possible to __7__ normal trade, cultural and diplomatic __8__ as soon as possible.

1. A) resume   B) agreement   C) link   D) split
2. A) celebration   B) protest
    C) agreement   D) disagreement
3. A) break off   B) break in   C) break out   D) break down
4. A) educational B) sanitary   C) ambassador   D) diplomatic

Everyday Vocabulary

5. A) presidents B) ministers C) ambassadors D) bureaucrats
6. A) palaces B) embassies C) centers D) hotels
7. A) resume B) give up C) cease D) halt
8. A) borders B) embassies C) links D) splits

AN ARREST

A policeman was sent to __1__ the disappearance of some property from a hotel. When he arrived, he found that the hotel staff had caught a boy in one of the rooms with a camera and some cash. When the policeman tried to __2__ the boy, he became violent and the policeman had to __3__ him. At the police station the boy could not give a satisfactory explanation for his actions and the police decided to __4__ him with the __5__ of the camera and cash. They took his __6__ locked him in a __7__ and __8__ him overnight. The next morning he appeared in __9__ before the __10__. He took a(an) __11__ and __12__ not guilty. Two __13__, the owner of the property and a member of the hotel staff, gave __14__. After both sides of the case had been heard the boy was __15__ guilty. He had to pay a(an) __16__ of £50 and he was given a __17__ of three months in prison suspended for two years.

1. A) arrest B) magistrate C) investigate D) detain
2. A) arrest B) investigate C) charge D) save
3. A) arrest B) plead C) handcuff D) detain
4. A) arrest B) sentence C) detain D) charge
5. A) thieving B) steal C) theft D) evidence
6. A) fingerprints B) tiptoes C) handcuffs D) witnesses
7. A) prison B) dungeon C) cell D) jail
8. A) took B) charged C) handcuffed D) detained
9. A) dungeon B) prison C) station D) court
10. A) criminal B) magistrate C) lawyer D) prosecutor
11. A) witness B) oath C) promise D) plead
12. A) asked B) pleaded C) promised D) begged
13. A) witnesses B) magistrates C) friends D) opponents
14. A) criminal B) magistrate
    C) investigations D) evidence
15. A) found B) sentenced C) celled D) charged
16. A) fine B) oath C) sentence D) money
17. A) word B) sentence C) fine D) charge

LAW AND PUNISMENT

If you want legal advice in Britain, you go to a __1__. At the end of the __2__, the judge orders the twelve men and women of the __3__ to retire and consider their __4__ guilty or not guilty. Men or women who look after prisoners in prison are called prison officers or __5__. If a person dies in unusual circumstances, a(an) __6__ is held at a special court, and the 'judge' is called a __7__. A policeman who investigates serious crime is called a __8__. He wears __9__ clothes, not uniform. In some countries murderers are executed but other countries have abolished the death __10__.

1. A) trial B) coroner C) solicitor D) prosecutor
2. A) trial B) event C) incident D) verdict
3. A) inquisitive B) team C) detectives D) jury
4. A) trial B) response C) answer D) verdict
5. A) detectives B) coroners C) warders D) soldiers
6. A) inquest B) trial C) verdict D) jury
7. A) warder B) coroner C) jury D) criminal
8. A) warder B) coroner C) detective D) jury
9. A) colorful B) plain C) detective D) jury
10. A) fine B) sentence C) punishment D) penalty

CLASSICAL MUSIC

While the concert __1__ was filling up and the __2__ were taking their seats, the __3__ were tuning their __4__. The famous __5__ entered. He gave the audience a low __6__, picked up his __7__, looked briefly at the __8__ which lay open in front of him, and raised his hands. The pianist placed her fingers ready over the __9__ of her piano. The __10__ section of the orchestra (violinists, cellists etc.) brought their __11__ up, ready to play. The concert was about to begin.

1. A) area B) saloon C) stadium D) hall
2. A) spectators B) musicians C) audience D) watchers
3. A) spectators B) musicians C) audience D) watchers
4. A) instruments B) tools C) devices D) apparatus
5. A) conductor B) singer C) director D) actor
6. A) hug B) bow C) greeting D) hello
7. A) stick B) string C) score D) baton
8. A) book B) notebook C) score D) baton
9. A) keys B) buttons C) switches D) strings
10. A) drum B) bow C) singer D) string
11. A) keys B) sticks C) bows D) batons

POPULAR MUSIC

After the Beatles, The Rolling Stones have probably been the most successful __1__ in Britain. Most of their records have gone into the __2__ ten and they've had many at __3__ one. But their records have usually been made in a recording __4__ and I always wanted to hear them __5__ at a __6__. I wanted to see them perform on __7__ in front of thousands of excited __8__. And I did, at Earls Court in 1990. It was great. And Mick Jagger, the __9__, sang all the old favorites. I couldn't hear the __10__ very well because of the noise, but somehow it didn't matter.

1. A) group B) team C) squad D) vocalists
2. A) upper B) bottom C) good D) top
3. A) top B) best C) number D) worst
4. A) center B) studio C) institution D) house
5. A) live B) living C) alive D) life
6. A) stage B) concert C) studio D) cinema
7. A) stage B) concert C) studio D) movie
8. A) watchers B) supporters C) fans D) spectators
9. A) vocal B) lyrics C) actor D) vocalist
10. A) letters B) lyrics C) words D) scripts

FAMINE AND FLOOD

If a country has no rain for a long time, this dry period is called a __1__. In countries dependent on their agriculture, this can lead to a period of __2__, when there is not enough food and people actually __3__ (die of hunger). They die of __4__. When it rains very heavily and the land is under water, this is called a __5__. In this situation people and animals can __6__. Sometimes __7__ have to __8__ food supplies to people in areas which are __9__.

1. A) famine B) drown C) drought D) flood
2. A) famine B) drown C) drought D) flood
3. A) survive B) starve C) drop D) extinct
4. A) starvation B) starve C) drown D) drought
5. A) famine B) drown C) drought D) flood
6. A) starve B) drown C) swim D) extinct
7. A) trains B) balloons C) parachutes D) helicopters
8. A) throw B) starve C) drop D) fly
9. A) cut up B) cut off C) cut down D) cut in

Everyday Vocabulary

EARTHQUAKE AND EPIDEMIC

In some parts of the world, the ground shakes from time to time. This is called a(an) __1__ and if it's a bad one, the number of __2__ (dead and injured people) is sometimes large. Buildings often __3__ and __4__ teams have to search for people who are __5__ under the __6__. Sometimes water supplies are affected and there is a(an) __7__ of disease, called a(an) __8__. __9__ teams are sent by the government to help the sick. The death __10__ can reach hundreds or even thousands.

1. A) casualty   B) outbreak   C) earthquake D) collapse
2. A) casualties   B) outbreaks   C) epidemics   D) wounded
3. A) tremble   B) outbreak   C) quake   D) collapse
4. A) epidemic   B) quake   C) rescue   D) saving
5. A) pressed   B) squeezed   C) rescued   D) trapped
6. A) rubble   B) toll   C) bubble   D) hole
7. A) casualty   B) outbreak   C) abundance   D) collapse
8. A) epidemic   B) disaster   C) illness   D) outbreak
9. A) epidemic   B) medical   C) rescue   D) quake
10. A) rubble   B) toll   C) result   D) outbreak

FIRE

During the night it was reported that a house was __1__ fire. Someone phoned the fire __2__ and a fire __3__ was sent to the house. One fire __4__ was __5__ by smoke and taken to hospital, but in half an hour the fire was __6__ control and after another half hour it was finally __7__. At first the police thought it was an accident, but later they found matches and a petrol can and began to suspect __8__.

1. A) under   B) in   C) on   D) out
2. A) team   B) brigade   C) police   D) bridge
3. A) engine   B) brigade   C) agent   D) car
4. A) engine   B) brigade   C) police   D) man
5. A) undercome   B) overgone   C) overcome   D) overwent
6. A) under   B) over   C) in   D) out
7. A) put in   B) put by   C) put off   D) put out
8. A) accident   B) arson   C) burglar   D) robbery

PUBLIC TRANSPORT

A taxi, sometimes called a __1__, is the most comfortable way to travel. You simply __2__ the taxi in the street or go to a taxi __3__, where there are several taxis waiting, for example at a station. At the end of your journey, you can see how much the __4__ is by looking at the __5__. You add a __6__ to this, and that's it. Very simple. But expensive! What about taking a bus? If it has- two floors, it's called a double- __7__ and you can get a good view from the top. If it has only one floor, it's called a(an) __8__-decker. Most buses have a two-person __9__ the __10__, who drives, of course, and the __11__, who takes your money. Keep your ticket because a(an) __12__ might want to __13__ it. You catch a bus by waiting at a bus __14__. You can see where a bus is going because the __15__ is written on the front. But try to avoid the __16__ hour. Quicker than the bus is the underground (called the __17__ in London, the __18__ in New York and the __19__ in Paris and many other cities). You buy your ticket at the ticket-office. Go down to the __20__ on the __21__ or in the __22__. The train comes. The __23__ doors open. You get on. You look at the map of the underground system. Very simple. For longer distances take a train or a long distance bus, usually called a __24__ which is slower but cheaper. The train is very fast. Put your luggage on the __25__ and sit and wait till you arrive.

1. A) rack   B) tip   C) lift   D) cab
2. A) coach   B) hail   C) tube   D) fare
3. A) rank   B) center   C) lift   D) platform
4. A) price   B) cost   C) fair   D) fare
5. A) crew   B) check   C) meter   D) metro
6. A) rack   B) tip   C) lift   D) cab
7. A) bus   B) floor   C) decker   D) storey
8. A) single   B) only   C) one   D) solo
9. A) crew   B) team   C) group   D) metro
10. A) rider   B) driver   C) writer   D) runner
11. A) accountant   B) performer   C) conductor   D) inspector
12. A) accountant   B) inspector   C) conductor   D) performer
13. A) crew   B) check   C) subway   D) metro
14. A) center   B) station   C) stop   D) platform
15. A) return   B) destination C) name   D) road
16. A) quick   B) rush   C) crowded   D) bad
17. A) floor   B) metro   C) tube   D) subway
18. A) subway   B) lift   C) metro   D) tube
19. A) crew   B) subway   C) tube   D) metro
20. A) rank   B) storey   C) stop   D) platform
21. A) escalator   B) cab   C) ladder   D) building
22. A) rack   B) ladder   C) lift   D) stairs
23. A) colorful   B) working   C) gliding   D) sliding
24. A) coach   B) hail   C) tube   D) rack
25. A) rack   B) tip   C) lift   D) cab

ROMANCE

Ann was a very __1__ girl who often dreamed of love and marriage. She was especially __2__ to a young man called Michael, who worked in the same office as she did, and he was very __3__ on her too. They became friendly and one day Michael asked her to go out with him. Their first __4__ was a visit to the cinema, and they both enjoyed the evening so much that they decided to __5__ together regularly. Michael was a bit untidy and rather young, and Ann's parents didn't __6__ of him at first, but Ann was a sensible, __7__ girl and they had confidence in her. For a year or so everything went well, but then somehow they slowly began to __8__, until finally they decided to __9__ their __10__.

1. A) realistic   B) romantic   C) mature   D) immature
2. A) approved   B) interested C) attracted   D) involved
3. A) keen   B) interested C) attracted   D) involved
4. A) engagement   B) dating   C) relationship D) date
5. A) go in   B) go out   C) go off   D) go up
6. A) approve   B) interest   C) attract   D) involve
7. A) immature   B) romantic   C) mature   D) crazy
8. A) settle down   B) drift apart C) break in   D) drift up
9. A) break down   B) drift apart C) break in   D) break off
10. A) relationship B) date   C) marriage   D) divorce

MARRIAGE

One evening, although he was nervous, Joe decided to __1__ to his girlfriend, Linda. She accepted his proposal, they became __2__ and he gave her a ring. After a year they had saved enough money to get married (they were both over 18 so they did not need their parents' __3__). Some people have a religious ceremony with a priest, but Joe and Linda decided on a __4__ ceremony in a registry office. On the day of the __5__ Linda, the __6__, was very calm, but Joe, the __7__, was nervous. Afterwards, at the __8__, speeches were made and the guests drank a __9__ to the happy couple, who finally left for a __10__ in Spain.

1. A) offer   B) engage   C) divorce   D) propose
2. A) married   B) engaged   C) divorced   D) parted

Everyday Vocabulary

3. A) answer B) reception C) welcome D) consent
4. A) civil B) reception C) honeymoon D) religious
5. A) engagement B) reception C) wedding D) propose
6. A) bride B) bridesmaid C) bridegroom D) wife
7. A) bride B) bridesmaid C) bridegroom D) husband
8. A) civil consent B) reception C) honeymoon D) engagement
9. A) juice B) toast C) water D) lemonade
10. A) wedding B) reception C) honeymoon D) engagement

GOING SHOPPING

If you want to buy a ready-made (or we sometimes say off the __1__) jacket, first find the jackets in the shop and look at the __2__ inside to see the size, material and make. For the price, look at the price-__3__. To see if it will __4__ you, you can __5__ the jacket in front of a mirror. If necessary a(an) __6__ will help you. You pay the __7__, who you will find at the __8__ desk. He or she will take your money, put it in the __9__ and give you your change. Make sure you also get a(an) __10__, which you should keep and bring back to the shop with the jacket if something is wrong with it and you want to __11__ it or ask for a(an) __12__ of your money. In clothes shops you pay the fixed price, of course. You don't __13__. Or you can wait until the __14__, when many goods are reduced in price. If you don't like shops, you can stay at home, look at catalogues and newspaper advertisements and do your shopping by __15__ order.

1. A) peg B) made C) record D) tag
2. A) list B) receipt C) bill D) label
3. A) paper B) receipt C) tag D) bill
4. A) go B) adapt C) tag D) fit
5. A) try up B) try in C) try on D) try out
6. A) cashier B) assistant C) worker D) bargain
7. A) assistant B) cashier C) worker D) bargain
8. A) cash B) refund C) order D) sales
9. A) till B) wallet C) bag D) case
10. A) receipt B) paper C) label D) tag
11. A) refund B) repay C) exchange D) label
12. A) repay B) refund C) order D) sale
13. A) agree B) bargain C) argue D) discount
14. A) refund B) bargain C) exchange D) sales
15. A) cash B) shop C) mail D) sales

SPORTS FACILITIES AND ATHLETICS

There's a big new sports centre near my home. There are football __1__ tennis and basketball __2__ swimming __3__ a sports hall with two boxing __4__ and even a skating __5__. There is also a separate athletics __6__, where 20,000 __7__ can watch the track __8__ on the track and the __9__ events such as jumping and throwing, in the grass centre. The __10__ get ready in modern changing rooms and the __11__ time and measure the events with modern equipment. A huge electronic __12__ shows the results.

1. A) courts B) rings C) pitches D) pools
2. A) pools B) courts C) rings D) pitches
3. A) pools B) courts C) rings D) pitches
4. A) pitches B) rings C) pools D) courts
5. A) pools B) courts C) stadium D) rink
6. A) pool B) court C) stadium D) ring
7. A) audience B) spectators C) watchers D) viewers
8. A) matches B) plays C) events D) shows
9. A) area B) central C) track D) field
10. A) athletes B) players C) gamblers D) officials
11. A) athletes B) viewers C) spectators D) officials
12. A) scoreboard B) television C) video D) cinema

FOOTBALL

I play football for my local __1__ against other sides in the area. Of course the __2__ aren't paid, we're just __3__. But anyway we __4__ very hard in the evenings and we're lucky because we can use the __5__ of a local school. On the day of the __6__ we arrive early, change, and put on __7__ suits to keep warm. Then the __8__, dressed in black, calls the two __9__ to the centre to __10__ a coin to decide who will play in which direction. Not many people come to watch the game. We usually have a(an) __11__ of only one or two hundred. But we enjoy it, whether we win, lose or __12__.

1. A) group B) team C) side D) squad
2. A) referees B) friends C) players D) spectators
3. A) specialists B) professionals C) referees D) amateurs
4. A) train B) try C) coach D) test
5. A) theater B) gymnasium C) pool D) court
6. A) contest B) team C) play D) match
7. A) track B) match C) play D) game
8. A) trainer B) player C) referee D) coach
9. A) trainers B) captains C) referees D) coaches
10. A) fling B) give C) toss D) throw
11. A) audience B) spectator C) group D) crowd
12. A) draw B) tie C) defeat D) beat

TELEVISION

Mass __1__ is a phrase often used to describe ways of giving information and entertainment to very large numbers of people. It includes newspapers, advertising and radio and, of course, television. In most countries people can __2__ to any of three or four different __3__. Do television programs influence our minds? Do they __4__ us? Is the news completely __5__ (neutral) or is it __6__ (considered from one particular point of view)? Don't the __7__ for alcohol, food and other goods condition our minds? Even the __8__ going on week after week telling the story of one family or group of people sometimes make us want to copy the life-style we see on the screen. Also __9__ which give people big prizes for answering simple questions can make us greedy. Some programs are watched by tens of millions of __10__.

1. A) press B) information C) media D) entertainment
2. A) button B) switch C) control D) change
3. A) channels B) objectives C) buttons D) medias
4. A) indoctrinate B) switch C) treat D) motivate
5. A) subjective B) objective C) partial D) biased
6. A) objective B) subjective C) fair D) impartial
7. A) products B) publications C) commercials D) comments
8. A) movies B) documentaries C) commercials D) soap operas
9. A) documentaries B) soap operas C) commercials D) quiz shows
10. A) viewers B) spectators C) audience D) crowd

Everyday Vocabulary

NEWSPAPERS

A newspaper makes its money from the price people pay for it and also from the __1__ it carries. A popular newspaper with a(an) __2__ of over five million daily makes a lot of money. Less serious newspapers are probably read just for __3__. They have big __4__ above the news stories, funny __5__ to look at and __6__ photos of violence. The __7__ columns are full of stories of the private lives of famous people. No one takes the political __8__ of such papers very seriously. On the other hand, in a free country where there is no __9__, serious newspapers are read principally for their news, sent to them by their __10__ round the world and by the big news __11__. People also *read* these newspapers for their __12__ of new books, films and plays and for their __13__, which represent the opinion of the newspaper itself about the important events and issues of the moment.

1. A) editorials B) advertising C) circulation D) censorship
2. A) editorial B) advertising C) circulation D) censorship
3. A) review   B) advertising
   C) entertainment   D) correspondent
4. A) reviews   B) headlines
   C) subtitles   D) gossip columns
5. A) cartoons   B) headlines
   C) gossip columns D) jokes
6. A) amusing B) funny C) hilarious D) sensational
7. A) cartoon B) view C) gossip D) circulation
8. A) circulation B) views
   C) entertainment D) sensations
9. A) editorial B) advertising C) circulation D) censorship
10. A) reviews   B) editorials
    C) speakers   D) correspondents
11. A) firms B) centers C) companies D) agencies
12. A) reviews   B) headlines
    C) entertainment D) correspondents
13. A) editorials B) advertisings
    C) circulations D) gossip columns

JOURNEYS

1. For general advice about travel, go to a travel _____.
   A) center B) agent C) place D) manager
2. One day I would like to do the _____ by train and ship across Russia to Japan.
   A) trip B) voyage C) journey D) cruise
3. We're going on a _____ of Europe, visiting 11 countries in five weeks.
   A) holiday B) tour C) voyage D) flight
4. We went on a three-week _____ round the Mediterranean. The ship called at Venice, Athens, Istanbul and Alexandria.
   A) trip B) holiday C) flight D) cruise
5. He once went by ship to Australia. The _____ took 4 weeks.
   A) travel B) tour C) voyage D) flight
6. I'm going on a business _____ to Paris next weekend.
   A) trip B) travel C) journey D) cruise
7. Air France _____ 507 from Paris to New York will be taking off in ten minutes.
   A) cruise B) tour C) voyage D) flight
8. The _____ from Heathrow Airport to the centre of London takes about 45 minutes by underground.
   A) flight B) trip C) journey D) cruise
9. On our first day in New York we went on a three-hour _____ of the city by bus, which showed us the main sights.
   A) cruise B) tour C) voyage D) flight
10. During our stay in Paris we went on a day _____ to Disneyland.
    A) trip B) travel C) journey D) cruise

ARGUMENT

I've always had a feeling of __1__ towards my older brother John, because he always received more attention from our parents. There has always been __2__ between us. And now that I'm more successful than he is in his job, he is __3__ of me. We've never actually had a __4__, just the occasional __5__, but we've never got on well. And his wife likes to make things worse. She's a real __6__, a nasty, argumentative, quarrelsome, __7__ woman. I've heard her __8__ John continually to get a better job, a bigger house, a nicer car.

1. A) disagreement B) agreement
   C) nag   D) resentment
2. A) jealous B) friction C) nag D) resentment
3. A) aggressive B) row C) troublemaker D) jealous
4. A) battle B) row C) war D) match
5. A) disagreement B) agreement
   C) nag   D) resentment
6. A) beautiful B) confused C) troublemaker D) sympathetic
7. A) aggressive B) humble C) modest D) thoughtful
8. A) agree B) tell C) nag D) resent

SADNESS

When Susan's cat was killed by a car she burst into __1__ and began to __2__ so loudly that the neighbors next door heard her. She was __3__ by the __4__. Her mother tried to __5__ her but Susan's __6__ was so great that it was three days (and three __7__ nights) before she began to __8__ enough to eat normally. Even then she talked to no one and was silent and __9__ for weeks. I think she'll always __10__ her pet.

1. A) sobers B) heart C) tears D) grief
2. A) sob B) tear C) giggle D) grief
3. A) heartdestroyed B) heartbroken
   C) heartburn   D) amazed
4. A) recovery B) loss C) lost D) lose
5. A) comfort B) recover C) withdraw D) miss
6. A) joy B) heart C) tear D) grief
7. A) sleepy B) sleepless C) asleep D) sleeping
8. A) recover B) comfort C) withdraw D) restore
9. A) bashful B) shy C) withdrawn D) outgoing
10. A) forget B) lose C) remind D) miss

BIRTH

When a woman is __1__ a baby, we say that she is __2__. Babies are __3__ either at home or in the maternity __4__ of a hospital. It is the job of a doctor or a __5__ to __6__ new babies. The proud __7__ must soon decide what to __8__ the child. For the first six months of their lives most babies are taken out in __9__ and sleep in __10__. At eight months or so they learn to __11__ along the floor, and they can usually walk soon after their first birthday.

1. A) delivering B) calling C) expecting D) parenting
2. A) pregnant B) midwife C) maternity D) crawling
3. A) expected B) born C) called D) crawled
4. A) ward B) center C) point D) institution
5. A) surgeon B) parent C) midwife D) nurse
6. A) deliver B) expect C) bear D) bring
7. A) pregnants B) surgeons C) midwife D) parents
8. A) deliver B) call C) tell D) say
9. A) cars B) prams C) trolleys D) streetcars
10. A) beds B) prams C) cots D) wards
11. A) sneak B) climb C) creep D) crawl

Everyday Vocabulary

DEATH

The body of a person who has died is taken in a special car called a __1__ to the __2__ service, which is conducted by a __3__. The relatives and friends of the __4__ person, who are called the __5__ are there. Then the wooden coffin is buried in a grave in the __6__ or cremated in a __7__. When people get older they usually make a __8__ and __9__ their money and other things to their family and friends. When a man dies, it is usually his __10__ who __11__ his property.

1. A) vehicle B) hearse C) coffin D) funeral
2. A) funeral B) cemetery C) wedding D) priest
3. A) mourner B) cemetery C) dead D) priest
4. A) mourners B) widow C) dead D) priest
5. A) mourners B) widows C) funerals D) priests
6. A) cemetery B) funeral C) deadgarden D) coffin
7. A) cemetery B) crematorium C) funeral D) vehicle
8. A) funeral B) cemetery C) widow D) will
9. A) sell B) deliver C) leave D) take
10. A) funeral B) hearse C) widow D) will
11. A) delivers B) owns C) leaves D) inherits

ADVERTISING

Advertisements are everywhere, from columns of small __1__ advertisements for houses, jobs cars etc. in newspapers to big __2__ on walls and enormous advertisements on __3__ by the side of the road. The job of the advertising __4__ is to __5__ the products of the firms who employ them. They design eye-__6__ advertisements and make television __7__ to __8__ us to buy, buy, buy.

1. A) classical B) class C) classified D) classic
2. A) hostels B) posters C) commercials D) agencies
3. A) hoardings B) commercials C) hostels D) agencies
4. A) centers B) agencies C) commercials D) agents
5. A) produce B) stick C) classify D) publicize
6. A) persuading B) keeping C) holding D) catching
7. A) classicals B) agencies
   C) commercials D) documentaries
8. A) persuade B) refuse C) accept D) publicize

ART

One of the most __1__ things anyone can do is to make a work of art, whether it's a/an __2__ making a __3__ or a __4__ painting pictures. __5__ artists do it for their own satisfaction and pleasure, but __6__ artists have to make a living from their art and they are dependent on __7__ to sell their __8__ in city __9__. I myself have three Picassos, a Botticelli and a Van Gogh. They're __10__ not originals, but they're all I can afford.

1. A) creature B) creative C) creation D) professional
2. A) carpenter B) painter C) architect D) sculptor
3. A) sculptor B) creature C) work D) sculpture
4. A) dealer B) painter C) sculptor D) architect
5. A) amateur B) specialist C) professional D) special
6. A) amateur B) novice
   C) professional D) non-professional
7. A) dealers B) painters C) architects D) sculptors
8. A) galleries B) creatures C) works D) workers
9. A) galleries B) centers C) shops D) stores
10. A) models B) reproductions
    C) genuine D) restores

PHOTOGRAPHY

A lot of people buy a/an __1__ just to take holiday __2__. They have __3__ made and put them in a/an __4__ or sometimes they prefer __5__ which they can show on the wall or screen with a/an __6__ Other people are more serious. They __7__ and print their films themselves in their own darkroom at home. If they want big pictures they make __8__.

1. A) printer B) scanner C) album D) camera
2. A) snaps B) slaps C) prints D) projects
3. A) prints B) slides C) albums D) cameras
4. A) printer B) slides C) album D) camera
5. A) prints B) slides C) albums D) cameras
6. A) snap B) scanner C) enlarger D) projector
7. A) build B) develop C) energize D) project
8. A) snaps B) developments
   C) enlargements D) projection

MILITARY SERVICE

In some countries military service is __1__. All young men and sometimes young women must spend a year or two in the __2__ (In most countries nowadays they don't have to. All members of the armed services are __3__) To be a soldier you join the __4__ to be a sailor you join the __5__ and to be an airman you join the __6__. If you are good at your job and can take responsibility, you might get __7__ and become a/an __8__.

1. A) comfortable B) compulsory C) free D) voluntary
2. A) forces B) powers C) strengths D) storehouse
3. A) non-willing B) opposed C) volunteers D) compulsories
4. A) army B) group C) navy D) battle
5. A) army B) battle C) navy D) war
6. A) airways B) air traffic C) air power D) air force
7. A) expansion B) growth C) increase D) promotion
8. A) private B) officer C) volunteer D) soldier

POLICE

Alan is now old enough and tall enough to __1__ the police __2__. At first, of course, he'll be an ordinary __3__ of the lowest __4__. He'll wear a/an __5__ and go out in the streets keeping in touch with the police station with his __6__. Then he'd like to be a/an __7__ in __8__ investigating serious crime.

1. A) enter B) join C) rank D) connect
2. A) center B) power C) rank D) force
3. A) lieutenant B) policeman C) detective D) soldier
4. A) point B) place C) rank D) row
5. A) clothes B) jacket C) suit D) uniform
6. A) walkie-talkie B) mobile phone
   C) camera D) telephone
7. A) private B) policeman C) detective D) officer
8. A) plain clothes B) uniform
   C) suit D) trousers

Everyday Vocabulary

SECURITY WORK

I run a __1__ firm which offers a complete range of security services. We have __2__ vehicles with special __3__ windows to transport money and other valuable items. We can supply trained __4__ to protect exhibits at art shows and jewelry displays. We can advise you if you think someone is trying to __5__ your phone or __6__ your private conversations at home or in the office with hidden microphones. We have ex-policemen whom you can hire as __7__ detectives and special __8__ to deliver your valuable parcels anywhere in the world. We can protect you or your children against possible __9__.

1. A) police   B) security   C) armored   D) crime
2. A) bombed   B) gunned   C) armored   D) weaponed
3. A) bullet-proof   B) gun-proof
   C) weapon-proof   D) army-proof
4. A) kidnappers   B) couriers   C) guards   D) burglars
5. A) pit   B) tip   C) pat   D) tap
6. A) ask   B) stop   C) cut   D) bug
7. A) separate   B) retired   C) private   D) self
8. A) kidnappers   B) couriers   C) guards   D) detectives
9. A) kidnappers   B) couriers   C) guards   D) detectives

THE SEASIDE

Many people's idea of relaxation is to sit on a sandy __1__ gazing at the broad __2__ or watching the __3__ roll in one after the other. But the sea can be dangerous and every year hundreds of bathers __4__ either when they are carried out to sea by strong __5__ or simply because they can't swim and find themselves out of their __6__ with their feet no longer touching the bottom. And hundreds more have to be rescued by __7__. If you want to __8__ into the sea, from rocks or some other high point, make sure it's deep enough. If it's __9__ you could seriously injure yourself. And finally, if you decide to walk along the high __10__ overlooking the beach and the sea, don't go too near the edge.

1. A) shore   B) beach   C) bank   D) land
2. A) waves   B) shallow   C) horizon   D) fish
3. A) waves   B) shallows   C) horizons   D) divers
4. A) hang   B) choke   C) suffocate   D) drown
5. A) cliffs   B) currents   C) horizons   D) beaches
6. A) mass   B) length   C) depth   D) weight
7. A) lifeguards B) bathers   C) lifesavers D) firefighters
8. A) swim   B) jump   C) drown   D) dive
9. A) deep   B) shallow   C) long   D) low
10. A) cliffs   B) currents   C) depths   D) beaches

MOUNTAINS

The Himalayas are the best-known mountain __1__ in the world and Mt Everest, with a __2__ of 8,880 meters is the highest mountain. Since Edmund Hillary made the first __3__ in 1953, __4__ from many countries have managed to __5__ to the __6__. Normally they need to take __7__ cylinders to help them breathe and other special __8__, including __9__ to connect themselves to each other. It's a dangerous sport and many people have lost their lives, not just on the way up but during the __10__ as well.

1. A) ascent   B) rage   C) descent   D) range
2. A) weight   B) height   C) length   D) descent
3. A) jump   B) peak   C) ascent   D) descent
4. A) mountaineers   B) jumpers
   C) athletes   D) cliffers
5. A) peak   B) climb   C) jump   D) descent

6. A) peak   B) bottom   C) surface   D) upwards
7. A) oxygen   B) air   C) water   D) hydrogen
8. A) tools   B) equipment   C) devices   D) apparatus
9. A) iron bars   B) strings   C) ropes   D) chains
10. A) attack   B) landing   C) decrease   D) descent

ELECTRICAL APPLIANCES

When you buy a television, radio or cassette recorder make sure it has a long enough __1__. __2__ it in at the most convenient __3__ in your room, and then __4__ on. You normally __5__ the volume by turning a/an __6__, and there are other __7__ as well. It is probably best to __8__ the appliance when it is not in use. If you have any trouble with it, ask a/an __9__ to look at it or take it back to the __10__ you bought it from.

1. A) lead   B) leave   C) control   D) plug
2. A) adjust   B) switch   C) plug   D) knob
3. A) control   B) socket   C) hole   D) plug
4. A) adjust   B) switch   C) plug   D) knob
5. A) adjust   B) switch   C) plug   D) knob
6. A) control   B) chain   C) plug   D) knob
7. A) leads   B) sockets   C) controls   D) plugs
8. A) lead   B) plug   C) control   D) unplug
9. A) fixer   B) electrician C) mechanic   D) repairmen
10. A) dealer   B) electrician C) repairmen   D) mechanic

THE TELEPHONE

How easy it is to use the telephone! Nowadays we usually don't need the __1__ to connect us to friends in other countries. We can __2__ the number in the telephone __3__, pick up the __4__ and __5__ the number, if the number is not __6__, we __7__ straightaway and if it's a good __8__ we can have a clear, easy conversation with people on the other side of the world.

1. A) dialer   B) directory   C) engager   D) operator
2. A) look on   B) look in   C) look up   D) look through
3. A) album   B) directory   C) agenda   D) operator
4. A) receiver   B) line   C) operator   D) director
5. A) dial   B) call   C) search   D) operate
6. A) receiver   B) available   C) free   D) engaged
7. A) get in   B) get out   C) get through   D) get by
8. A) rope   B) line   C) wire   D) net

COMPUTERS

So you only have a pocket __1__ to do additions, multiplications and so on, and you want to know about real __2__? Right. Well, the machines themselves are called the __3__ and the programs that you feed into them are called the __4__. If you want to see the results of what you are doing, you'll need a __5__ or you'll have to plug in to a television set. You'll operate your machine like a typewriter by pressing keys on the __6__. If you want a record on paper of what you're doing, you'll need a __7__, and if you want a machine which will enable you to see, arrange, re-arrange and then print a page of material, then the machine you want is a word __8__. You want color? Well, you can

1. A) hardware   B) calculator   C) keyboard   D) printer
2. A) software   B) screen
   C) computers   D) word processor
3. A) hardware   B) software   C) driver   D) printer
4. A) software   B) hardware   C) adapter   D) scanner
5. A) software   B) screen   C) keyboard   D) scanner

Everyday Vocabulary

6. A) hardware B) calculator C) keyboard D) printer
7. A) hardware B) calculator C) keyboard D) printer
8. A) software B) screen C) writer D) processor

SOUNDS

1. We heard a _____ of tires. It was a police-car turning a corner at top speed.
   A) squeal B) clatter C) roar D) splash
2. The plates and glasses fell to the floor with a _____.
   A) whistle B) rustle C) crash D) bang
3. We live near the airport and there's a terrible _____ every time a plane goes overhead.
   A) squeal B) clatter C) roar D) splash
4. The day was very quiet and we could hear the _____ of leaves in the wind.
   A) whistle B) rustle C) crash D) bang
5. He fell into the water with a great _____.
   A) squeal B) clatter C) roar D) splash
6. I heard a _____. It sounded like a gun-shot.
   A) whistle B) rustle C) crash D) bang
7. It was an enormous, heavy, old, wooden door and it used to _____ loudly when anyone opened it.
   A) rumble B) creak C) whistle D) rustle
8. It was the best football match I've ever seen. Both teams played hard until the final _____.
   A) rumble B) creak C) whistle D) rustle
9. The metal tray fell down the stone stairs with a _____.
   A) squeal B) clatter C) roar D) splash
10. I could hear the _____ of thunder in the distance.
    A) rumble B) creak C) whistle D) rustle
11. There was no sound except the quiet _____ of the air-conditioning.
    A) hum B) peal C) crack D) tick
12. At every hour on the radio there are six _____ so that people can check the precise time.
    A) squeaks B) pops C) pips D) cracks
13. The champagne cork finally came out with a loud _____.
    A) squeak B) pop C) pips D) jingle
14. Be careful. The ice is very thin and I think I heard it _____.
    A) hum B) peal C) crack D) tick
15. To celebrate the happy event, all the church bells in the town began to _____.
    A) hum B) peal C) crack D) tick
16. I must oil my bike. There's a _____ somewhere in the back wheel.
    A) squeak B) pop C) pip D) jingle
17. The engine of a Rolls Royce is so quiet that even when the car is going fast you can hear the clock _____.
    A) hum B) peal C) crack D) tick
18. The animals had small bells round their necks, which used to _____ when they moved.
    A) squeak B) pop C) pips D) jingle

ANIMAL SOUNDS

Match each animal with the sound it makes.

___ 1- monkey   a) roar
___ 2- lion   b) cluck
___ 3- dog   c) meow, purr
___ 4- cat   d) chatter
___ 5- horse   e) crow
___ 6- hen   f) bark, growl
___ 7- cock   g) moo
___ 8- bee   h) neigh
___ 9- cow   i) buzz
___ 10- sheep   j) bleat
___ 11- elephant   k) bray
___ 12- pig   l) hiss
___ 13- donkey   m) trumpet
___ 14- frog   n) grunt, squeal
___ 15- snake   o) squeak
___ 16- duck   p) howl
___ 17- wolf   q) quack
___ 18- mouse   r) croak

HUMAN SOUNDS

- He was so nervous he could only __1__, 'I...I...I... I'm please to meet you.'
- Don't __2__ all the time. Use a handkerchief and blow your nose.
- If we are out of breath after running we __3__ and __4__.
- It is said that people __5__ if they sleep with their mouths open and on their backs.
- He drank a lot of beer quickly and began to __6__.
- If you have a cold and you __7__ we often say, 'Bless you'.
- Don't speak so loud! Just __8__. The children are asleep.
- I always used to __9__ in history lessons. They were so boring.
- He can't stop talking. We always __10__ with relief when he goes away.
- Smoking always makes me __11__.
- My children __12__ when I tell them they must go to bed.

1. A) stammer B) hiccup C) cough D) yawn
2. A) sigh B) pant C) sniff D) puff
3. A) sigh B) pant C) sniff D) puff
4. A) sigh B) pant C) sniff D) puff
5. A) whisper B) groan C) snore D) sneeze
6. A) stammer B) hiccup C) cough D) yawn
7. A) whisper B) groan C) snore D) sneeze
8. A) whisper B) groan C) snore D) sneeze
9. A) stammer B) hiccup C) cough D) yawn
10. A) sigh B) pant C) sniff D) puff
11. A) stammer B) hiccup C) cough D) yawn
12. A) whisper B) groan C) snore D) sneeze

WAYS OF LOOKING

1. That man does look rather strange but you shouldn't _____ at him.
   A) glare B) blink C) stare D) frown
2. He made a hole in the fence so that he could _____ through without being seen.
   A) peer B) blink C) wink D) peep
3. If you go out into bright sunlight after being in the dark, you sometimes _____.
   A) peer B) blink C) glare D) peep
4. Small boys often stand outside the bicycle shop and _____ at the wonderful machines in the window.
   A) glare B) gaze C) wink D) frown

Everyday Vocabulary

5. We _____ if we are rather annoyed or if we are concentrating.
   A) peer   B) gaze   C) stare   D) frown

6. Did you _____ someone pass the window a moment ago? I thought I just saw someone.
   A) wink   B) glimpse   C) glare   D) frown

7. I thought he was serious until I saw him _____ at me to show he was joking.
   A) wink   B) glimpse   C) glance   D) frown

8. Grandfather has very bad eyes. He has to _____ at the newspaper to read it.
   A) peer   B) blink   C) wink   D) peep

9. I saw the motorist get out of his car and _____ furiously at the other driver who had run into the back of him.
   A) glare   B) gaze   C) blink   D) wink

10. I saw him _____ quickly at his watch.
    A) wink   B) gaze   C) glance   D) stare

WALKING

1. He was completely drunk. I watched him _____ across the road and fall down.
   A) crawl   B) trip   C) wander   D) stagger

2. It's very pleasant for a tourist to _____ round a new city with no particular purpose or destination.
   A) crawl   B) trip   C) wander   D) stagger

3. It was a lovely day so we decided to _____ in the park for an hour.
   A) stroll   B) stray   C) creep   D) limp

4. His injured foot made him _____ badly.
   A) stroll   B) stray   C) creep   D) limp

5. Be careful or you'll _____ on this icy bit of pavement.
   A) trudge   B) dash   C) slip   D) march

6. Everyone was asleep when I returned so I had to _____ to my room without making a noise.
   A) stroll   B) stray   C) creep   D) limp

7. If you join the army, you'll have to learn to _____.
   A) trudge   B) stagger   C) slip   D) march

8. Please don't _____ away from the main group or you'll get lost.
   A) stroll   B) stray   C) creep   D) limp

9. Before babies can walk, they can only _____ on their hands and knees.
   A) crawl   B) trip   C) wander   D) stagger

10. I'm afraid someone will _____ over that piece of wood and fall.
    A) crawl   B) trip   C) wander   D) stagger

11. It began to rain and we had to _____ into a shop to keep dry.
    A) trudge   B) dash   C) slip   D) stray

12. The exhausted men had to _____ for five miles through the snow.
    A) trudge   B) dash   C) slip   D) wander

BODY MOVEMENTS 1

Match each item on the left with the most suitable phrase on the right

___ 1. He flexed   a) his head in disagreement
___ 2. He shook   b) his fists angrily
___ 3. He clenched   c) his neck to see better.
___ 4. He craned   d) his muscles proudly
___ 5. He snapped   e) his forehead with a handkerchief
___ 6. He shrugged   f) his foot in time to the music
___ 7. He wiped   g) his shoulders
___ 8. He folded   h) his breath under water.
___ 9. He scratched   i) his knee because it was painful
___ 10. He held   j) his arms and relaxed.
___ 11. He tapped   k) his head thoughtfully
___ 12. He rubbed   l) his fingers to get attention.

BODY MOVEMENTS 2

Match each item on the left with the most suitable phrase on the right

___ 1. He trembled
___ 2. He shivered
___ 3. He sweated
___ 4. He blushed
___ 5. He sobbed
___ 6. He startled
___ 7. He dozed
___ 8. He fainted

a) in the hot sun.
b) with embarrassment
c) with fear
d) when he heard the sad news
e) with-cold
f) after going without food for three days
g) in surprise at the sudden noise.
h) in his armchair after a hard day's work

BODY MOVEMENTS 3

Match each item on the left with the most suitable phrase on the right

___ 1. She nodded
___ 2. He bowed
___ 3. She curtseyed
___ 4. She waved
___ 5. He smiled
___ 6. He saluted
___ 7. She fidgeted
___ 8. He pointed

a) when she saw her friend getting off the bus.
b) when his commanding officer entered the room.
c) in agreement.
d) when she was introduced to the Queen
e) when he was introduced to the Queen
f) to show the shop assistant what he wanted
g) because he was happy
h) after sitting in the same position for so long.

CONNECTORS

We sew cloth with a __1__ and __2__. We tie up a parcel with __3__. Mountaineers use __4__ to keep together and avoid falling. To keep a baby's nappy in place we use __5__. We use a hammer to knock a __6__ into wood. To pin a notice to a notice board we use a paper __7__. To keep pieces of cloth together in dressmaking we use __8__. We keep pieces of paper together firmly with a paper __9__. Different parts of a bicycle and other machines are kept together with __10__ and __11__. We use a screwdriver to put in or take out __12__.

Large ships in port are kept in place with heavy iron __13__. The postman keeps all the letters for one street together with a __14__, made of elastic.

1. A) nail   B) rope   C) chain   D) needle
2. A) rope   B) thread   C) chain   D) string
3. A) rope   B) thread   C) chain   D) string
4. A) rope   B) thread   C) wire   D) string
5. A) drawing pin B) paper clip C) safety pin D) rubber band
6. A) pin   B) nail   C) nut   D) bolt
7. A) drawing pin B) paper clip C) safety pin D) rubber band
8. A) pins   B) nails   C) nuts   D) bolts
9. A) pin   B) clip   C) bolt   D) band
10. A) pins   B) nails   C) nuts   D) clips

Everyday Vocabulary

11. A) pins   B) nails   C) clips   D) bolts
12. A) pins   B) needles   C) bolts   D) screws
13. A) ropes   B) threads   C) chains   D) clips
14. A) drawing pin   B) paper clip   C) safety pin   D) rubber band

TOOLS

1. We cut paper or cloth with a pair of _____.
   A) penknives   B) knives   C) scissors   D) axes
2. We put in and take out screws with a _____.
   A) drill   B) chisel   C) screwdriver   D) hammer
3. We dig holes in the ground with a _____.
   A) rake   B) spade   C) penknife   D) fork
4. We make holes in wood, metal or stone with a _____.
   A) drill   B) chisel   C) screwdriver   D) hammer
5. We raise a car to change a wheel with a _____.
   A) spanner   B) saw   C) jack   D) mallet
6. We knock nails into wood with a _____.
   A) drill   B) chisel   C) screwdriver   D) hammer
7. We cut down trees with a/an _____.
   A) penknife   B) scissor   C) scissors   D) axe
8. We carve wood or stone with a _____.
   A) drill   B) chisel   C) screwdriver   D) hammer
9. We hit a chisel with a _____.
   A) spanner   B) saw   C) jack   D) mallet
10. We collect dry leaves and make earth level with a _____.
    A) rake   B) spade   C) penknife   D) fork
11. To cut string and other things, we carry in our pocket a folding _____.
    A) rake   B) spade   C) penknife   D) fork
12. We turn the earth over in the garden with a spade or _____.
    A) rake   B) spade   C) penknife   D) fork
13. We saw wood with a _____.
    A) spanner   B) saw   C) jack   D) mallet
14. We tighten or loosen nuts and bolts with a _____.
    A) spanner   B) saw   C) jack   D) mallet

COLLECTIVE NOUNS

1. The _____ of the British Royal Navy was very strong in the nineteenth century.
   A) mob   B) fleet   C) crew   D) shoal
2. Disease reduced the farmer's _____ from 90 to 65 cows.
   A) flock   B) bundle   C) herd   D) stack
3. She was attacked by a _____ of wasps.
   A) pack   B) swarm   C) suite   D) congregation
4. A _____ of shouting people overturned cars, set fire to shops and attacked a police station.
   A) mob   B) fleet   C) crew   D) shoal
5. The Irish Prime Minister occupied a _____ of rooms at the hotel.
   A) pack   B) swarm   C) suite   D) congregation
6. Some spectators in the _____ disagreed with the referee's decision.
   A) bunch   B) crowd   C) audience   D) set
7. He bought a large _____ of bananas.
   A) bunch   B) crowd   C) audience   D) set
8. The priest was very sad to see his _____ getting smaller week by week.
   A) pack   B) swarm   C) suite   D) congregation
9. Fishing boats use modern equipment to locate the _____ of fish.
   A) mob   B) fleet   C) crew   D) shoals
10. She lost her balance and fell down a _____ of steps.
    A) gang   B) flight   C) clump   D) set
11. He was the leader of a well-known _____ of criminals.
    A) gang   B) flight   C) clump   D) set
12. We sat down in the shade of a _____ of trees.
    A) gang   B) flight   C) clump   D) set
13. In spring _____ of birds arrive back in Europe after spending the winter in Africa.
    A) flocks   B) bundles   C) herds   D) stacks
14. Our picnic was completely ruined by a _____ of ants.
    A) pack   B) swarm   C) suite   D) congregation
15. He gave her a _____ of flowers.
    A) bunch   B) crowd   C) audience   D) set
16. British Airways has a _____ of 26 Boeing 747s.
    A) mob   B) fleet   C) crew   D) shoal
17. She gave a _____ of old clothes to a charity organization.
    A) flock   B) bundle   C) herd   D) stack
18. The _____ applauded the new play enthusiastically.
    A) bunch   B) mob   C) audience   D) set
19. Has anyone seen a _____ of keys? I left them somewhere.
    A) bunch   B) crowd   C) stack   D) set
20. Golf is an expensive game. You'll need a _____ of clubs.
    A) bunch   B) crowd   C) audience   D) set
21. The books were arranged in a _____ one on top of the other.
    A) flocks   B) bundle   C) herd   D) stack
22. They've bought a leather three-piece _____ - a sofa and two armchairs.
    A) pack   B) swarm   C) suite   D) congregation
23. Let's play a game. Who's got a _____ of cards?
    A) pack   B) swarm   C) suite   D) congregation
24. The cruise ship carries 150 passengers and a _____ of 85.
    A) mob   B) fleet   C) crew   D) shoal
25. The _____ of sheep was controlled by a shepherd and two dogs.
    A) herd   B) bundle   C) set   D) stack
26. For their wedding I gave them a _____ of cutlery (6 knives, 6 spoons, 6 forks etc.).
    A) bunch   B) crowd   C) audience   D) set

LAW BREAKERS 1

Match each person on the left with the correct definition on the right.

___ 1. an arsonist
___ 2. a shoplifter
___ 3. a mugger
___ 4. an offender
___ 5. a vandal
___ 6. a burglar
___ 7. a murderer
___ 8. a kidnapper
___ 9. a pickpocket
___ 10. an accomplice
___ 11. a drug dealer
___ 12. a spy
___ 13. a terrorist

a) attacks and robs people, often in the street
b) sets fire to property illegally
c) is anyone who breaks the law
d) breaks into houses or other buildings to steal
e) steals from shops while acting as an ordinary customer
f) kills someone
g) deliberately causes damage to property
h) steals things from people's pockets in crowded places
i) gets secret information from another country
j) buys and sells drugs illegally
k) takes away people by force, demanding money for their return
l) helps a criminal in a criminal act
m) uses violence for political reasons

Everyday Vocabulary

LAW BREAKERS 2

Match each person on the left with the correct definition on the right.

___ 1. an assassin
___ 2. a hooligan
___ 3. a stowaway
___ 4. a thief
___ 5. a hijacker
___ 6. a forger
___ 7. a robber
___ 8. a smuggler
___ 9. a traitor
___ 10. a gangster
___ 11. a deserter
___ 12. a bigamist

a) causes damage or disturbance in public places
b) hides on a ship or plane to get a free journey
c) takes control of a plane by force & makes the pilot change course
d) murders for political reasons or a reward
e) is someone who steals
f) makes counterfeit (false) money or signatures
g) is a member of a criminal group
h) steals money etc. by force from people or places
i) marries illegally, being married already
j) is a soldier who runs away from the army
k) brings goods into a country illegally without paying tax
l) betrays his or her country to another state

OCCUPATIONS 1

Match each person or on the left with the correct definition on the right.

___ 1. a traffic warden
___ 2. a dustman
___ 3. a window dresser
___ 4. an estate agent
___ 5. a secretary
___ 6. an undertaker
___ 7. a bricklayer
___ 8. a civil servant
___ 9. a vet
___ 10. a newsagent
___ 11. a midwife

a) arranges shop-window displays
b) makes brick buildings and walls
c) works in a government ministry
d) controls parking and parking meters
e) collects rubbish from people's houses
f) treats sick animals
g) helps people buy and sell houses
h) sells newspapers and magazines from a shop
i) delivers babies
j) makes arrangements for funerals
k) deals with office correspondence and records

OCCUPATIONS 2

Match each person or on the left with the correct definition on the right.

___ 1. a chef
___ 2. an architect
___ 3. a librarian
___ 4. a fishmonger
___ 5. a miner
___ 6. a curator
___ 7. an interior decorator
___ 8. a typist
___ 9. a chauffeur
___ 10. a surgeon

a) drives someone's car for them
b) types letters in an office
c) designs buildings
d) operates on sick people
e) cooks in a restaurant or hotel
f) designs the insides of houses, hotels etc.
g) runs a museum
h) works in a library
i) gets coal from under the ground
j) sells fish from a shop

OCCUPATIONS 3

Match each person or on the left with the correct definition on the right.

___ 1. an optician
___ 2. a clown
___ 3. a jockey
___ 4. an auctioneer
___ 5. an editor
___ 6. a docker
___ 7. a chiropodist
___ 8. a butcher
___ 9. a reporter
___ 10. a diplomat
___ 11. a florist

a) rides racehorses
b) loads and unloads ships in a port
c) sells valuable objects at an auction
d) makes people laugh at a circus
e) tests people's eyes and sells glasses
f) writes for a newspaper
g) sells flowers from a shop
h) represents his or her country at an embassy
i) sells meat
j) prepares books, newspapers etc. for publication
k) treats people's feet

PEOPLE

Match each item on the left with the most suitable phrase on the right.

1. a chatterbox
2. a highbrow
3. a nosey parker
4. a bookworm
5. a film fan
6. a slowcoach
7. a lazybones
8. a scatterbrain
9. a workaholic
10. a fresh air fiend
11. a high flier
12. a troublemaker
13. a killjoy

a) is inquisitive and pokes his or her nose into other people's business
b) can't stop talking
c) loves reading books
d) is confused and forgetful
e) is intellectual and likes serious literature, art, music
f) loves to work
g) is very keen on the cinema
h) is not very active or energetic
i) is slow
j) causes difficulties between people
k) seems to enjoy preventing others from enjoying themselves
l) likes to open the windows or be outside
m) is clever and ambitious and will get promotion and success

Everyday Vocabulary

QUANTITIES

We buy things in different units. Match each item on the left with the most suitable item on its right.

1. a bar   a) of matches
2. a pair   b) of soap
3. a box   c) of potatoes
4. a pound   d) of cloth
5. a roll   e) of shoes
6. an ounce   f) of milk
7. a yard   g) of tobacco
8. a pint   h) of film
9. an acre   i) of flowers
10. a bottle   j) of toothpaste
11. a gallon   k) of land
12. a bunch   l) of wine
13. a tin   m) of sardines
14. a tube   n) of petrol
15. a packet   o) of jam
16. a jar   p) of cigarettes

SLANG

Replace each slang word with a word or phrase from the list.

- He smokes 30 fags __1__ a day. Too many!
- He drinks a lot. He must spend twenty quid __2__ a week on booze __3__.
- He thought his meal was overcooked. When the waiter brought his bill he kicked up __4__ a fuss and would not pay.
- I lost £500 at a casino last night. I'm absolutely skint __5__.
- My mate __6__ stole a car. Now he's in the nick __7__.
- She got bored with her boyfriend and ditched __8__ him.
- There's a good film on the telly __9__ tonight, but I've got to go out. What a drag! __10__
- I wouldn't like to be a copper __11__ directing traffic in the street in this bad weather.

a) alcohol
b) made
c) pound(s)
d) friend
e) cigarettes
f) television
g) policeman
h) discarded
i) nuisance
j) prison
k) without money

AMERICAN WORDS 1

The American words in the sentences below *are* printed in bold. Replace each American word or phrase with a British word or phrase from the following list.

- His mother thought he was at school but in fact he was playing hookey __1__. He'll probably flunk __2__ his exams.
- The kitchen faucet __3__ in my apartment __4__ isn't working. I'll tell the janitor __5__. He'll get it fixed.
- Blue-collar workers are asking for a pay-hike __6__ and longer paid vacations __7__.
- The dog attacked the mailman __8__ and tore his pants __9__.
- Do you have a railroad schedule __10__? I want an early train for Chicago tomorrow.
- A patrolman __11__ reported a light-blue sedan __12__ parked right across the sidewalk __13__ on 3rd Street.
- She has a little baby so she has to make regular visits to the drugstore __14__ to buy diapers __15__.
- When the waiter handed me the check __16__ after the meal, I found that I had no money!
- How much does it cost to mail __17__ a letter to Australia?

a) fail
b) bill
c) tap
d) postman
e) rise
f) flat
g) trousers
h) holidays
i) caretaker
j) playing truant
k) nappies
l) pavement
m) saloon car
n) railway timetable
o) chemist
p) ordinary uniformed policeman
q) post

AMERICAN WORDS 2

Replace each American word or phrase with a British word or phrase from the following list.

- We had to stand in line __1__ at the movie-theater __2__ last night.
- Our back yard __3__ looks lovely in the fall __4__. The leaves on the trees turn brown and red.
- He wants to major __5__ in math __6__ at college __7__ when he leaves high school __8__.
- When you stop for gas __9__ at a gas station __10__, they sometimes clean your windshield __11__.
- We had to buy a lot at the stores __12__, then we took the subway __13__ home.
- The elevator's __14__ broken down again, but it doesn't matter. We live on the first floor __15__.
- She likes candy __16__, and bread and butter with jelly __17__ on it. They're bad for her teeth.
- The only money I have is a twenty dollar bill __18__.
- In this district they only collect the garbage __19__ once a week.

a) petrol
b) queue
c) rubbish
d) autumn
e) sweets
f) jam
g) garden
h) note
i) lift
j) shops
k) underground
l) cinema
m) petrol station
n) ground floor
o) windscreen
p) specialize
q) mathematics
r) secondary school
s) university

Everyday Vocabulary

PART C: PHRASAL VERBS — CLASSIFIED PHRASAL VERBS

Expressions with Break

1. The firefighters had to break the door _____ to rescue the little girl.
   A) into B) out C) down

2. The burglar broke _____ the house and stole all their money and jewelry.
   A) away B) into C) forth

3. I don't know why their marriage is breaking _____.
   A) through B) in C) up

4. After two hours of hard work, we decided to break _____ for a little cup of coffee.
   A) off B) up C) into

5. We have to break _____ all our emotional barriers to feel free.
   A) away B) down C) into

6. When he spread the news, panic broke _____ in the city.
   A) in B) away C) out

7. Scientists will break _____ in their search for new sources of energy.
   A) up B) through C) out

8. Mary feels miserable, for she's just broken _____ her boyfriend.
   A) with B) up C) down

Expressions with Bring

9. Does this bring _____ memories?
   A) in B) on C) back

10. She had to bring _____ the children by herself.
    A) on B) up C) out

11. Did he ever bring _____ that book?
    A) back B) up C) on

12. Can I bring _____ my friend?
    A) up B) along C) out

13. Being a teacher doesn't bring _____ much money
    A) up B) back C) in

Expressions with Come

14. The idea came _____ her while she was reading "Hamlet".
    A) to B) about C) before

15. The farmer himself came _____ the intruders.
    A) before B) along C) after

16. I came _____ Schumacher at that big hotel.
    A) about B) apart C) across

17. The terrible scene of the crime continues to come _____ to me now and then.
    A) back B) between C) down

18. The properties will come _____ him on his father's death.
    A) after B) to C) on

19. Nobody wants to come _____ as a witness of the crime.
    A) over B) forward C) at

20. The Canadian swimmer came _____ first.
    A) in B) round C) off

21. I wonder why his experiment never came _____.
    A) from B) upon C) off

22. Look how beautiful it is! All the flowers are coming _____. It's springtime.
    A) out B) off C) down

23. He came _____ with a good solution to the problem.
    A) apart B) out C) up

24. He was lucky to come _____ without any scratches.
    A) through B) under C) by

25. Be careful! It's really fragile. I don't want it to come _____ in your hands.
    A) away B) out C) apart

26. Will the stain come _____ if I wash it?
    A) out B) in C) up

27. His aunt just died so he will come _____ a lot of money.
    A) out B) up C) into

28. The question didn't come _____ so I was happy.
    A) up B) in C) down

29. That book will come _____ very useful.
    A) up B) in C) down

30. She said she would come _____ and visit today.
    A) for B) over C) through

Expressions with Down

31. To be hit by a car or bus is the same as to be _____ down.
    A) cooled B) marked C) knocked

32. To reduce the amount you do something is the same as to _____ down.
    A) cut B) tear C) fall

33. To fail to do something when someone is relying on you is the same as to _____ down someone.
    A) let B) quieten C) sit

34. To let something become less hot is the same as to let it _____ down.
    A) lie B) cool C) tone

35. If it is raining very heavily, it is the same as to _____ down rain.
    A) pour B) cut C) tear

36. To have a lot of stress is similar to being _____ down by a lot of problems.
    A) poured B) cut C) weighted

37. To pass things from father to son is the same as to _____ down from generation to generation.
    A) calm B) hand C) climb

38. To relax from stress is the same as to _____ down.
    A) wind B) lie C) let

39. To write a note is the same as to _____ down something.
    A) jot B) scale C) tie

40. To make something appear less serious than it is the same as to _____ down something.
    A) slam B) set C) play

Expressions with Get

41. The manager failed to get his ideas _____ to the employees.
    A) across B) down C) in

42. I don't think they can easily get _____ from prison.
    A) away B) into C) down

43. She is very well-paid, so she can get _____ without any help from him.
    A) about B) over C) by

44. Ok. It's time to get _____ to business.
    A) in B) down C) away

45. I hope you don't get _____ trouble again.
    A) into B) on C) in

46. The teacher was lucky to get the truth _____ of him.
    A) up B) out C) away

47. Stop getting _____ my nerves!
    A) on B) at C) down

48. I doubt she'll ever get _____ her trauma.
    A) out B) over C) in

49. I can't get _____ all this work. I need some help.
    A) about B) away C) through

50. What time do you usually get _____?
    A) on B) up C) about

51. The rumors of his dismissal will soon get _____.
    A) along B) away C) about

52. If you're in trouble, get _____ to a lawyer.
    A) by B) on C) in

Classified Phrasal Verbs

Expressions with Give

53. The little boy was forced to give _____ to his brother's wishes.
    A) in   B) for   C) down
54. I give _____. This problem is too difficult to solve.
    A) down   B) away   C) up
55. He gave _____ all his fortune to charities.
    A) down   B) away   C) up
56. Don't forget to give my books _____. I need to study for my exams.
    A) out   B) back   C) up
57. After a week camping, all our food supplies gave _____.
    A) down   B) out   C) in
58. Remember to give all your papers _____ by Monday morning so that I can grade them.
    A) in   B) up   C) out
59. This must be a special type of writing paper, for it gives _____ a very pleasant smell.
    A) on   B) off   C) up
60. His time after school was given _____ to sports.
    A) in   B) over   C) down

Expressions with Go

61. Why did he go _____ on his word?
    A) after   B) back   C) away
62. I don't think you should go _____ a job in that company.
    A) after   B) in   C) to
63. Time goes _____ quickly, my dear.
    A) by   B) for   C) in
64. The price of gas did not go _____ as we expected.
    A) off   B) about   C) down
65. My complaint goes _____ you, too.
    A) on   B) for   C) in
66. John is not happy because his son went _____ the Army.
    A) for   B) forward   C) into
67. I believe she'll never go _____ for sewing.
    A) in   B) down   C) out
68. What's going _____ here!
    A) round   B) in   C) on
69. Don't you think we should go _____ our plans again?
    A) down   B) through   C) on
70. Love and hate normally go _____.
    A) together   B) about   C) forth
71. What he said goes _____ his principles.
    A) against   B) off   C) ahead
72. What color did he go _____?
    A) over   B) with   C) for
73. Let's go _____ for dinner tonight?
    A) in   B) around   C) out
74. Why did the alarm go _____ like that?
    A) out   B) off   C) through
75. Put the milk in the fridge or it will go _____.
    A) out   B) off   C) down
76. Let's go _____ to the river to swim.
    A) out   B) down   C) through

Expressions with Into

77. To inherit money is the same as to _____ into money.
    A) come   B) move   C) keep
78. To join the army is the same as to _____ into the army.
    A) go   B) let   C) look
79. To make a quick decision about something is the same as to _____ into something.
    A) look   B) rush   C) break
80. To meet someone unexpectedly is the same as to _____ into someone.
    A) bump   B) get   C) check
81. To fit into something later is the same as to _____ into it.
    A) let   B) make   C) grow
82. To suddenly cry is the same as to _____ into tears.
    A) fly   B) burst   C) run
83. To drive off the road into a gasoline station is the same as to _____ into the gas station.
    A) pull   B) get   C) let
84. To go and register at a hotel is the same as to _____ into a hotel.
    A) look   B) tune   C) check
85. To have to borrow money is the same as to _____ into debt.
    A) get   B) make   C) crowd
86. To check and find out what happened is the same as to _____ into something.
    A) look   B) make   C) pull

Expressions with Keep

87. She couldn't keep _____ the payments so she lost the house.
    A) on   B) off   C) up
88. She likes to keep _____ with the latest fashions.
    A) away   B) off   C) up
89. The doctor said that I have to keep _____ alcohol.
    A) on   B) off   C) up
90. This spray will keep _____ the bugs.
    A) away   B) off   C) on
91. She keeps _____ about him even though he has left.
    A) away   B) back   C) on
92. Shut the door and keep the dogs _____ of the house.
    A) away   B) off   C) out
93. Try to keep the children _____ from the fire. They may get burn.
    A) away   B) out   C) off
94. She always reads the paper and watches TV to keep _____ with the latest news.
    A) up   B) in   C) at
95. If he doesn't keep _____ the expenses, he'll go bankrupt.
    A) off   B) in   C) down
96. You will succeed if you keep _____ doing it well.
    A) in   B) with   C) on
97. He never let us down, for he always kept _____ his promises.
    A) at   B) to   C) back
98. Bob is trying hard to keep _____ with the rest of his class.
    A) up   B) on   C) in
99. We should advise children to keep _____ drugs.
    A) out   B) off   C) away
100. She couldn't keep the secret _____ from her parents.
    A) out   B) away   C) back
101. Look! The sign says: "Keep _____ the grass".
    A) out   B) off   C) away
102. If you keep _____ your work, you'll like it.
    A) in   B) with   C) at

Expressions with Look

103. Who is going to look _____ the child while her mother is away?
    A) after   B) for   C) at
104. When she got the promotion, she started to look _____ on the people she used to work with.
    A) up   B) for   C) down
105. At this moment, it's nonsense to look _____ results.
    A) about   B) for   C) in
106. We must look _____ all the applications before we decide to hire someone.
    A) for   B) up   C) over

Classified Phrasal Verbs

107. People looked _____ him as a great leader.
    A) on   B) forward   C) in

108. I'm looking _____ to visiting my relatives in California.
    A) for   B) forward   C) up

109. He is really lucky! He got a room that looks _____ on the sea.
    A) up   B) over   C) out

110. I'm sure you have written that down. Look _____ your notes and you will find it.
    A) round   B) in   C) up

111. Students usually look _____ the counselor to help them choose a career.
    A) at   B) to   C) into

112. If you don't know the word, look it _____ in the dictionary.
    A) up   B) for   C) at

Expressions with Make

113. If there is an earthquake, you should make _____ the park.
    A) out   B) up   C) for

114. It was so foggy that she couldn't make _____ the road ahead.
    A) out   B) over   C) up

115. It took 20 years for them to make _____ after their fight.
    A) up   B) over   C) out

116. The man made _____ with all her money.
    A) for   B) off   C) up

117. I wish she wouldn't make _____ stories like that.
    A) for   B) up   C) over

118. The room was big, so they made it _____ a conference room.
    A) into   B) of   C) on

119. The police don't know who made _____ with the money of that big company.
    A) for   B) out   C) off

120. I have already made _____ my mind about it.
    A) over   B) into   C) up

121. Nothing will make _____ for their inefficiency.
    A) in   B) out   C) up

122. Before going to the supermarket, make _____ a list of items you want to buy.
    A) into   B) out   C) for

123. How is he making _____ with his new girlfriend?
    A) out   B) off   C) away

124. Don't trust him. He always makes _____ stories.
    A) up   B) out   C) after

125. The thief ran but the police made _____ him and caught him.
    A) up   B) off   C) after

126. Only good employer-employee relationships can make _____ good production.
    A) at   B) for   C) after

127. I can hardly make _____ the letters on that sign. They are too small.
    A) in   B) off   C) out

Expressions with Pass

128. When he sees blood, he passes _____.
    A) over   B) out   C) on

129. I'm so sorry to hear that your father has passed _____.
    A) by   B) away   C) off

130. He tried to pass himself _____ as the leader of the community.
    A) up   B) out   C) off

131. He's passed _____ bad moments in his life.
    A) through   B) out   C) away

132. If you're clever, you should never pass _____ an opportunity.
    A) up   B) out   C) on

133. He is too young to pass _____ a member of this committee.
    A) into   B) off   C) for

134. The children remained quiet as the parade passed _____.
    A) in   B) by   C) off

135. Read the book and then pass it _____ to a friend.
    A) in   B) on   C) off

Expressions with Pull

136. Can you help me pull _____ these boots?
    A) off   B) our   C) in

137. The doctors think she can't pull _____ another heart attack.
    A) back   B) through   C) out

138. I think I just saw dad's car pull _____ the driveway.
    A) into   B) over   C) by

139. The sun is so bright. Do you mind if I pull _____ the blinds.
    A) in   B) over   C) down

Expressions with Put

140. She doesn't exercise anymore so she has put _____ weight.
    A) on   B) in   C) by

141. He put _____ for a transfer, but it was refused.
    A) on   B) in   C) by

142. My father put _____ the money to buy the house.
    A) up   B) in   C) on

143. Taxes are going to be put _____ next year.
    A) in   B) up   C) over

144. My back is really painful, since I put it _____.
    A) out   B) on   C) down

145. I told her she couldn't come down until all her clothes were put _____.
    A) off   B) in   C) away

146. People often put _____ her opinions.
    A) down   B) in   C) out

147. The game was put _____ until next month.
    A) over   B) off   C) away

148. Will you help me put _____ this poster?
    A) over   B) through   C) up

149. Will the last one to leave please put _____ the candles?
    A) out   B) in   C) by

Expressions with Run

150. Why did he try to run _____ from home?
    A) off   B) out   C) away

151. I always run _____ old students of mine when I go to that cafeteria.
    A) after   B) across   C) over

152. He runs _____ every pretty girl he sees at school.
    A) on   B) after   C) in

153. Yesterday I ran _____ an old friend of mine at the supermarket.
    A) for   B) down   C) into

154. He ran _____ with his best friend's girlfriend.
    A) off   B) into   C) on

155. The police ran _____ all the people who were near the scene of the horrible crime.
    A) in   B) over   C) on

156. The thief ran _____ with all the money and jewelry he found in the house.
    A) away   B) after   C) at

157. That man runs _____ his monthly salary in less than a week.
    A) at   B) through   C) in

158. I don't know how many candidates are running _____ President.
    A) up   B) for   C) off

159. They ran _____ against several problems when they tried to build the bridge in that area.
    A) off   B) on   C) up

160. We ran _____ of beer when the party was half over.
    A) away   B) out   C) off

161. John didn't notice he had run _____ his neighbor's little dog.
    A) over   B) on   C) off

Expressions with Take

162. Don't forget to take _____ notes of everything he says at the conference.
    A) down   B) over   C) on

163. The shop owner decided to take US$5.00 _____ the price.
    A) out   B) off   C) away

164. John did not accept the job, for he did not want to take _____ all those responsibilities.
    A) on   B) out   C) for

165. How can I take all these stains _____ from my tablecloth?
    A) apart   B) away   C) out

166. I know you are tired and disappointed, but don't take it _____ on me.
    A) off   B) out   C) after

167. Have the children taken _____ their new teacher?
    A) up   B) to   C) over

168. You should take your brother _____ on his offer to help you do it.
    A) up   B) in   C) at

169. The plane will take _____ in ten minutes.
    A) out   B) in   C) off

170. These big books shouldn't be taken _____ from the library.
    A) after   B) in   C) away

171. Take _____ account everything he's done for us.
    A) into   B) for   C) after

172. Don't let yourself be taken _____ by anyone.
    A) into   B) in   C) on

Expressions with Up

173. To stick a poster to a wall is the same as to _____ up a poster.
    A) liven   B) put   C) stand

174. To go from sitting to standing is the same as to _____ up.
    A) shoot   B) speak   C) stand

175. To go from being a child to being an adult is the same as to _____ up.
    A) heal   B) grow   C) hurry

176. To ask someone to talk loudly so that you can hear them is the same as to _____ up.
    A) talk   B) ask   C) speak

177. To rush so that you aren't late is the same as to _____ up.
    A) hurry   B) fill   C) cheer

178. To become happy after being sad or miserable is the same as to _____ up.
    A) put   B) look   C) cheer

179. To put nice clothes on and look smart is the same as to _____ up.
    A) stand   B) lock   C) dress

180. To clean a room is the same as to _____ up.
    A) clean   B) seal   C) cheer

181. To explode a bomb in a building is the same as to _____ up a building.
    A) blow   B) mess   C) make

182. To not go to bed early is the same as to _____ up.
    A) look   B) stay   C) lock

183. To go faster and faster is the same as to _____ up.
    A) shoot   B) call   C) speed

184. If a problem suddenly happens, it is the same as a problem has just _____ up.
    A) lit   B) beat   C) cropped

185. To divide into groups is the same as to _____ up.
    A) screw   B) split   C) beat

186. To admit you have done something wrong is the same as to _____ up.
    A) own   B) dig   C) lighten

187. To fasten your coat is the same as to _____ up your coat.
    A) sum   B) tighten   C) do

188. To make or create trouble is the same as to _____ up trouble.
    A) try   B) stir   C) liven

189. To try to find some information or thing from the past is the same as to _____ up something.
    A) try   B) hold   C) dig

190. To redo your lipstick and tidy up your hair and appearance is the same as to _____ up.
    A) pull   B) freshen   C) kick

191. To make something louder is the same as to _____ up the volume.
    A) turn   B) polish   C) call

192. If you hit, punch or kick someone, it's the same as to _____ up someone.
    A) pull   B) bottle   C) beat

193. To finish your drink quickly because you are leaving is the same as to _____ up.
    A) keep   B) kick   C) drink

194. If you form a queue to get something, it is the same as to _____ up.
    A) line   B) hold   C) call

195. To not share your feeling with anyone is the same as to _____ up your feelings.
    A) bottle   B) sum   C) pile

196. To stop outside of somewhere is the same as to _____ up outside.
    A) turn   B) fold   C) pull

197. To make a mistake is the same as to _____ up.
    A) screw   B) hang   C) flare

198. To practice a skill you have already is the same as to _____ up a skill.
    A) fold   B) kick   C) polish

199. To not be able to speak or move because of fright or worry is the same as to _____ up.
    A) keep   B) freeze   C) hang

200. To support something or stop something is the same as to _____ it up.
    A) hold   B) kick   C) brush

201. To appear uninvited is the same as to _____ up.
    A) draw   B) hold   C) turn

202. I am so tired today because I _____ up early.
    A) built   B) cheer   C) got

203. I missed a lot of classes so I have to work hard to _____ up.
    A) save   B) catch   C) lock

204. I don't know the telephone number so I'll have to _____ it up.
    A) mix   B) look   C) use

205. If you don't _____ up, we will be late.
    A) hurry   B) bring   C) draw

206. Her husband died so she had to _____ up the children alone.
    A) blow   B) bring   C) crop

207. The traffic was _____ up because of road work.
    A) held   B) freshened   C) kept

208. The police _____ up the political demonstration.
    A) got   B) turned   C) broke

209. You should always _____ up any words you don't know in a dictionary.
    A) get   B) look   C) cheer

210. I can't believe he _____ up the bill and paid for our dinner.
    A) set   B) put   C) picked

211. The boy _____ up his seat to the old lady.
    A) made   B) gave   C) came

Classified Phrasal Verbs

Expressions about Crime

212. To get into a building or car using force is to _____.
    A) break out   B) break down   C) break in

213. To steal money from a bank by using force is a _____.
    A) hold in   B) hold down   C) hold up

214. To steal or take something without asking is to _____.
    A) run off with   B) do without   C) do over

215. To hurt someone badly by hitting or kicking is to _____.
    A) pull them over   B) beat them up   C) put one over

216. To kill someone in informal English is to _____ with them.
    A) do away   B) have away   C) stay

217. To destroy something with a bomb is to _____.
    A) beat it up   B) blow it up   C) knock it over

218. To take a criminal to the police is to _____.
    A) turn them over   B) turn them in
    C) turn them down

219. To put someone in prison is to _____.
    A) lock them up   B) do them in   C) blow them up

220. To not punish someone for their crime is to _____.
    A) give them over   B) let them off   C) put them away

221. To succeed in not being punished for a crime is to _____ it
    A) get away with   B) make off with   C) pick through

Expressions about Emotions

222. To make someone unhappy is to _____.
    A) get over them   B) get on with them   C) get them down

223. To make someone feel upset or angry is to _____.
    A) jump them   B) get to them   C) do them in

224. To make someone feel good is to __.
    A) perk them up   B) peep them in   C) rack them up

225. To stop feeling upset or angry about something is to _____.
    A) clam up   B) wash out   C) calm down

226. To be so excited that you lose control is to get _____.
    A) carried away   B) carried off   C) carried over

227. To start behaving in a violent or strange way is to _____.
    A) liven up   B) freak out   C) throw out

Expressions about Food and Drink

228. To eat food very quickly is to _____.
    A) bolt it down   B) pig out   C) whip it up

229. If you only eat a small amount of a meal, you _____.
    A) gnaw it   B) bolt it down   C) pick at it

230. To eat a lot of food is to _____.
    A) pig out   B) roll out   C) wear out

231. To eat less of something to improve your health is to _____ on it.
    A) strip down   B) cut back   C) run

232. To drink a lot of alcohol is to _____.
    A) knock it over   B) knock it in   C) knock it back

233. To heat food again that has already been cooked is to _____.
    A) ruffle it up   B) warm it up   C) pick it up

Expressions about Illness

234. To get an illness from someone is to _____.
    A) pick it up   B) truck it in   C) take it away

235. To try hard to get rid of an illness is to _____.
    A) tide it over   B) cave in   C) fight it off

236. If a part of your body gets bigger and rounder because of injury or illness it _____.
    A) comes out   B) kicks in   C) swells up

237. Another expression for vomiting is to _____.
    A) throw up   B) toss out   C) pass out

238. To be able to eat or drink without vomiting is to _____.
    A) keep it down   B) get over it   C) dip into

239. To become unconscious is to _____.
    A) go out   B) black out   C) knock over

Expressions about Speaking

240. If you speak for a long time, you _____.
    A) get on   B) go on   C) edge on

241. If you talk too long on one subject, you _____.
    A) run out   B) run over   C) run on

242. If you talk too long on one subject, you _____.
    A) tread on   B) unwind   C) ramble on

243. If you say something you have learned quickly and without stopping, you _____.
    A) knock down   B) rattle off   C) rabbit on

244. If you say something you have learned quickly and without stopping, you _____.
    A) reel off   B) rope off   C) tie off

245. To say something while another person is talking is to _____.
    A) butt in   B) figure out   C) go over

246. To say something suddenly and without thinking is to _____.
    A) ease up   B) rub in   C) blurt out

247. To make someone stop talking is to _____.
    A) shut up   B) shut out   C) shut in

248. To speak to someone without letting them answer is to _____.
    A) talk over   B) talk at   C) talk to

249. To suddenly stop talking in the middle of a speech because you have forgotten what to say it to _____.
    A) wipe out   B) dry up   C) go over.

Expressions about Thinking

250. To think carefully about an idea before making a decision is to _____.
    A) figure out   B) think over   C) chip in

251. To think of a suggestion, a solution or plan is to _____.
    A) come up with   B) come out with   C) come over

252. To think about something that has happened is to _____.
    A) run over   B) go over   C) go with

253. To create an idea, or plan using your imagination is to _____.
    A) work out   B) think over   C) think up

254. To stop yourself from thinking about something is to _____.
    A) think it out   B) bring it out   C) shut it out

255. To think of a very imaginative and not really possible plan is to _____.
    A) dream it up   B) go over it   C) come out with

256. To think about an idea, but not seriously is to _____.
    A) toy with it   B) dream about it   C) work it out

257. To find the answer to something through deep thinking is _____.
    A) think it up   B) figure it out   C) play with it

Expressions about Travel

258. To go on holiday especially because you need a rest is to _____.
    A) get over   B) go off   C) get away

259. To show your ticket and get your seat at the airport is to _____.
    A) check out   B) check off   C) check in

260. When the aircraft leaves the ground it _____.
    A) takes off   B) takes over   C) takes in

261. To start on a journey is to _____.
    A) set in   B) set by   C) set off

262. The time a train, bus or plane arrives is when it _____.
    A) gets away   B) gets in   C) gets over

263. To visit somewhere for a short time when you are going somewhere is to _____.
    A) stop off   B) stop away   C) stop on

264. To stay somewhere for a length of time when you are on a long journey is to _____.
    A) stop by   B) stop over   C) stop on

PHRASAL VERBS

TEST - 1

1. While they were on holiday their house was broken _____ and some valuable paintings were stolen.
   A) down   B) into   C) about   D) away

2. By the way, I've just heard that Sally and Chris have _____ their engagement.
   A) broken into   B) broken down   C) broken away   D) broken up

3. After a bitter discussion they went _____ each other.
   A) to   B) at   C) off   D) over

4. A: The new boss looks a bit serious, doesn't he? I don't think I'm going to like him.
   B: Oh, come on, Joyce, you can't go _____ appearances. He's probably very nice.
   A) after   B) by   C) out   D) over

5. No one really believed it when the news came that Titanic had _____.
   A) gone away   B) gone down   C) gone out   D) gone by

6. I've been afraid of dogs ever since a large Canine _____ me when I was a child.
   A) went for   B) went after   C) went to   D) went over

7. By the way, Bill, how much did that Regency desk go _____ in the auction on Saturday?
   A) away   B) for   C) in   D) off

8. The dog went _____ the beggar and he shouted " help!".
   A) over   B) off   C) for   D) down

9. A: And another thing I'd like to say is that...
   B: Sorry to _____, Mr. Green, but you're wanted on the phone. It's your wife.
   A) butt in   B) get throuh   C) stop over   D) go over

10. I'm afraid Mr Brown's been _____ (asked to go somewhere else) on business.
    A) put on   B) called away   C) got in   D) called for

11. By the way, Clive _____ (paid a short visit) but you were out. So I told him to come and see you tomorrow.
    A) fall for   B) called by   C) get by   D) cut down in

12. Shall I _____ (collect) you on my way to work?
    A) call off   B) bring down   C) call for   D) call away

13. I was just getting out of the bath when the lights _____.
    A) went up   B) went off   C) went away   D) went down

14. A bomb _____ (exploded) in the town center, killing three people and injuring twenty-five others.
    A) went on   B) went off   C) set on   D) set off

15. Don't eat that cheese - it's _____!
    A) gone away   B) gone out   C) gone off   D) gone down

16. It's difficult to see through this windscreen - I can't even make _____ where the road is.
    A) up   B) out   C) into   D) over

17. He had such a strong accent that it was very difficult to _____ what he was saying.
    A) make up   B) make out   C) make over   D) make for

18. A sudden draught caused the candle to _____ (stop burning).
    A) put off   B) cut off   C) go off   D) go out

19. When the meeting had finished, they went _____ the plan once again.
    A) up   B) on   C) over   D) down

20. Have a piece of cake, everyone. There should be enough to _____.
    A) go down   B) go along   C) go round   D) go over

21. Lucille is _____ a difficult period at work right now.
    A) going into   B) going over   C) going out of   D) going through

22. I know you've got it - so come on, _____!
    A) hand it on   B) hand it out   C) hand it over   D) hand it in

23. Could you hand _____ a minute? I'll be right back.
    A) on   B) in   C) up   C) on to

24. I'll have to _____ now, I'm afraid; there is someone at the door.
    A) hang on   B) hang up   C) hang out   D) hang back

25. Now, James, are you quite sure that I'm not putting you _____ (putting you to any trouble)?
    A) after   B) by   C) out   D) over

26. When a fire _____ at least ten priceless paintings were completely destroyed.
    A) broke out   B) broke off   C) broke down   D) broke through

27. The tree prisoners who _____ jail last weekend have finally been recaptured.
    A) broke away from   B) broke out in
    C) broke out of   D) broke up into

28. I took the doctor's prescription to the chemist's to be _____.
    A) made out   B) made up   C) made over   D) made into

29. My boss has _____ playing golf three afternoons a week.
    A) taken over   B) taken to   C) taken for   D) taken out

30. Children usually _____ after an illness much more quickly than adults.
    A) pick up   B) pick over   C) pick on   D) pick out

31. The police are still looking for the three prisoners who _____ (escaped from) jail at the weekend.
    A) broke out of   B) set off   C) take up   D) cross out

32. I'm not surprised that Tom and Julie have _____. They were never really suited.
    A) broken down   B) broken off
    C) broken up   D) broken away

33. By the way, Sally, I'm _____ one or two friends _____ on Saturday and I was wondering if you and Peter would like to come too?
    A) having / in   B) having / on
    C) having / round   D) having / up

34. Are you sure you aren't holding your stomach _____, Charles? Your waist was two inches more than this the last time I measured it.
    A) away   B) for   C) in   D) off

35. Would you _____ a minute please, I'll try to connect you.
    A) keep on   B) stay on   C) hold on   D) stop on

36. It's really windy today, so _____ your hat!
    A) hold on to   B) hold down to
    C) hold by   D) hold for

37. I hope help comes soon, Julie. I don't think we can _____ much longer.
    A) hold back   B) hold over   C) hold in   D) hold out

38. I'm sorry I'm late. I was _____ in the traffic.
    A) held back   B) held down   C) held over   D) held up

39. John won't be arriving until later, I'm afraid. His train's been _____.
    A) held up   B) held off   C) held back   D) held in

Test 1

40. In some parks visitors are requested to keep _____ the grass.
    A) off   B) aside   C) out   D) away

41. Keep _____ alcohol and don't smoke.
    A) at   B) with in   C) away   D) off

42. He kept _____ trying to annoy me and in the end I just hit him.
    A) in   B) on   C) at   D) with

43. If you want to make a good impression, it's important to _____ your colleagues.
    A) keep away from   B) keep in with
    C) keep out of   D) keep on at

44. This nuclear power station let _____ a cloud of dangerous gases.
    A) down   B) in   C) off   D) out

45. Instead of being sent to prison, The shoplifter was _____ with a fine.
    A) let away   B) let off   C) let loose   D) let out

46. The children had great fun _____ fireworks.
    A) letting out B) letting in   C) letting down D) letting off

47. I've just heard that John Parker - you remember who robbed a house a few years ago- is being _____ this weekend.
    A) let down   B) let out   C) let through D) let off

48. The dog let _____ a yowl of pain when accidentally stepped on its tail.
    A) out   B) off   C) up   D) through

49. As the doctor arrived to attend to the girl who had fainted, the crowd moved to one side to _____.
    A) let him off   B) let him through
    C) let him down   D) let him out

50. If you don't know what the word means, you'd better _____ in the dictionary.
    A) look it over B) look for it C) look it up   D) look into it

51. Our living room looks _____ the mountains.
    A) up to   B) at   C) to   D) on to

52. _____ ! (Be careful) There is a car coming!
    A) look at   B) look out   C) hold up   D) keep up

53. I'd like to _____ the house before I decide to rent it.
    A) look over   B) look into   C) look out   D) look up

54. I _____ the paper for news of the proposed strike, but didn't find anything.
    A) looked over   B) looked into
    C) looked on   D) looked through

55. Was that true or did you _____ ?
    A) make it up   B) make it out
    C) make it off   D) make it over

56. I was _____ (moving towards) the post office when it suddenly started to rain.
    A) running down   B) taking up
    C) get through   D) making for

57. I must get a new pair of boots. I've _____ my old ones.
    A) worn off   B) worn down   C) worn out   D) worn away

58. After working all day in the garden Homer was _____.
    A) worn out   B) worn down   C) worn off   D) worn away

59. Looking carefully, we made _____ a tall figure in the darkness.
    A) out   B) over   C) up   D) off

60. We must _____ our minds about where to go for our holidays this year.
    A) make out   B) make off   C) make up   D) make for

61. Can you make _____ this prescription, please?
    A) up   B) over   C) for   D) off

62. Some working parents _____ being absent all day by giving their children lots of presents.
    A) make out   B) make out of C) make up   D) make up for

63. Heidi and John had a big quarrel but later _____.
    A) made over   B) made off   C) made up   D) made out

64. I don't believe a word you're saying. I think you've made the whole thing _____.
    A) for   B) up   C) out   D) down

65. The other day I came _____ an advert for a job you might be interested in.
    A) through   B) over   C) across   D) around

66. How did you come _____ that cut on your chin?
    A) by   B) down   C) in for   D) across

67. How is the new book coming _____, (progressing) Simon?
    A) along   B) down   C) in   D) up

68. The policeman told the people to _____ when they stopped to watch the accident.
    A) hurry up   B) get away   C) go off   D) move along

69. Although she was only sixteen she looked a lot older. In fact, she could easily pass _____ twenty-one.
    A) away   B) for   C) in   D) off

70. We _____ from the hotel early the following morning.
    A) called off   B) passed out   C) set off   D) turned off

71. Before we start the meeting today I'd like to _____ (distribute) some notes I've made about the forthcoming advertising campaign.
    A) let down   B) send out   C) pass out   D) give on

72. He stole one of the officers' uniforms and managed to escape by passing himself _____ as a guard.
    A) by   B) out   C) through   D) off

73. All my hard work paid _____ in the end - I came top of the class in the exam.
    A) up   B) off   C) out   D) in

74. He put six rings on the table and told her to _____ the one she liked best.
    A) pick off   B) pick out   C) pick at   D) pick on

75. Excuse me, sir, but may I ask how you came _____ (obtained) these goods?
    A) after   B) by   C) out   D) over

76. Laughing Boy (horse) _____ second in the 2.15 race at Ascot.
    A) came in   B) came by   C) came over   D) came out

77. He _____ quite a lot of money when his parents died.
    A) came over   B) came down   C) came into   D) came on

78. There were so many people leaving the hotel that it took nearly an hour to _____.
    A) check up   B) check out   C) check in   D) check over

79. The police will check _____ your story, so tell the truth.
    A) in to   B) out of   C) over   D) up on

80. Rosemary _____ a beautiful necktie for her husband's birthday.
    A) picked over B) picked on   C) picked out   D) picked off

81. Do you ever pick _____ hitch-hikers?
    A) along   B) down   C) in   D) up

82. A: He still sucks his thumb, darling.
    B: Yes, I know. It's strange. I thought he'd have _____ it by now.
    A) stop off at   B) get out of
    C) grown out of   D) turn away from

Test 1

83. He ran for the bus but it pulled _____ from the stop just as he got there.
    A) up   B) over   C) back   D) away

84. I try to keep _____ the latest fashions by going lots of shows in London.
    A) up with   B) along with C) up to   D) next to

85. Manchester United's chances of going to the final of the F.A. Cup were ended when they were knocked _____ by Liverpool in the semi-final.
    A) back   B) up   C) out   D) away

86. Sales were down so they had to _____ some of their staff.
    A) put out   B) get out   C) lay off   D) turn down

87. It took the soldier a long time to _____ the death of his comrade.
    A) get round B) get over   C) get across D) get through

88. The fact is, doctor, I just can't _____ this dreadful cough.
    A) get out of B) get rid of C) get down to D) get round to

89. It's an excellent story, and in the end it turns _____ that everyone had a part in the murder.
    A) out   B) up   C) in   D) away

90. The car _____ after the crash but fortunately no one was killed.
    A) turned down   B) turned back
    C) turned over   D) turned away

91. In court, she was so upset that she broke _____.
    A) out   B) in   C) up   D) down

92. I think I'll have to sell my car. It keeps _____.
    A) breaking off   B) breaking up
    C) breaking down   D) breaking in

93. I think she's coming _____! Thank God for that! I thought she was dead!
    A) up   B) away   C) back   D) round

94. It took him a long time to come _____ our way of thinking.
    A) across to B) round to   C) down to   D) in at

95. Birthdays seem to _____ much quicker nowadays than when I was a child.
    A) come up   B) come over   C) come out   D) come round

96. Sorry I'm late but I was _____ by traffic.
    A) held up   B) held in   C) held over   D) held out

97. A: I thought you said you weren't going to let Sally go to that pop concert in Brighton.
    B: Yes, but you know Sally - she always finds a way to get _____ me in the end.
    A) after   B) by   C) out   D) round

98. He was going to reply her letter, but for various reasons he never got _____ it.
    A) up to   B) round to   C) over   D) out of

99. It was a very difficult problem - one which no one could see a way of _____.
    A) getting through   B) getting out
    C) getting over   D) geting round

100. You look very unhappy, Dorris. What's the matter? Is something getting you _____?
    A) along   B) down   C) in   D) up

TEST - 2

1. I'll _____ in my car on the way to work.
   A) take you out   B) bring you up
   C) let you off   D) pick you up

2. They _____ us just because we're poor.
   A) look down at   B) look down for
   C) look down on   D) look down over

3. We look _____ to receiving a prompt reply to our letter.
   A) round   B) through   C) after   D) forward

4. My wife _____ a squirrel on her way to work this morning.
   A) ran over B) ran up   C) ran out of D) ran off

5. I can hardly hear that radio. Could you _____ (increase/raise) the volume please.
   A) put up   B) switch on   C) give out   D) turn up

6. I'd ask you to marry me but I'm sure you'd turn me _____.
   A) around   B) down   C) off   D) over

7. I'm pretty tired so if you don't mind, I'll _____ for the night.
   A) hold on   B) work on   C) work out   D) turn in

8. Before you go to bed don't forget to _____ all the lights.
   A) turn over B) turn away   C) turn out   D) turn in

9. Before we start the lesson, I'd like to _____ what we did yesterday.
   A) run up   B) run through C) run along   D) run into

10. We shall have to _____ if we want to go to Florida this summer.
    A) save up   B) put away   C) put aside   D) lay up

11. I went to the Train Station to see my uncle _____ to Dublin.
    A) off   B) across   C) home   D) through

12. The children were playing the new teacher _____.
    A) along   B) down   C) in   D) up

13. James is threatening to resign, but I don't think he will _____ it really.
    A) go on with   B) go in for
    C) go along with   D) go through with

14. What a lovely tie! And it _____ (matches) your jacket too!
    A) goes off B) goes with   C) makes out   D) gets over

15. I had to put _____ having the party because I was ill.
    A) up   B) through   C) off   D) on

16. We'll have to sell the piano, darling. It _____ (occupies) too much room.
    A) makes out B) takes up   C) takes away D) fills in

17. I was _____ with Alvin for arguing with the waiter about our bill.
    A) put out   B) put off   C) put down   D) put on

18. Most schools in England _____ at the end of July.
    A) break up B) break down C) break off   D) break with

19. It's a great shame that you _____ with each other as you used to be such good friends.
    A) came out B) fell out   C) set out   D) turned out

20. Our plan to increase the productivity fell _____.
    A) off   B) through   C) in   D) back

21. Janet and Peter broke _____ a few months ago and are living apart.
    A) into   B) out   C) up   D) away

22. Several students fainted during the display but they were soon brought _____ .
    A) round   B) at   C) under   D) up

23. We live in a friendly community and everyone _____ each other very well.
    A) gets on with   B) gets up to
    C) gets out of   D) gets down to

24. How are you _____ your studies? Do you feel that you are making headway?
    A) getting down to   B) getting ahead of
    C) getting on with   D) get up to

25. How's Pauline _____ in her new job?
    A) getting by   B) getting through
    C) getting on   D) getting along with

26. I _____ (visited) for a chat on my way home from work.
    A) called in   B) got in   C) turned back   D) fell in

27. Do you think you could _____ the cleaner's on your way home tonight?
    A) call down on   B) call in at
    C) call away to   D) call out to

28. I've just heard that they're _____ (increasing/raising) my rent at the end of next month.
    A) turning up   B) taking up   C) putting up   D) holding up

29. They _____ (erected/built) that block of flats two years ago.
    A) set up   B) turned up   C) put up   D) put on

30. I find her husband unbearable, and I can't imagine how she can put _____ his awful behaviour.
    A) on to   B) up with   C) down on   D) away from

31. I _____ (ordered by post) the catalogue two weeks ago, but it still hasn't arrived.
    A) passed out   B) sent for   C) called for   D) wrote for

32. Be careful with the bomb! The slightest touch might _____!
    A) set it up   B) set it off   C) set it out   D) set it down

33. This strike has set us _____ months.
    A) up   B) down   C) back   D) off

34. We _____ (began our journey) at 6.30 in the morning.
    A) broke out   B) got away   C) set off   D) went off

35. Hello! Is that the Grand Hotel? Could you _____ the manager, please?
    A) put me up with   B) put me on to
    C) put me in for   D) put me through to

36. The idea of a balanced diet is difficult to _____ to those who know little about food values.
    A) come across   B) take in   C) make over   D) put across

37. A: Who was on the phone?
    B: I don't know. He _____ before I could ask.
    A) hold back   B) rang off   C) got down   D) went off

38. My father was _____ (hit/knocked down) by a bus on his work to work.
    A) gone by   B) broken down   C) got down   D) run down

39. The battery has run _____.
    A) down   B) out   C) over   D) about

40. Because of possible bomb threats, the Queen has decided to _____ her proposed visit to Northern Ireland next month.
    A) call out   B) call away   C) call up   D) call off

41. My father was called _____ halfway through the Second World War.
    A) in   B) over   C) up   D) off

42. Do you think you could _____ these figures for me, just to make sure they're correct.
    A) check over   B) check off
    C) check in   D) check through

43. I hope the weather will _____ before we leave for Brighton.
    A) clear off   B) go off   C) clear up   D) go away

44. Oh, Miss Jones, would you mind _____ these figures again, please?
    A) going by   B) going into   C) going over   D) going after

45. Help yourself to an apple. I think there are enough to _____.
    A) hand in   B) go round   C) have on   D) fix up

46. It looks as if the weather is beginning to _____ at last.
    A) clear off   B) clear out   C) clear away   D) clear up

47. This is a word I have never come _____ before.
    A) across   B) on   C) through   D) to

48. It must be spring; the leaves have started _____ (appearing) on all the trees in the park.
    A) breaking up   B) bringing up   C) coming out   D) coming down

49. The government may be hiding the facts now, but they are bound to _____ sooner or later.
    A) come back   B) come in   C) come out   D) come up

50. Why don't you _____ (visit us) on Friday?
    A) ring up   B) turn up   C) get back   D) come round

51. By the way, Jill, Gregory was asking _____ you (asking how you are).
    A) after   B) by   C) out   D) over

52. I'm afraid you've signed the agreement now, Mr. Blake. It's too late to back _____ it.
    A) out of   B) away from   C) away with   D) down to

53. I tried hard but I simply couldn't break _____ from my old habits.
    A) into   B) away   C) down   D) off

54. How did you managed to come _____ even without a scratch?
    A) round   B) out with   C) off   D) through

55. Many people _____ meditation to relax.
    A) give up   B) make   C) take up   D) take out

56. I took _____ tennis again at the beginning of this year.
    A) on   B) with   C) by   D) up

57. Which shirt shall I _____ (wear) tonight?
    A) take on   B) get on   C) go with   D) put on

58. Until I repay my bank loan, I'll have to _____ my living expenses.
    A) call off   B) cut down on   C) get round   D) turn down

59. If you want to lose weight, you should _____ the number of sweets and chocolates you eat.
    A) come down with   B) take out of
    C) cut down on   D) watch out for

60. The nights are beginning to draw _____ again. It was light this time last week.
    A) away   B) for   C) in   D) off

61. He drew all his money _____ the bank before he left.
    A) of   B) off   C) out of   D) to

62. The taxi _____ (came to a stop) outside the station and an old lady got out.
    A) drew out   B) drew up   C) gave in   D) get down

63. I don't think they'd really like it if we just _____ them (visited them without telling them first). You know how they like to tidy up before visitors come.
    A) run out on   B) drop in on   C) call by   D) go along

Test 2

64. A: Where do you want me to _____ you _____ Jane?
    B: Outside the station, if its all right.
    A) take / off B) bring / off C) drop / off D) leave / off

65. Mr. Brown still hadn't faced _____ the fact that they're never going to make him Assistant Manager.
    A) up to B) down in C) on in D) round to

66. Sooner or later he will have to _____ his responsibilities.
    A) take account B) look after C) see into D) face up to

67. The attack was so fierce that the enemy soldiers had to fall _____.
    A) down B) behind C) away D) back

68. They had a plan to trick him, but he didn't fall _____ it.
    A) for B) to C) at D) by

69. After a lot of persuasion, he finally agreed to fall _____ our plans.
    A) across to B) down in C) in with C) up to

70. David, do you think you could _____ a meeting with Mr. Brown for one day next week?
    A) catch up B) have round C) fix up D) work out

71. The Prime Minister had difficulty in _____ his message to the nation.
    A) getting through B) getting across
    C) getting out D) getting on

72. It is difficult to get _____ people how dangerous smoking is to their health.
    A) down in B) in at C) across to D) in with

73. It's too far away - I can't _____ (reach) it.
    A) get together B) go after C) get through D) get at

74. The thieves _____ (escaped) by rushing into the underground.
    A) got back B) got away C) picked up D) got through

75. I don't know how they _____ (manage/survive financially) now that Harry's out of work.
    A) go on B) get by C) get over D) pass out

76. I simply cannot get _____ such a low salary.
    A) by on B) at C) along D) down

77. She never really got _____ the shock of her son's death.
    A) into B) around C) up to D) over

78. I hear they're going to _____ (demolish) those old houses in Church Lane and build a new supermarket there instead.
    A) clear up B) leave out C) put away D) pull down

79. I hear they are going to _____ the old Variety Theatre at the end of George street.
    A) pull away B) pull out C) pull up D) pull down

80. I think we'd better pull _____ the next garage to check the oil.
    A) pull round to B) up to C) in at D) out to

81. They surrounded the enemy and forced them to _____.
    A) give in B) give out C) give up D) give over

82. The unknown substance was giving _____ an unpleasant smell.
    A) out B) up C) over D) off

83. The policeman asked the driver to _____ to the side of the road.
    A) pull out B) pull in C) pull through D) pull round

84. They say that it takes smokers longer to _____ a cold than non-smokers.
    A) get across B) get off C) get out of D) get over

85. Although I hadn't worked very hard, I still managed to _____ (pass) the exam.
    A) put up B) come round C) get through D) pick up

86. I don't really think I'll _____ the exam this summer.
    A) get through B) get away with
    C) get up D) get in

87. It took us nearly half an hour to _____ the hill. It was so steep.
    A) get on B) get up C) get away D) get through

88. I don't like my children going to parties. You never know what young people _____ these days.
    A) get on with B) get up to
    C) get through to D) get in with

89. What have you been getting _____ recently? - Oh nothing much.
    A) through to B) out of C) over D) up to

90. I don't seem to be making any progress and it's beginning to _____ me down.
    A) carry B) get C) pull D) take

91. If she hadn't given him _____, the police would never have found him.
    A) away B) for C) in D) off

92. The teacher asked the students to _____ (hand in) their homework at the end of the lesson.
    A) give back B) give in C) turn back D) bring about

93. In winter this town is often cut _____ by heavy snowfalls.
    A) off B) back C) out D) dead

94. I think your essay would be much better if you cut _____ these two lines here.
    A) in B) through C) off D) out

95. A: Oh, I could really _____ a cigarette now! Have you got one Pete?
    B: Sorry Bob, I stopped smoking two weeks ago.
    A) do with B) do without
    C) make up with D) hang on with

96. The terrorists were forced to give _____.
    A) off B) out C) in D) away

97. Oh, Charles, could you _____ (distribute) the books, please?
    A) give out B) give in C) put away D) put out

98. It was given _____ on the news that an assassination attempt had been made on the Prime Minister.
    A) out B) off C) away D) up

99. I wonder if you'd help me to _____ some anti-nuclear power leaflets this weekend, Jim?
    A) give out B) give over C) give in D) give off

100. After failing his driving test four times, he finally _____ trying to pass.
    A) gave up B) gave away C) gave off D) gave in

TEST - 3

1. There was a robbery at the bank, and the police are looking _____ the matter.
   A) up to   B) in on   C) into   D) through

2. At least half a dozen people _____ (watched without doing anything) while the man was being attacked.
   A) looked at   B) looked on   C) looked over   D) looked into

3. I've been trying to phone to Charles all evening, but there must be something wrong with the line; I can't seem to _____.
   A) get down   B) get together   C) get out   D) get through

4. My sister was very cruel when she was a child. She used to catch spiders and _____ their legs one by one.
   A) pull up   B) pull away   C) pull off   D) pull out

5. I nearly fainted when my dentist told me that he'd have to _____ two of my teeth.
   A) pull off   B) pull away   C) pull up   D) pull out

6. The lorry _____ at the traffic lights.
   A) pulled off   B) pulled up   C) pulled out   D) pulled through

7. The operator _____ me _____ (connected me) almost immediately.
   A) put / through   B) put / on   C) picked / up   D) called / for

8. Would you _____ (like) something to eat, Mrs. Brown?
   A) care for   B) take up   C) look for   D) make for

9. It took my mother quite a while to catch _____ that we were only joking.
   A) away   B) for   C) in   D) on

10. When Joan returned to school after her illness, she had to work really hard to catch _____ the others.
    A) in with   B) up to   C) up with   D) roun to

11. Thieves held _____ a bank in Manchester and got away with 50,000 pounds.
    A) on   B) out   C) over   D) up

12. Summer time ends tomorrow, so don't forget to _____ your clock tonight.
    A) put on   B) put down   C) put back   D) put out

13. She is very important to him. He wouldn't get _____ without her.
    A) over   B) by   C) down   D) round

14. I tried to _____ everything he said, but he spoke so quickly that it was impossible.
    A) get up   B) get over   C) get away   D) get down

15. Right, if you're really ready, I think it's time to get _____ some work.
    A) round to   B) down in   C) on in   D) down to

16. What time did you _____ last night? It must have been quite late because when I phoned you at 11:30 your mother said you were still out.
    A) get away   B) get in   C) get by   D) get down

17. I think we'll have to get _____ more drink for the party.
    A) off   B) over   C) on   D) in

18. Let's _____ the subject of nuclear war. It's beginning to make me feel very depressed.
    A) get off   B) get over   C) get through   D) get out

19. How is Janet _____ (progressing) in her new school?
    A) coming round   B) getting on   C) going on   D) getting in

20. The teacher asked the class to _____ (write down) the school telephone number.
    A) get down   B) put down   C) hold on   D) keep out

21. She put _____ an interesting proposal.
    A) to   B) against   C) forward   D) backwards

22. I want to put _____ the position you advertised.
    A) off   B) out   C) up   D) in for

23. It's very kind of you to put me _____ for the night, James.
    A) along   B) down   C) in   D) up

24. I'm feeling _____ and could do with a holiday.
    A) run across   B) run down   C) run out   D) run over

25. We should finish today, but as the time running _____ we may have to continue tomorrow.
    A) out   B) down   C) away   D) off

26. You'll have to get a new television license. This one isn't valid. It _____ two weeks ago.
    A) ran up   B) ran out   C) ran off   D) ran away

27. I'm making you responsible for this project. Please see _____ it that it is finished.
    A) to   B) into   C) for   D) on

28. We decided to _____ early to avoid the rush-hour traffic.
    A) set down   D) set on   C) set back   D) set out

29. The government wants people to set _____ their own businesses.
    A) off   B) in   C) up   D) down

30. There is a certain amount of evidence to suggest that violence on television and in films _____ (causes) violence among young people.
    A) breaks down   B) gives out   C) brings about   D) makes for

31. Seeing the couple walking hand in hand _____ memories of his own first love.
    A) brought up   B) brought back   C) brought out   D) brought on

32. It was walking home in the rain that must have _____ your cold.
    A) brought up   B) brought on   C) brought out   D) brought on

33. We shall bring _____ the question of the new swimming-pool at the next committee meeting.
    A) about   B) up   C) round   D) off

34. She set _____ in business on her own and was very successful.
    A) by   B) aside   C) up   D) off

35. The Government is planning to _____ (establish) a new department to be responsible for what people do in their leisure time. It is to be called the Ministry of Leisure.
    A) bring up   B) put up   C) set up   D) hold on

36. The government has _____ an inquiry to investigate bribery in local elections.
    A) set out   B) set to   C) set up   D) set about

37. A: Would it be all right if I _____ you on Friday, Mr. Brown?
    B: Yes of course, Mrs. Price. You can pay me any time.
    A) get on with   B) settle up with   C) get up to   D) get along with

38. Don't take any notice on him, Janet. He's only trying to show _____.
    A) away   B) for   C) in   D) off

39. Catherine promised to _____ at Josie's luncheon in time for dessert.
    A) show up   B) show off   C) show down   D) show through

Test 3

40. A good friend will always _____ you when you're in trouble.
    A) stand by   B) stand up
    C) stand for   D) stand up against

41. In her first year in business, my aunt came _____ more problems than she had expected.
    A) down on   B) out of   C) in to   D) up against

42. You can count _____ me if you ever want any help.
    A) in   B) on   C) up   D) by

43. If you're sure the trip isn't going to cost more than ten pounds, then you can count me _____.
    A) in   B) off   C) up   D) with

44. We'll get home much quicker if we _____ this field.
    A) cut across   B) cut down   C) cut out   D) cut off

45. Your wife is so rude. If I were you, I wouldn't stand _____ her.
    A) by   B) to   C) at   D) for

46. You mustn't let him treat you so badly; you must stand _____ him and be strong.
    A) for   B) by   C) up to   D) down

47. If you _____ (subtract) twenty-five from a hundred, you are left with seventy-five.
    A) put down   B) take away   C) take off   D) cross out

48. I was feeling rather tired, so I didn't really _____ what the teacher was saying.
    A) take up   B) take in   C) take over   D) take away

49. I'm very flattered that you want me to make the speech at the end-of-term party, but, to be honest with you, I don't really _____ it (think I'm capable of doing it).
    A) feel up to   B) feel for   C) feel on to   D) feel by

50. The landlord threatened to evict her when she fell _____ her rent.
    A) behind with   B) down in   C) out of   D) behind for

51. We were both completely taken _____ by the car salesman, who turned out to be a crook.
    A) out   B) up   C) in   D) down

52. I knew from the start he was dishonest so I wasn't taken _____ by him, but some of my friends lost money.
    A) in   B) down   C) at   D) to

53. The plane _____ late because of the terrible weather.
    A) blew up   B) grew up   C) went on   D) took off

54. I think it's a lot more difficult to _____ children nowadays than it used to be.
    A) bring out   B) bring off   C) bring on   D) bring up

55. How many more times have I got to tell you not to _____ here without knocking?
    A) burst out   B) burst on   C) burst in   D) burst off

56. The present situation calls _____ prompt action.
    A) on   B) by   C) off   D) for

57. Anyway, John, _____ (remove) your coat and come through and meet the others.
    A) take off   B) get together   C) hold up   D) put on

58. They always _____ extra staff in the summer.
    A) put on   B) take in   C) put in   D) take on

59. The company has had a bad year, and will therefore not be taking _____ any new workers.
    A) up   B) off   C) after   D) on

60. I'm going to the bank to _____ some money.
    A) take in   B) take out   C) take on   D) take back

61. The marriage will _____ next Monday at noon.
    A) take place   B) go off
    C) come together   D) carry on

62. I really thought he was telling the truth. He certainly took me _____.
    A) away   B) for   C) in   D) off

63. When I retire I think I'll _____ (start/begin) painting.
    A) set off   B) break in   C) get in   D) take up

64. My doctor advised me to get some exercise, so I've decided to _____ tennis.
    A) take up   B) take after   C) take on   D) take down

65. When he came back to England, he _____ up the job he had had before.
    A) got   B) took   C) made   D) set

66. I'm afraid I can't give you an answer straight away, Mr. Green. I'd like to _____ for a day or two.
    A) think of it   B) think it up   C) think it over   D) think it out

67. I'll be back soon; I'm just going to _____ my new bike.
    A) try for   B) try out   C) try over   D) try on

68. Oh, blast! The button's has just _____ my dress.
    A) come down   B) come out   C) come round   D) come off

69. There was an expectant hush from the audience as the leading actor _____ stage.
    A) came into   B) came on   C) came by   D) came off

70. I think I'll go to bed. I can feel a headache _____.
    A) coming on   B) coming over   C) coming out   D) coming on

71. In order to be able to afford a holiday every summer I have to try to put _____ some money each month.
    A) away   B) for   C) in   D) off

72. If Diane doesn't turn _____ in the next five minutes, then we'll have to go without her.
    A) out   B) up   C) off   D) in

73. They turned _____ at the party, despite the bad weather.
    A) round   B) in   C) back   D) up

74. The effects of the anesthetic used for the operation take quite time to _____ off.
    A) wear   B) turn   C) give   D) move

75. Our school _____ for the summer holidays on 10th July.
    A) breaks up   B) breaks down   C) breaks in   D) breaks off

76. When you come to London, I can _____ for the night.
    A) put you down   B) put you off
    C) put you up   D) put you right

Choose the best alternative to replace the underlined words.

77. Robert started to get out of bed, but he was so weak from his illness that he <u>fainted</u> on the floor.
    A) passed out   B) passed down
    C) passed away   D) passed over

78. Poor old Mr. Lonely <u>died</u> peacefully on Tuesday.
    A) passed out   B) passed away
    C) passed down   D) passed over

79. Low pressure coming in from the Mediterranean will <u>cause</u> a change in the weather.
    A) bring round   B) bring down   C) bring up   D) bring about

80. Is he going to <u>participate in</u> the 5000 meters race this year?
    A) go on   B) go in   C) go in for   D) go for

81. She's got very light hair. She <u>resembles</u> her mother.
    A) takes back   B) takes after   C) takes down   D) takes apart

Test 3

82. He's started school, hasn't he? How is he doing?
    A) getting on   B) looking after   C) showing up   D) taking up

83. This factory can produce fifty cars a day.
    A) turn over   B) turn off   C) turn out   D) turn up

84. When do you expect to finish?
    A) get over   B) get out   C) get through   D) get down

85. You may omit the second question.
    A) hand in   B) leave out   C) take off   D) put out

86. Robert wanted to discuss a problem with his advisor.
    A) take up   B) look up   C) talk over   D) get through

87. The tailor let out the waist of the jacket.
    A) enlarged   B) shortened   C) shrank   D) set free

88. She passed out in a crowded bus.
    A) got on   B) got out   C) fainted   D) stood

89. The municipality pulled down much of Ankara in the 1980s.
    A) misused   B) suppressed   C) discovered   D) demolished

90. He proposed a very good suggestion.
    A) put in   B) put down   C) put out   D) put forward

91. I refuse to put up with his actions any longer.
    A) pretend   B) support   C) endure   D) consider

92. The meeting was postponed until next week.
    A) put off   B) put away   C) put out   D) put up

93. My headache isn't serious. It will disappear gradually.
    A) break off   B) wear off   C) tear off   D) put off

94. To me it was a very funny story, but when I told it nobody seemed to catch on.
    A) laugh   B) be pleased   C) understand   D) listen to it

95. Their rear windows overlook a lovely garden.
    A) look out on   B) are opposite   C) take in   D) are close to

96. The effects of the drug will wear off soon.
    A) disappear   B) tolerate   C) heal   D) prevent

97. This opportunity is too good to refuse.
    A) turn down   B) turn away   C) turn off   D) turn over

98. The design of the new car seems excellent, but we haven't tested it on the road.
    A) tried it out   B) traded it in   C) tuned it up   D) thrown it off

99. He said he wasn't interested in helping out, but I'll try to talk him round.
    A) persuade   B) scold   C) argue with   D) employ

100. Whenever George starts talking, Jim simply switches off.
    A) falls asleep   B) leaves the room   C) stops listening   D) interrupts him

TEST - 4

1. If the car _____ once more, I'm going to get a new one.
   A) breaks down   B) comes about   C) gives in   D) changes down

2. Not one of the girl's teachers could _____ her poor examination results.
   A) act out   B) answer back   C) account for   D) ask after

3. New students spend the first few days _____ themselves _____ the layout of the university.
   A) calling / out   B) bringing / about   C) acquainting / with   D) carrying / on

4. You go now and I'll _____ you later.
   A) catch up with   B) back up   C) go back on   D) come about

5. We certainly didn't _____ all this rain when we booked the holiday.
   A) hold out   B) back up   C) figure out   D) run into

6. If you will just _____ me for a few moments, I'll explain the reasons behind the decision.
   A) turn over to   B) take up with   C) bear with   D) care for

7. He was glad he had _____ the first question.
   A) took up with   B) disposed of   C) run into   D) got ahead

8. Our advisors _____ the plan, saying that it would be too costly.
   A) got over   B) got through with   C) got out of   D) came out against

9. His new novel _____ in the fall.
   A) shows up   B) takes up   C) sets out   D) comes out

10. She could _____ a year's salary in a week if you let her.
    A) put up with   B) run through   C) put aside   D) carry out

11. A row of back-to-back houses is being _____ to make way for new flats.
    A) pulled down   B) held up   C) closed down   D) turned up

12. I always try to _____ my friends when they're ill.
    A) care for   B) change up   C) call on   D) live on

13. How do you manage to _____ such a small salary?
    A) live on   B) put down   C) keep on   D) hold on to

14. He often _____ his dinner so that he can get more work done.
    A) hangs on   B) goes without   C) eats away   D) ends up

15. The river is _____ the bank _____ in several places.
    A) eating / away   B) embarking / on   C) handing / over   D) letting / in

16. He was living in El Salvador when the war _____.
    A) broke out   B) broke down   C) broke up   D) broke into

17. If you have any questions while I'm talking, feel free to _____.
    A) look on   B) come up   C) break in   D) look for

18. In both physical appearance and personality, John _____ his father.
    A) takes up   B) looks after   C) takes after   D) looks in

19. I was quite sad about my friend's death, but slowly I _____ it.
    A) got over   B) got out   C) got out of   D) came to

20. While he was looking on at the football game he _____ an old classmate from high school days.
    A) ran over   B) ran after   C) ran across   D) went into

Test 4

21. If you _____ your promise to stop smoking, you'll feel better and live longer.
    A) go into   B) stick to   C) turn into   D) come to
22. Many poor people in the world have to _____ life's necessities.
    A) go without   B) got over   C) come to   D) part with
23. Because of inflation, my weekly food bill now _____ $ 25.
    A) parts with   B) gets over   C) comes to   D) goes through
24. Save your money. Don't _____ it too quickly.
    A) go through   B) die down   C) hold on   D) touch on
25. He had an appointment with me but he never _____.
    A) turned into   B) showed up   C) came to   D) look into
26. You really cough too much; you should _____ smoking.
    A) cut down on   B) go through
    C) get around   D) try for
27. I didn't know you were in town. It's strange to _____ you like this.
    A) look forward to   B) run after
    C) run across   D) put up with
28. To lose weight, you have to _____ sugar and other sweet things.
    A) cut down on   B) look up to
    C) come up with   D) be in on
29. If a child does not _____ his parents, they probably are not very good to him.
    A) come up with   B) get rid of
    C) look up to   D) get through with
30. The police are trying to _____ crime, but the underworld is very strong.
    A) do away with   B) run around with
    C) be in on   D) work up to
31. If you do your homework every day, you can _____ your classmates.
    A) look forward to   B) live up to
    C) run around with   D) keep up with
32. When I _____ my college years, I'm surprised that I graduated.
    A) look forward to   B) look back on
    C) look out for   D) do away with
33. It's bad habit to _____ lies about things which you know are wrong; no one will believe you.
    A) give away   B) carry out   C) bring up   D) make up
34. Do you ever fail to do your duties or do you always _____ them?
    A) believe in   B) live up to   C) carry out   D) clear up
35. When the noise _____ I began to speak.
    A) died down   B) went without
    C) broke in   D) made up
36. I tried to get through to him, but I couldn't _____ his misunderstanding.
    A) catch on   B) clear up   C) work up to   D) catch up with
37. Despite his dislike of Jack, he had always _____ him if some other boy at school attacked him.
    A) kept up with   B) carried out
    C) settled down   D) stood up for
38. Did the committee _____ the problem carefully before deciding on it?
    A) get on   B) touch on   C) clear up   D) talk over
39. Because of inflation, salaries can't _____ the high cost of living.
    A) hold on   B) get ahead   C) keep up with   D) catch on
40. Right before a test, you should _____ your notes briefly to refresh your memory.
    A) touch on   B) run across   C) turn to   D) run over
41. It's difficult for a person with a broken leg to _____.
    A) get ahead   B) go around   C) come about   D) stand out
42. The staff meeting _____ just before lunch.
    A) broke out   B) broke into   C) broke up   D) brought out
43. The children were very well _____.
    A) gave up   B) got off   C) brought up   D) gave up
44. The meeting was _____ as the chairman was ill.
    A) called for   B) called off   C) called up   D) called out
45. He's a very bright boy, he's sure to _____ in his job.
    A) get about   B) come out   C) get out   D) get ahead
46. He _____ all the doctors in the district with medical samples.
    A) called on   B) was over   C) broke up   D) come into
47. Don't trust her, she always _____ her word.
    A) goes back   B) goes back on
    C) gets over   D) gets round
48. Is there enough coffee to _____ or shall I make some more?
    A) put forward   B) make up   C) set in   D) go round
49. You must _____ with the sunray treatment, it's doing you good.
    A) make up   B) go up   C) go on   D) put up
50. He's very bright, and _____ all the competitions.
    A) goes into   B) gives out   C) gives in   D) goes in for
51. Time's up. You must _____ your examination papers now.
    A) get in   B) go in for   C) come up   D) give in
52. He speaks very badly, I can't _____ what he is saying.
    A) make out   B) put down   C) go over   D) get out
53. He's a terrible liar, he's always _____ stories.
    A) getting up   B) putting through
    C) making up   D) going over
54. He _____ everything I said.
    A) put down   B) set out   C) picked up   D) looked to
55. The chairman _____ a very controversial idea which had little chance of being accepted.
    A) got on   B) came up   C) made for   D) put forward
56. You're very late now we'll have to work very hard to _____ lost time.
    A) put off   B) make up for   C) make up   D) set back
57. Most girls _____ their faces.
    A) make up for   B) make up   C) make for   D) make off
58. The meeting has been _____ until next week.
    A) put off   B) gone through
    C) set out   D) taken off
59. George _____ a difficult period shortly after his marriage broke down, but after a year or so his health and spirits picked up.
    A) went out   B) ran after
    C) put back   D) passed through
60. The hospital was near a main road so the patients had to _____ a lot of noise.
    A) made up for   B) went down with
    C) put up with   D) got over
61. She's very much fatter. I wonder how much weight she has _____.
    A) gone up   B) made up   C) put on   D) taken on
62. The telephone operator _____ me _____ almost immediately.
    A) went / through   B) put / through
    C) took / to   D) got / into

Test 4

63. When the chief surgeon suddenly announced he was going to leave, we were all _____.
    A) gone off   B) put through   C) set back   D) taken aback

64. What do you _____ me _____ a fool?
    A) take / for   B) take / in   C) look / for   D) look / after

65. When his father died he _____ the family business.
    A) went on   B) put back   C) turned out   D) took over

66. I wasn't listening very attentively and suddenly realized I hadn't _____ what the doctor said.
    A) turned out   B) made up for   C) taken in   D) put forward

67. His decision to close the factory _____ a series of protest meetings.
    A) set off   B) put out   C) put back   D) turned out

68. When the man _____ after the operation he found himself back in bed.
    A) came on   B) came in   C) came out   D) came round

69. Hospital doctors don't go out very often as their work _____ all their time.
    A) takes away   B) takes in   C) take on   D) takes up

70. I'm afraid that old man won't live much longer, he seems to have _____ the struggle.
    A) given out   B) given up   C) given away   D) given back

71. I was very _____ by the nurse's attitude, it really annoyed me.
    A) put out   B) put up   C) put by   D) put aside

72. The secretary said she would _____ duty at seven o'clock this evening.
    A) be through   B) be after   C) be off   D) be over

73. The old lady couldn't _____ because she had rheumatism.
    A) get about   B) get in   C) get on   D) get behind

74. As there was a power cut in the hospital, the surgeon had to _____ the operation.
    A) call off   B) call up   C) call on   D) call out

75. How many words _____ this sentence?
    A) go up   B) fill up   C) make up   D) call up

76. More Turkish students should _____ a foreign language and follow it through until they know it well.
    A) take for   B) take after   C) take on   D) take up

77. A week-old garbage usually _____ a terrible stink.
    A) give up   B) gives off   C) give on   D) give in

78. This skirt is too long. I must _____ it _____.
    A) take / up   B) turn / off   C) get / over   D) make / for

79. Her dress was too wide on the waist so she _____ it _____.
    A) took / up   B) turned / away   C) got / in   D) took / in

80. She _____ the radio before answering the phone.
    A) took in   B) turned down   C) turned back   D) put through

81. He couldn't find his keys so he _____ his pockets _____.
    A) turned / upside down   B) took / out   C) turned / on   D) turned / inside out

82. Why don't you _____ your proposal at the next meeting?
    A) come to   B) get over   C) call up   D) bring up

83. We have to _____ the first five lessons before the test.
    A) go over   B) get over   C) look up to   D) turn into

84. The morning was wet, but _____ fine in the afternoon.
    A) turned out   B) came to   C) went into   D) came back

85. After he got knocked down by the champion in the third round, it took him five minutes to _____.
    A) turn out   B) go in for   C) come to   D) get rid of

86. I trusted him to pay me back but he _____ me _____.
    A) let / down   B) put / down   C) left / over   D) kicked / off

87. We _____ at noon to have lunch.
    A) broke up   B) broke off   C) came about   D) went over

88. I couldn't _____ all of it _____.
    A) bring / round   B) get / on   C) take / in   D) go / over

89. Can you try to _____ what time the play starts on Saturdays?
    A) pick out   B) pull up   C) find out   D) hold up

90. You might _____ your ideas much better if you planned what you wanted to say.
    A) get on   B) look up   C) carry out   D) put across

91. When she heard the death of her husband, she _____ and cried.
    A) broke down   B) broke off   C) broke up   D) broke out

92. I must _____. I'll call you again at the same time tomorrow.
    A) break off   B) ring off   C) answer back   D) hang about

93. Let's _____ to work now.
    A) get on   B) get down   C) get off   D) get up

94. The whole area was _____ by the storms and floods.
    A) cut off   B) cut down   C) cut through   D) cut into

95. I wouldn't have noticed the mistake if you hadn't _____ it _____.
    A) looked / after   B) put / off   C) pointed / out   D) checked / out

96. I can't _____ what the sign says. It is too far away.
    A) pass out   B) cut out   C) make out   D) stand out

97. I want you to _____ the talking right now; I'm trying to read.
    A) run out   B) carry out   C) break out   D) cut out

98. When the two of you have _____ your problems, we'll start again. I can't work with people who are arguing.
    A) drop out   B) iron out   C) dry up   D) eat away

99. Five minutes after take off, the aircraft _____ at 30.000 feet.
    A) leveled out   B) lifted of   C) lined up   D) made up

100. Is he telling the truth, or _____ it all _____?
    A) picking / up   B) putting / up   C) making / up   D) taking / up

101. Two prisoners _____ of Midford Prison last night. They are armed and dangerous.
    A) ran out   B) passed out   C) broke out   D) made out

102. She _____ when she heard the bad news. It must have been a terrible shock to her.
    A) passed out   B) worn out   C) called off   D) bottled up

103. The article _____ the problem, but it did not discuss it in detail.
    A) brought on   B) passed on   C) called on   D) touched on

104. His cold was _____ by the unexpected change in temperature.
    A) broken up   B) brought on   C) broken away   D) broken down

105. The offer was so good that I couldn't _____ it _____.
    A) turn / down   B) clear / up   C) make / out   D) hand / out

106. A bus crashed on the main highway this morning and _____ traffic for hours.
    A) held up   B) cleared up   C) made up   D) blew up

107. It would be a good idea to discuss the plan. Why don't you _____ a meeting.
    A) take up   B) set up   C) make out   D) pick out

Test 4

108. You should _____ an insurance policy.
    A) take up   B) give up   C) break off   D) take out

109. The troops easily _____ the rebellion.
    A) went in for   B) took over   C) put down   D) showed up

110. The plane is almost taking _____ . We had better be quick.
    A) off   B) in   C) on   D) up

111. How are you _____ with your new job? Do you like it?
    A) looking for   B) getting along
    C) waiting on   D) taking over

112. The game was _____ on account of darkness.
    A) got over   B) taken off   C) put out   D) called off

113. I want to _____ these exercises before I give them to the teacher.
    A) keep on   B) count on   C) look over   D) point out

114. The travel agent managed to _____ the problems about my ticket.
    A) stick to   B) go with   C) make out   D) sort out

115. Peggy wants to _____ ceramics when she retires.
    A) look after   B) take up   C) wear out   D) do over

116. The gun _____ while he was cleaning it; it really frightened him.
    A) went off   B) cut off   C) ran over   D) put up

117. Susan works so hard that no one in the office can _____ her.
    A) put up with   B) go without
    C) get along with   D) keep up with

118. They _____ the old building and built a new one.
    A) tried out   B) put off   C) cut off   D) tore down

119. So many people came that there were not enough sandwiches to _____.
    A) go around   B) pass for   C) show off   D) put on

120. We seem to have _____ your size. Can you come back next week?
    A) sold out of   B) keep up with
    C) sent out for   D) given away

Choose the best alternative to replace the underlined words.

121. We had to cancel the party last week.
    A) break off   B) let off   C) put off   D) call off

122. Let's postpone the meeting till Friday.
    A) put off   B) call off   C) hold off   D) carry out

123. I've had flu for a week now: I just can't get rid of it.
    A) shake it off   B) shake it out
    C) shake it down   D) shake it up

124. His father often criticizes him.
    A) takes him off   B) runs him down
    C) puts him off   D) lets him down

125. My father was raised in a small village.
    A) called up   B) brought up   C) taken off   D) come out

126. You are never too late to start a new sport.
    A) set up   B) take in   C) call up   D) take up

127. The meeting ended in disorder.
    A) broke out   B) broke down   C) broke up   D) broke off

128. His project has failed to be completed.
    A) fallen through   B) fallen behind
    C) fallen back   D) fallen off

129. She pretended that she couldn't swim.
    A) turned out   B) made out   C) turned up   D) made up

130. My father has stopped smoking.
    A) taken out   B) turned down   C) given up   D) given back

131. When you make a promise you must fulfill it.
    A) carry it out   B) carry it on   C) carry it off   D) carry it over

132. When she got thinner she had to make her dress smaller.
    A) make for   B) put off   C) make over   D) take in

133. He called me a liar and I told him if he didn't apologize I'd punch him on the nose.
    A) make it out   B) make it over   C) put it back   D) take it back

134. I am getting fat; I ought to start tennis.
    A) take up   B) make up   C) put up   D) set out

135. He was so astonished that for a moment he was lost for words.
    A) worn out   B) taken aback   C) brought up   D) break down

136. I have so much work to do that I can't accept any more.
    A) take in   B) take after   C) take up   D) take on

137. I didn't feel like going to the dentist's so I delayed going there until I had a really bad toothache.
    A) put off   B) put by   C) put on   D) put out

138. I really must buy a car so I'm going to save some money every month until I can afford one.
    A) put by   B) put up   C) put off   D) put on

139. His father died of lung cancer and the doctor attributed it to the fact that he was a heavy smoker.
    A) took it off   B) carried it back
    C) thought it over   D) put it down

140. He just seems to spend money like water these days.
    A) fall through   B) go through   C) put off   D) give out

141. I had a wonderful idea to save money but it didn't succeed.
    A) catch up   B) bring out   C) come off   D) come up

142. Please visit me when you come to Ankara.
    A) call me up   B) stand for me
    C) look me up   D) look for me

143. That looks a nice flat. Shall we inspect it if it is for sale?
    A) look on   B) look over   C) look to   D) look through

144. Being the second child of three, he tends to admire his elder brother and despise his younger sister.
    A) look over / look up   B) make up to / make over
    C) make for / make up to   D) look up to / look down on

145. As we had a long way to go, we left at five in the morning.
    A) set off   B) put up   C) stood for   D) set about

146. The Prime Minister established a committee to discuss ways of improving the Turkish economy.
    A) set up   B) put out   C) kept up   D) found out

147. The factory has reduced its workforce by 50%.
    A) cut back   B) cut off   C) set off   D) taken in

148. The editor had to omit several articles because of lack of space.
    A) cut down   B) cut out   C) cut off   D) cut away

149. He gave a lift to three students outside London and dropped them off in Watford.
    A) called up   B) brought up   C) took up   D) picked up

150. Our radio can receive the Voice of America very clearly.
    A) get on   B) take off   C) pick out   D) pick up

TEST 1

1. Apart from those three very cold weeks in January, it has been a very _____ winter.
   A) plain   B) soft   C) pale   D) mild   E) calm

2. The best student in each class will _____ a prize at the end of term.
   A) catch   B) receive   C) possess   D) prove   E) reward

3. There is real concern that food supplies will not be _____ to feed the increasing world population.
   A) sufficient   B) satisfactory   C) equal   D) measured   E) effective

4. The police _____ her for helping the murderer to escape.
   A) caught   B) prevented   C) searched   D) brought   E) arrested

5. The children will not be allowed to come with us if they don't _____ themselves better.
   A) direct   B) accustom   C) behave   D) declare   E) compose

6. You must obtain _____ from the landowner to fish in this river.
   A) permit   B) freedom   C) permission   D) right   E) allowance

7. The local tourist bureau will send you _____ about hotels in the area.
   A) knowledge   B) information   C) news   D) notice   E) advertisement

8. The use of plastic for shoes _____ of leather has ruined shoe repairing as a business.
   A) although   B) as well   C) else   D) instead   E) outside

9. Her husband felt it would be silly to _____ the color of the curtains before they had painted the room.
   A) change   B) find   C) choose   D) lose   E) charge

10. The _____ of ice-cream sold increases sharply in the summer months.
    A) account   B) amount   C) count   D) number   E) size

11. It will _____ time if we make the sandwiches the day before the picnic.
    A) earn   B) spare   C) lower   D) save   E) win

12. I haven't got enough string to _____ up this parcel.
    A) stick   B) fold   C) close   D) shut   E) tie

13. Bill doesn't _____ what people say about him.
    A) concern   B) care   C) matter   D) disturb   E) depend

14. Although the false banknotes fooled many people, they did not _____ to close examination.
    A) keep up   B) put up   C) stand up   D) pay up   E) look up

15. When he beat the carpet, the _____ rose in clouds.
    A) dust   B) soil   C) mud   D) earth   E) powder

16. _____ of money prevented us from taking a holiday this year.
    A) Limit   B) Freeze   C) Emptiness   D) Expense   E) Lack

17. This blue-flower is known by _____ names in other parts of England.
    A) severe   B) difference   C) various   D) separate   E) usual

18. Why can't you do this small _____ for me? I've helped you often enough in the past.
    A) command   B) demand   C) effort   D) favor   E) influence

19. When there was a short _____ in the conversation, I asked if anyone would like anything to drink.
    A) fall   B) blank   C) wait   D) pause   E) place

20. While I am on holiday, ring me at my hotel only if there are any _____ messages for me.
    A) urgent   B) hasty   C) valuable   D) early   E) confident

21. This _____ is not big enough to cut down a tree.
    A) axe   B) hammer   C) screw   D) knife   E) spade

22. He must give us more time _____ we shall not be able to make a good job of it.
    A) whether   B) otherwise   C) consequently   D) therefore   E) doubtless

23. I should be very _____ if you would post this letter for me.
    A) grateful   B) pleasant   C) accepted   D) pleasing   E) thanking

24. When you get to the motorway, follow the _____ for London.
    A) masks   B) points   C) signs   D) plans   E) ways

25. The garden _____ as far as the river.
    A) advances   B) extends   C) lies   D) develops   E) enlarges

26. It is time to _____ the table for dinner.
    A) place   B) lay   C) lay out   D) put out   E) serve

27. I have always _____ you my best friend.
    A) regarded   B) considered   C) trusted   D) hoped   E) liked

28. He lost his _____ when the policeman stopped him.
    A) temper   B) language   C) spirit   D) character   E) pride

29. He won't _____ to buy some bread unless I tell him again.
    A) remind   B) realize   C) remember   D) forget   E) record

30. Because of the fine weather, we had all our classes in the _____ air.
    A) full   B) clear   C) open   D) thin   E) outside

31. Will you be taking my previous experience into _____ when you fix my salary?
    A) possession   B) account   C) mind   D) salesmanship   E) scale

32. If it wasn't an accident, he must have done it on _____.
    A) mistake   B) purpose   C) himself   D) fault   E) intention

33. Most things are now mass-produced rather than _____.
    A) hand-made   B) by hand   C) single   D) selected   E) detailed

34. The office lifts are out of _____ again.
    A) operating   B) order   C) work   D) working   E) movement

35. Let me know if any difficulties _____.
    A) find   B) arise   C) come   D) rise   E) happen

36. I can't _____ to have a holiday abroad on my salary.
    A) spend   B) think   C) afford   D) help   E) spare

37. They are twins and look very _____.
    A) alike   B) same   C) like   D) likely   E) identical

38. It is a very popular play, and it would be wise to _____ seats well in advance.
    A) engage   B) book   C) buy   D) occupy   E) preserve

39. He's not _____ of learning German in six months.
    A) possible   B) interested   C) inclined   D) able   E) capable

40. There was a large box behind the door and John could not _____ falling over it.
    A) prevent   B) avoid   C) fail   D) resist   E) save

TEST 2

1. Although I spoke to him many times, he never took any _____.
   A) notice   B) remark   C) warning
   D) observation   E) attention

2. The house was sold for £60000, which was far more than its real _____.
   A) cost   B) value   C) price
   D) sum   E) expense

3. This morning, drivers were warned of _____ fog in all industrial areas.
   A) deep   B) important   C) thick
   D) cloudy   E) great

4. I can't find the scissors anywhere. What have you done _____ them?
   A) with   B) to   C) of
   D) by   E) for

5. You couldn't _____ any secrets even for an hour in that little town.
   A) keep   B) net   C) take
   D) learn   E) hear

6. The workers went on strike because they thought their wages were too _____.
   A) little   B) few   C) short
   D) low   E) small

7. The explorer _____ all the way to the source of the river by boat.
   A) drove   B) traveled   C) rode
   D) followed   E) tracked

8. When the bill came, he had to _____ money from his brother to pay it.
   A) borrow   B) lend   C) loan
   D) ask   E) let

9. Because the company was doing more business it was necessary to _____ the factory.
   A) extend   B) increase   C) broaden
   D) grow   E) magnify

10. The farmer had to wear heavy boots in the winter because the fields were so wet and _____.
    A) earthy   B) soiled   C) dusty
    D) greasy   E) muddy

11. Very few scientists _____ with completely new answers to the world's problems.
    A) come to   B) come around   C) come up
    D) come in   E) come on

12. When John _____ in London, he went to see the Houses of Parliament.
    A) came   B) reached   C) arrived
    D) got   E) stood

13. He climbed up into the tree and picked all the fruit _____ reach.
    A) near   B) inside   C) within
    D) at   E) beyond

14. I was not _____ that I had cut myself until I saw the blood all over my hand.
    A) familiar   B) awake   C) disturbed
    D) astonished   E) conscious

15. Tropical diseases are comparatively _____ in Britain.
    A) scarce   B) rare   C) less
    D) slight   E) scattered

16. If you want to telephone him you will have to _____ the number in the book.
    A) look at   B) look to   C) look through
    D) look up   E) look after

17. She began to feel nervous when the train pulled up at the _____ between Austria and Yugoslavia.
    A) limit   B) edge   C) bar
    D) border   E) division

18. Margaret proudly showed her mother the toy cat she had _____ in the competition.
    A) gained   B) won   C) caught
    D) rewarded   E) taken

19. He asked us if we would _____ to share a room.
    A) accept   B) consider   C) agree
    D) admit   E) approve

20. Students are expected to _____ their classes regularly.
    A) assist   B) frequent   C) attend
    D) follow   E) present

21. The _____ charged by the lawyer for his services was unusually high.
    A) fee   B) fare   C) debt
    D) hire   E) prize

22. He was pleased to have the _____ to hear such a fine musician play hit favorite piece of music.
    A) occasion   B) possibility   C) fate
    D) opportunity   E) space

23. He tried to _____ his daughter of the dangers of spending more than she earned.
    A) remember   B) remain   C) warn
    D) realize   E) threaten

24. We had a marvelous holiday: only the last two days were slightly _____ by the weather.
    A) damaged   B) hurt   C) ruined
    D) spoiled   E) wasted

25. Dearer electricity will mean _____ bills for most families.
    A) dear   B) difficult   C) expensive
    D) hard   E) heavy

26. These figures give a rough guide to the cost of _____ your car.
    A) controlling   B) handling   C) keeping
    D) managing   E) running

27. It was the longest film I've ever seen; it _____ four hours.
    A) ended   B) finished   C) lasted
    D) stayed   E) was

28. The information-office at the station _____ that all trains were running about one hour behind time.
    A) advertised   B) decided   C) explained
    D) promised   E) told

29. Ann is so _____ to succeed that I am sure nothing will stop her.
    A) determined   B) willing   C) strong
    D) patient   E) obvious

30. It takes six weeks to _____ a man to do this job.
    A) train   B) guide   C) lead
    D) raise   E) learn

31. On Sundays the business center of the city was usually quite _____.
    A) left   B) deserted   C) unpopular
    D) unattended   E) alone

32. In today's paper, it _____ that there will be a new government soon.
    A) tells   B) states   C) stands
    D) writes   E) records

33. Before you sign anything important, pay careful _____ to all the conditions.
    A) notice   B) attention   C) regards
    D) reference   E) study

34. When I came through the customs at the airport I had to pay _____ on a clock I had bought.
    A) taxes   B) duty   C) fines
    D) rates   E) allowance

35. It was after dark when the two children were both _____ on the safety-crossing by a lorry.
    A) knocked down   B) knocked out   C) run across
    D) run out   E) run in

36. The rising _____ of living is as hard on country families as on city families.
    A) amount   B) cost   C) expense
    D) increase   E) price

37. When it was time for our tickets to be _____, I couldn't find mine.
    A) controlled   B) bought   C) checked
    D) overlooked   E) served

38. Will you _____ my essay, please, to find out whether I made any mistakes?
    A) see through   B) look through   C) look up
    D) look into   E) see to

39. At the moment my car is at the garage being made ready for a _____ across Europe.
    A) journey   B) route   C) travel
    D) progress   E) voyage

40. He asked an artist to _____ some drawings to illustrate what he had written.
    A) show   B) make   C) paint
    D) describe   E) picture

TEST 3

1. When he was a student, his father gave him a monthly _____ towards his expenses.
   A) salary   B) permission   C) allowance   D) wage   E) money

2. It seemed as if all of a _____ the animal had smelt danger in the air.
   A) sudden   B) moment   C) minute   D) once   E) shot

3. What do you think would be the _____ of this ring, if I were to sell it?
   A) worth   B) value   C) cost   D) good   E) importance

4. Police officers working on the murder have _____ hundreds of families.
   A) asked   B) demanded   C) enquired   D) questioned   E) requested

5. The thief was _____ to prison for two years.
   A) brought   B) put   C) sent   D) taken   E) judged

6. He was a much older tennis player but he had the great _____ of experience.
   A) advantage   B) deal   C) help   D) value   E) profit

7. To get my travelers' cheques I had to _____ a special cheque to the Bank for the total amount.
   A) make for   B) make off   C) make out   D) make over   E) make up

8. He began to take politics _____ only when he left school.
   A) carefully   B) bravely   C) seriously   D) solemnly   E) strictly

9. Unless the workers' demands are _____ soon there will be a strike.
   A) given   B) met   C) paid   D) permitted   E) replied

10. The children thought that the cream was deliciously _____ and they finished it all.
    A) famous   B) chosen   C) flavored   D) hungered   E) favorable

11. The two scientists disagreed and a _____ argument developed.
    A) wet   B) bitter   C) salty   D) sour   E) bare

12. This theory _____ from the work of certain early 20th century scientists.
    A) resists   B) returns   C) raises   D) insults   E) results

13. Fear showed in the eyes of the young man, while the old man looked tired and _____.
    A) watery   B) wearing   C) weary   D) wandering   E) wondered

14. As he had no friends or relatives in the town, the traveler tried to find a _____ somewhere.
    A) log   B) lodge   C) landing   D) lodging   E) stay

15. After his journey, Gerard hoped to find an inn in which to _____ the night.
    A) shelter   B) waste   C) lose   D) spend   E) pay

16. In the central region the dry season is long and severe, and the _____ annual rainfall is only about 70 cm.
    A) refreshing   B) general   C) average   D) longest   E) greatest

17. George took an eager look at the _____ meal, which everyone was looking forward to, and sat down with the rest of the family.
    A) dusty   B) crusty   C) pasty   D) nasty   E) tasty

18. Owing to an accident, traffic had to be _____ to another route.
    A) redirected   B) turned   C) extended   D) sent   E) misled

19. Well-mannered children have usually been properly _____ by their parents.
    A) raised up   B) borne up   C) brought up   D) got up   E) put up

20. He said he had every _____ in his secretary; she would do the right thing.
    A) belief   B) dependence   C) thought   D) knowledge   E) confidence

21. Can you _____ me £5 until next week?
    A) borrow   B) let   C) hire   D) rent   E) lend

22. It is not _____ for you to eat too much.
    A) kind   B) good   C) well   D) useful   E) fit

23. The next _____ of the committee will take place on Thursday.
    A) seating   B) group   C) collection   D) meeting   E) gathering

24. Many kinds of _____ animals are disappearing or have already disappeared from the earth.
    A) brave   B) untamed   C) unfriendly   D) angry   E) wild

25. I am sorry that I can't _____ your invitation.
    A) take   B) except   C) agree   D) have   E) accept

26. I forgot to _____ him to buy some bread.
    A) remember   B) repeat   C) remind   D) let   E) make

27. The soldiers were put in prison because they _____ to obey orders.
    A) refused   B) rejected   C) denied   D) objected   E) disliked

28. I don't want to wait until tomorrow; I _____ go at once.
    A) prefer   B) would rather   C) want   D) like   E) am willing

29. When you are riding a bicycle you should _____ the handlebars firmly.
    A) handle   B) hold   C) hand   D) have   E) control

30. I had _____ decided to take a coat when it started to rain.
    A) already   B) yet   C) still   D) never   E) always

31. There is _____ that I may have to go into hospital next week.
    A) an opportunity   B) bad luck   C) a possibility   D) fate   E) an occasion

32. _____ what he says, he wasn't even there when the crime was committed.
    A) Following   B) Listening to   C) According to   D) Fearing   E) Meaning

33. If you _____ your money to mine, we shall have enough.
    A) add   B) combine   C) join   D) unite   E) bank

34. This young tree could not have been damaged by accident. I believe it was done _____.
    A) in fact   B) on purpose   C) by appointment   D) by plan   E) by understanding

35. How much would you _____ for repairing my watch?
    A) charge   B) cost   C) pay   D) spend   E) demand

36. After the battle, the _____ soldiers were helped by those who could walk.
    A) damaged   B) wounded   C) broken   D) killed   E) blessed

37. If we are thinking of having a day in the country, I should like to listen to a weather _____.
    A) statement   B) spell   C) forecast   D) recording   E) news

38. I do _____ I could speak English well.
    A) know   B) want   C) wish   D) like   E) hope

39. Where do you _____ going for your holidays this year?
    A) intend   B) expect   C) pretend   D) mean   E) guess

40. He hoped the appointment would enable him to gain greater _____ in publishing.
    A) experience   B) work   C) jobs   D) employment   E) hope

Test 3

TEST 4

1. He grew very angry when he realized how he had been _____ out of his money.
   A) tricked   B) played   C) deceived
   D) robbed   E) stolen

2. The cow had lost its own calf, but the farmer persuaded it to _____ one whose mother had died.
   A) choose   B) adopt   C) undertake
   D) collect   E) educate

3. When my aunt lost her cat last summer, it turned _____ a week later at a house in the next village.
   A) in   B) on   C) over
   D) out   E) up

4. The funeral will be _____, and only members of the dead man's family will attend.
   A) peculiar   B) particular   C) private
   D) alone   E) personal

5. They were making enough noise at the party to wake the _____.
   A) people   B) population   C) living
   D) company   E) dead

6. I can't advise you what to do. You must use your own _____.
   A) opinion   B) guesswork   C) justice
   D) judgment   E) ideal

7. It isn't quite _____ that he will be present at the meeting.
   A) sure   B) right   C) exact
   D) certain   E) formal

8. The _____ from the forest fire could be seen ten miles away.
   A) mist   B) smell   C) spark
   D) steam   E) smoke

9. The house was so damp that it was _____ to live in.
   A) sickly   B) unhealthy   C) unwell
   D) diseased   E) infectious

10. There are usually at least two _____ of looking at every question.
    A) means   B) directions   C) views
    D) opinions   E) ways

11. He spoke so quickly that I didn't _____ what he said.
    A) receive   B) accept   C) listen
    D) take   E) catch

12. I have such a bad cold that I have lost all _____ of smell.
    A) degree   B) sense   C) strength
    D) skill   E) scent

13. Peter begged his neighbor to _____ him five pounds until the weekend.
    A) lend   B) supply   C) borrow
    D) provide   E) hire

14. The lorry driver was badly _____ when his lorry crashed into a wall.
    A) pained   B) hit   C) hurt
    D) harmed   E) damaged

15. Although John was the eldest in the family, he always let his sister _____ charge of the house.
    A) take   B) hold   C) make
    D) get   E) be

16. The policeman _____ everything he had noticed to the inspector.
    A) reviewed   B) accounted   C) reported
    D) informed   E) said

17. These trees cannot be grown in such a cold _____ as ours.
    A) weather   B) climate   C) air
    D) season   E) space

18. The audience waited until the curtain had risen and then _____ into applause.
    A) flooded   B) cheered   C) started
    D) burst   E) went

19. _____ up children properly is mainly their parents' duty.
    A) growing   B) rearing   C) breeding
    D) raising   E) bringing

20. When he makes a _____ by car, he takes his family with him.
    A) travel   B) course   C) passage
    D) voyage   E) journey

21. Science has made great _____ during the past 30 years.
    A) increases   B) motions   C) advances
    D) advantages   E) opportunities

22. People who live in a small village are bound to see a good _____ of each other.
    A) sum   B) quantity   C) deal
    D) portion   E) degree

23. As soon as the children were _____, their mother got them out of bed and into the bathroom.
    A) woke   B) awoke   C) wake
    D) awake   E) waken

24. This blue door was _____ painted green.
    A) lastly   B) before   C) firstly
    D) originally   E) presently

25. Her shoes _____ her gloves; they look very well together.
    A) suit   B) match   C) fit
    D) compare   E) color

26. If you have a _____ to make about the food, I am willing to listen.
    A) dislike   B) trouble   C) complaint
    D) discontent   E) fault

27. His father had _____ him how to make model airplanes.
    A) planned   B) guided   C) taught
    D) learnt   E) described

28. The old man got into the _____ of storing money under the bed.
    A) tradition   B) manner   C) use
    D) harvest   E) habit

29. Violent programs on television may have a bad _____ on children.
    A) affection   B) pressure   C) influence
    D) control   E) power

30. The shoes fitted her _____.
    A) perfectly   B) justly   C) fairly
    D) rightly   E) finely

31. Could you please _____ an appointment for me to see Mr. Smith?
    A) manage   B) arrange   C) do
    D) take   E) have

32. Tell your brother to come _____, because it's going to rain in a minute or two.
    A) indoors   B) outdoors   C) within
    D) inwards   E) homewards

33. As he was ill, he had to _____ the party.
    A) miss   B) avoid   C) regret
    D) lack   E) fail

34. When he was at school, he won the first _____ for good behavior.
    A) reward   B) prize   C) price
    D) present   E) praise

35. Can't you _____ your chief to let you have a holiday?
    A) overcome   B) make   C) succeed
    D) persuade   E) reason

36. The girl's father _____ to buy her a car if she passed her examination.
    A) admitted   B) accepted   C) agreed
    D) approved   E) afforded

37. The carriage was _____ by four horses.
    A) tired   B) rolled   C) pushed
    D) driven   E) drawn

38. He ate what he could, and gave the _____ of the food to the birds.
    A) remain   B) uneaten   C) waste
    D) part   E) rest

39. They decided to leave the waiter a big _____ because the food and service had been excellent.
    A) note   B) addition   C) tip
    D) gift   E) reward

40. As it had not rained for several months, there was a _____ of water.
    A) waste   B) shortage   C) drop
    D) loss   E) desert

TEST 5

1. The disease _____ widely, all over the country.
   A) sprang   B) sped   C) spread
   D) spilt   E) spun

2. If we _____ the plan you suggest, we are more likely to be successful.
   A) decide   B) elect   C) command
   D) vote   E) adopt

3. After years of war, the whole nation wanted to make _____ with their enemies.
   A) piece   B) peace   C) pace
   D) pact   E) peas

4. She chose cushions of a color which would _____ her carpet.
   A) equal   B) agree   C) help
   D) match   E) pair

5. She opened the packet and emptied the _____ into a saucepan.
   A) fullness   B) insides   C) container
   D) refills   E) contents

6. After trying several times, I _____ to see him.
   A) managed   B) succeeded   C) won
   D) attempted   E) became

7. He offered to _____ her a hand as the suitcase was too heavy for her to carry.
   A) lend   B) help   C) show
   D) loan   E) borrow

8. She is making herself ill with _____ over her son's future.
   A) trouble   B) annoyance   C) disgust
   D) worry   E) consideration

9. The government has lost a great deal of _____ because of the large increase in food prices.
   A) strength   B) support   C) agreement
   D) vote   E) progress

10. Because of the strong sun Mrs. Williams' new blue dining-room curtains _____ to gray within a year.
    A) faded   B) fainted   C) paled
    D) bleached   E) grew

11. A _____ from the local paper asked for details of the accident.
    A) salesman   B) newsagent   C) reporter
    D) typewriter E) broadcaster

12. She looked everywhere for her book but _____ had to return home without it.
    A) lastly   B) at the end   C) in the end
    D) in the finish E) at the last

13. I'm sorry but what he thinks is not of the _____ importance to me.
    A) merest   B) lowest   C) last
    D) worst   E) least

14. It was _____ by the railways board that the cost of rail fares would be increased by ten per cent.
    A) noticed   B) stated   C) suggested
    D) noted   E) spoken

15. When replying to this advertisement, please _____ a stamped addressed envelope.
    A) present   B) contain   C) enclose
    D) envelop   E) introduce

16. Every time he tried to start the car, the wheels _____ deeper into the mud.
    A) stayed   B) hollowed   C) feel
    D) dropped   E) sank

17. When are you going to begin to _____ that animal?
    A) direct   B) drive   C) teach
    D) train   E) get

18. They gave _____ looking for her when it grew dark.
    A) up   B) in   C) off
    D) out   E) away

19. There's no need to be frightened of the dog; he's quite _____.
    A) happy   B) eager   C) weak
    D) cheerful   E) harmless

20. His _____ had always been to become an architect.
    A) study   B) want   C) ambition
    D) imagination E) direction

21. Be quiet! It's rude to _____ people when they are speaking.
    A) interfere B) interrupt   C) prevent
    D) introduce E) block

22. Children _____ good food if they are to be healthy.
    A) have   B) receive   C) eat
    D) need   E) desire

23. After a lot of difficulty, he _____ to open the door.
    A) managed   B) succeeded   C) obtained
    D) realized   E) gained

24. I have been looking for this book for months, and _____ I have found it.
    A) at least   B) in time   C) at the end
    D) at present E) at last

25. The teacher _____ them the answer to the question.
    A) exclaimed B) told   C) said
    D) described E) declared

26. I have never _____ any experience of living in the country.
    A) had   B) seen   C) done
    D) made   E) got

27. The child was told to _____ for being rude to his uncle.
    A) excuse   B) apologize   C) punish
    D) confess   E) pardon

28. Throughout his childhood, he suffered from _____ illnesses.
    A) import   B) serious   C) solemn
    D) great   E) strong

29. The _____ of trees in the water was very clear.
    A) mirror   B) sight   C) reflection
    D) shadow   E) picture

30. That cupboard must always be _____ carefully locked.
    A) guarded   B) shut   C) closed
    D) kept   E) held

31. His name was on the _____ of my tongue, but I just couldn't remember it.
    A) end   B) point   C) edge
    D) tip   E) top

32. You should be very _____ to your teachers for their help.
    A) thankful   B) thanking   C) grateful
    D) considerate E) gracious

33. When can the students _____ for next year's evening classes?
    A) assist   B) enroll   C) join
    D) inscribe   E) subscribe

34. The policeman stopped him when he was driving home and _____ him of speeding.
    A) charged   B) accused   C) blamed
    D) warned   E) arrested

35. His new appointment takes _____ from the beginning of next month.
    A) place   B) effect   C) post
    D) possession E) position

36. I _____ her not to walk on the thin ice but she wouldn't listen to me.
    A) warned   B) guarded   C) suggested
    D) persuaded E) taught

37. After dinner the minister made a short _____ to the guests.
    A) delivery   B) pronunciation C) conversation
    D) piece   E) speech

38. He couldn't _____ the thought of leaving his home town for ever.
    A) support   B) bear   C) carry
    D) think   E) hold

39. On my present salary, I just can't _____ a car which cost over £3,000.
    A) pretend   B) allow   C) elect
    D) afford   E) adopt

40. He looked rather untidy as there were two buttons _____ from his coat.
    A) loosing   B) losing   C) off
    D) away   E) missing

Test 5

TEST 6

1. What measures have been _____ to control the crowd at Saturday's football match?
   A) imagined   B) made   C) given
   D) described   E) taken

2. He left in such a hurry that I _____ had time to thank him.
   A) almost   B) even   C) nearly
   D) scarcely   E) least

3. He gave me some very _____ advice on buying a house.
   A) precious   B) wealthy   C) dear
   D) prized   E) valuable

4. To get my travelers' cheques I had to _____ a special cheque to the Bank for the total amount.
   A) make for   B) make off   C) make out
   D) makeover   E) make up

5. If we can _____ our present difficulties, then everything should be all right.
   A) get off   B) come across   C) come over
   D) get over   E) get away

6. I'm _____ to get the tickets for the show today, as there are hardly any left.
   A) worried   B) curious   C) anxious
   D) afraid   E) troubled

7. His landlady gave him a week's _____ to leave the flat.
   A) threat   B) notice   C) advice
   D) caution   E) dismissal

8. We forgave his bad temper because we knew that his son's illness had put him under great _____.
   A) emotion   B) excitement   C) crisis
   D) stress   E) nervousness

9. A completely new situation is likely to _____ when the school leaving age is raised to 16.
   A) affect   B) rise   C) arise
   D) raise   E) happen

10. A competitor may submit any number of entries _____ each one is accompanied by a registration fee.
    A) guaranteeing   B) insuring   C) allowing
    D) providing   E) notwithstanding

11. Enquiries _____ the condition of patients may be made personally or by telephone.
    A) revealing   B) concerning   C) affecting
    D) for   E) following

12. Tenants are _____ to beware of paying rent to unknown persons.
    A) commanded   B) informed   C) notified
    D) advised   E) suggested

13. He tries to _____ up his lessons by telling a few jokes.
    A) raise   B) inspire   C) stimulate
    D) snap   E) liven

14. Many university courses are not really _____ to the needs of students or their future employers.
    A) associated   B) relative   C) geared
    D) sufficient   E) qualified

15. The noise of the traffic _____ Paul from his work.
    A) prevented   B) annoyed   C) obstructed
    D) upset   E) distracted

16. The plan was _____ when it was discovered just how much the scheme would cost.
    A) resigned   B) abandoned   C) surrendered
    D) released   E) disused

17. We finally managed to _____ the committee's approval of our plans.
    A) secure   B) arouse   C) acquire
    D) exert   E) execute

18. We are paying for the car in 24 monthly _____ of £55.
    A) fragments   B) parts   C) installments
    D) refunds   E) credits

19. Violence in the local prison has _____ two lives.
    A) removed   B) taken   C) cost
    D) murdered   E) spilt

20. The main road through Littlebury was blocked for three hours today after an accident _____ two lorries.
    A) containing   B) connecting   C) involving
    D) including   E) combining

21. Since any answer was likely to cause embarrassment to his party the politician tried to _____ the question.
    A) delude   B) seclude   C) pervade
    D) evade   E) elude

22. Only two of the candidates can be seriously _____ for this post.
    A) contemplated   B) commended   C) considered
    D) reviewed   E) entertained

23. When I went into the dining room next morning, the _____ of the dinner were still on the table.
    A) remains   B) results   C) remnants
    D) surplus   E) relics

24. She's a very selfish person who doesn't show much _____ for others.
    A) consternation   B) consideration   C) humanity
    D) estimation   E) complacency

25. The unpleasant taste _____ in his mouth for hours.
    A) insisted   B) prolonged   C) waited
    D) lingered   E) rested

26. His _____ book will deal with industrial relations.
    A) eventual   B) actual   C) prompt
    D) forthcoming   E) following

27. Hotel rooms must be _____ by noon, but luggage may be left with the porter.
    A) vacated   B) departed   C) abandoned
    D) discharged   E) displaced

28. Every citizen has the _____ to assist in the prevention of crime.
    A) duty   B) right   C) effort
    D) trouble   E) force

29. He couldn't _____ his father that he was telling the truth.
    A) admit   B) convince   C) believe
    D) confide   E) ensure

30. He began _____ absurd plans for escaping.
    A) doing   B) settling   C) hitching
    D) devising   E) thinking

31. He didn't intend to _____ this conversation further himself, for he disliked his aunt's patronizing tone.
    A) prosecute   B) pursue   C) push
    D) follow   E) enter

32. We aren't very busy in the shop at the moment. In fact we're quite _____.
    A) contrary   B) lazy   C) slack
    D) rare   E) opposite

33. Color-blind people often find it difficult to _____ between blue and green.
    A) separate   B) compare   C) distinguish
    D) contrast   E) relate

34. The completion of the new Town Hall has been _____ owing to a strike.
    A) held off   B) held down   C) held in
    D) held up   E) held on

35. It has always been the _____ of our firm to encourage workers to take part in social activities.
    A) plan   B) campaign   C) procedure
    D) policy   E) rule

36. Mr. Sanders has been asked to _____ the next meeting of the Library Committee.
    A) manage   B) chair   C) take
    D) lead   E) direct

37. The Jury gave a unanimous _____ of Not Guilty.
    A) decision   B) opinion   C) verdict
    D) judgment   E) assessment

38. I fear you can't count on him; he's liable to _____ out when things become difficult.
    A) be   B) let   C) opt
    D) take   E) stop

39. The 1950s were the _____ of this cult but one still hears references to it today.
    A) top   B) heyday   C) summit
    D) pick   E) pitch

40. What _____ of car do you run?
    A) fabrication   B) species   C) fabric
    D) mark   E) make

Test 6

TEST 7

1. Many poets have _____ the beauties of the countryside.
   A) applauded B) enthused C) enamored
   D) appealed E) extolled

2. When the student graduated, he got his _____.
   A) paper B) degree C) license
   D) pension E) bachelor

3. She didn't _____ doing the washing up, as she hadn't wanted to go out anyway.
   A) object B) care C) matter
   D) care for E) mind

4. The tremor in his voice _____ his nervousness.
   A) affirmed B) pronounced C) disguised
   D) represented E) revealed

5. Although I tried to concentrate on the lectures, I was _____ by the noise from the next room.
   A) dissuaded B) averted C) repressed
   D) distracted E) interfered

6. I _____ what her name is; I'm sure I know her face.
   A) remember B) wonder C) guess
   D) suspect E) suppose

7. 'I _____ that one', said the tourist, pointing for the benefit of the uncomprehending shopkeeper.
   A) want B) wish C) take
   D) desire E) become

8. I do not _____ to be clever but I am not stupid.
   A) permit B) classify C) confess
   D) claim E) compare

9. After the Cabinet reshuffle, the Minister wasn't very happy at his new _____.
   A) job B) post C) work
   D) shift E) place

10. Children under the age of 16 are not _____ to enter for the competition.
    A) enabled B) empowered C) capable
    D) eligible E) permissible

11. I was so _____ in my book that I didn't hear the doorbell ring.
    A) settled B) concentrated C) absorbed
    D) engaged E) occupied

12. Motorists _____ of speeding may be banned from driving for a year.
    A) convicted B) arrested C) charged
    D) judged E) condemned

13. In the medical profession, men _____ women by five to one.
    A) increase B) outnumber C) supersede
    D) overcome E) outclass

14. He has told us so many lies that we can no longer place any _____ on what he says.
    A) conviction B) reliance C) reputation
    D) credibility E) regard

15. Pools of water lay trapped among the rocks as the tide _____.
    A) removed B) refilled C) returned
    D) receded E) retired

16. He bought that house, _____ that he would inherit money under his uncle's will.
    A) speculating B) considering C) assuming
    D) estimating E) allowing

17. A _____ change in policy is needed if relations are ever to improve.
    A) severe B) violent C) drastic
    D) strict E) wide

18. He wrote the text book in _____ with his brother.
    A) harmony B) collaboration C) unison
    D) connection E) communion

19. His country cottage _____ the amenities of his London flat.
    A) missed B) overlooked C) neglected
    D) ignored E) lacked

20. The victory was _____ annually by a ten-gun salute.
    A) memorized B) commemorated C) reminded
    D) recapitulated E) remembered

21. He _____ the figures carefully before making any comment.
    A) estimated B) scrutinized C) watched
    D) remarked E) visualized

22. He couldn't explain the problem well, as he had only a _____ knowledge of the subject.
    A) profound B) primary C) rudimentary
    D) fundamental E) superfluous

23. His account must be true, because the evidence he gave _____ that of two other witnesses.
    A) collaborates B) consists C) coincides
    D) condones E) corroborates

24. We must hear the _____ of the last meeting before we proceed.
    A) minutes B) protocol C) reportage
    D) agenda E) items

25. Many road accidents occur because motorists cannot _____ the speed of approaching vehicles.
    A) conclude B) count C) gauge
    D) value E) number

26. The rainbow _____ as the sun came fully out from behind the clouds.
    A) dissolved B) removed C) dispersed
    D) retired E) disappeared

27. The boy, wanting to be independent, _____ his father's offer of help.
    A) turned away B) turned from C) turned down
    D) turned against E) turned up

28. It is not profitable to provide bus services in districts where the population is widely _____.
    A) scattered B) dismissed C) separated
    D) spaced E) divided

29. There is a _____ of a thousand pounds offered for the capture of the murderer.
    A) reward B) prize C) price
    D) grant E) credit

30. They always kept on good _____ with their next-door neighbors for the children's sake.
    A) friendship B) relations C) intentions
    D) terms E) will

31. She had clearly no _____ of doing any work, although she was very well paid.
    A) desire B) ambition C) willingness
    D) intention E) meaning

32. The car salesman took the customer for a drive in the new model in order to _____ its improved features.
    A) advocate B) demonstrate C) exhibit
    D) reveal E) expound

33. The actual _____ by which coal is extracted is well worth watching.
    A) conduct B) process C) procession
    D) pattern E) fashion

34. If we _____ the plan you suggest, we are more likely to be successful.
    A) decide B) elect C) command
    D) vote E) adopt

35. The child was _____ for getting his shoes and socks wet.
    A) corrected B) remonstrated C) suffered
    D) scolded E) complained

36. Certainly man must _____ the future, and find ways of providing for his needs.
    A) look to B) look up C) look after
    D) look for E) look on

37. He took the day off work to _____ his aunt's funeral.
    A) accompany B) regard C) assist
    D) attend E) follow

38. His energetic efforts met with only _____ success.
    A) particular B) proportionate C) partial
    D) entire E) complete

39. My rifle was not _____, so I did not hit anything.
    A) from the best B) for the better C) of the best
    D) for the best E) of the better

40. Any student who _____ his homework is unlikely to pass his examination.
    A) reduces B) neglects C) practices
    D) denies E) offends

TEST 8

1. Yesterday the pound fell to a _____ low level against the dollar, according to this morning news.
   A) final   B) major   C) record
   D) remote   E) last

2. Even the most detached and indifferent spectator can be _____ away by enthusiasm at a horserace.
   A) carried   B) moved   C) excited
   D) stirred   E) swept

3. The young performers _____ and held the audience's attention from the moment the curtain went up.
   A) caught   B) gathered   C) snatched
   D) took   E) trapped

4. She was very _____ when I told her my pet dog had died.
   A) sympathetic   B) just   C) helpful
   D) pitiful   E) friendly

5. What were John and Mary _____ about when you came into the room?
   A) speaking   B) discussing   C) saying
   D) telling   E) talking

6. I don't smoke, but I don't object to _____ people smoking.
   A) different   B) another   C) other
   D) alternative   E) unlike

7. I like your new red dress, the color _____ you.
   A) fits   B) looks   C) suits
   D) likes   E) seems

8. Mr. Jones wants to know if he can have a _____ with you.
   A) argument   B) word   C) lecture
   D) speech   E) conversation

9. Mrs. Brown has cleaned the house from _____ to bottom.
   A) attic   B) first floor   C) top
   D) roof   E) upstairs

10. Alice is tall and slim and has a beautiful _____.
    A) position   B) shape   C) form
    D) figure   E) size

11. Mrs. Brown's children have very good manners because they have been well _____.
    A) brought out   B) brought in   C) brought together
    D) brought up   E) brought round

12. My father is very _____ with his hands.
    A) curious   B) interested   C) interesting
    D) intelligent   E) clever

13. Mrs. Brown is offering a _____ of £50 to anyone who finds her diamond ring.
    A) prize   B) price   C) reward
    D) money   E) total

14. I should be _____ if you would answer my letter by return.
    A) nice   B) good   C) glad
    D) cheerful   E) kind

15. He will pass his examination if he works _____.
    A) quietly   B) strongly   C) hard
    D) cleverly   E) loudly

16. Mary is very _____ because she has failed her examination.
    A) excited   B) afraid   C) sensitive
    D) sensible   E) upset

17. My father told me never _____ a lie.
    A) to do   B) to make   C) to tell
    D) to recount   E) to relate

18. Mrs. Brown's children are always as good as _____.
    A) butter   B) gold   C) milk
    D) silk   E) silver

19. My cousin, who lives in France, is _____ me French.
    A) learning   B) teaching   C) helping
    D) assisting   E) instructing

20. Peter has not got the right _____ for that job.
    A) knowledge   B) learning   C) qualifications
    D) abilities   E) examinations

21. The Stephenson's' house was _____ by thieves last night.
    A) broken into   B) broken up   C) broken off
    D) broken down   E) broken in

22. The fishermen said that the high wind had made the sea very _____.
    A) calm   B) uneven   C) undulating
    D) rough   E) hard

23. Three masked men _____ the city bank early this morning.
    A) robbed   B) attacked   C) stole
    D) took   E) spoilt

24. I can't remember _____ told me Mary had gone to Spain.
    A) which   B) what   C) that
    D) who   E) whose

25. Can you tell the _____ between margarine and butter?
    A) opposite   B) change   C) alteration
    D) difference   E) sameness

26. Could you give me a _____? I've forgotten my matches.
    A) flame   B) light   C) fire
    D) illumination   E) flare

27. The Company gave my father a gold watch when he _____.
    A) replaced   B) reformed   C) retired
    D) retreated   E) rearranged

28. You can't _____ how frightened I was when I first saw an elephant.
    A) suppose   B) assume   C) propose
    D) wonder   E) imagine

29. When my sister was in hospital, she was _____ by a well-known surgeon.
    A) worked on   B) carried on   C) operated on
    D) turned on   E) passed on

30. If you ask Martin, he will explain _____ of cricket to you.
    A) the orders   B) the arrangements   C) the regulations
    D) the preparations   E) the rules

31. We arrived late because there was a traffic _____.
    A) stop   B) jam   C) holding
    D) suspension   E) confusion

32. I had to wait _____ for an answer to my letter.
    A) a long day   B) a period   C) an interval
    D) a stage   E) a long while

33. Call for me at any time that _____ you.
    A) fits   B) likes   C) suits
    D) does   E) meets

34. I am very _____ in architecture.
    A) interested   B) interesting   C) concerned
    D) informed   E) intelligent

35. The Meeting has been _____ till next Thursday.
    A) put by   B) put off   C) put over
    D) put in   E) put away

36. A circle is a different _____ from a square.
    A) shape   B) shade   C) sign
    D) style   E) number

37. Could you _____ me £5? I'll pay you back tomorrow.
    A) pay   B) borrow   C) lend
    D) provide   E) donate

38. You can't smoke here. It's _____.
    A) prevented   B) allowed   C) stopped
    D) prohibited   E) ceased

39. I don't believe you, you must be _____ my leg.
    A) grasping   B) holding   C) handling
    D) pulling   E) stretching

40. It's very cold, the temperature is several _____ below zero.
    A) ounces   B) inches   C) numbers
    D) degrees   E) figures

TEST 9

1. _____ you hurry up, you'll miss the bus.
   A) Because B) If C) Also
   D) Except E) Unless

2. The man jumped out of the window and committed _____.
   A) murder B) death C) sin
   D) suicide E) homicide

3. I was walking along the street when I accidentally _____ my friend.
   A) bumped into B) moved into C) came into
   D) fell into E) saw into

4. The doctor took his temperature and felt his _____.
   A) vein B) nerve C) blood
   D) pulse E) muscle

5. It's my _____ that it's going to rain.
   A) option B) opinion C) intention
   D) decision E) thought

6. This book is too _____, I don't understand it.
   A) secret B) opaque C) dark
   D) obscure E) blank

7. She was very inquisitive and she didn't _____ to hide her curiosity.
   A) effect B) affect C) attempt
   D) discover E) find

8. She wanted to buy a modern dress, she didn't want an old-_____ one.
   A) styled B) formed C) looked
   D) fashioned E) shaped

9. What _____ is your car?
   A) manufacture B) construction C) make
   D) mark E) assembly

10. He was a very _____ driver and had a lot of accidents.
    A) careful B) careless C) correct
    D) cautious E) conscientious

11. The _____ gave the new film a very good review.
    A) critics B) reporters C) announcers
    D) interviewers E) translators

12. Grandmother lets the children do anything they like, so they are completely _____.
    A) spoilt B) damaged C) hurt
    D) injured E) destroyed

13. The Manager asked me to _____ the contract for my new job.
    A) write B) describe C) sign
    D) disagree E) design

14. _____ for the post of Senior Clerk must be received by March 10th.
    A) Proposals B) Descriptions C) Possibilities
    D) Applications E) Offerings

15. Mr. Hobson has had to _____ his job because of ill-health.
    A) give in B) give up C) give away
    D) give out E) give over

16. My English teacher _____ me to try for a place at University.
    A) insisted B) persisted C) proposed
    D) convinced E) encouraged

17. I _____ you £5 that Peter will win the race on Saturday.
    A) gamble B) bet C) offer
    D) give E) risk

18. Mary had to be taken to hospital after her _____.
    A) dilemma B) distraction C) happening
    D) accident E) occurrence

19. I shall never _____ the time when I was lost in London without any money.
    A) remember B) recall C) forget
    D) recollect E) imagine

20. Mary is almost well again now, but she still looks rather _____.
    A) faded B) light C) poor
    D) transparent E) pale

21. I feel so sleepy, I can hardly _____ my eyes open.
    A) make B) keep C) pull
    D) take E) bring

22. After walking four miles in the pouring rain, the children were _____.
    A) moist B) damp C) drowned
    D) humid E) drenched

23. The Grand Hotel _____ five pounds for a single room with bath.
    A) pays B) prices C) charges
    D) expends E) spends

24. The thief _____ my handbag and ran off down the street.
    A) caught B) snatched C) picked
    D) disconnected E) detached

25. I thought the problem of pollution would _____ at the meeting but no one mentioned it.
    A) come in B) come over C) come to
    D) come up E) come round

26. Jane's new blue dress _____ her coat perfectly.
    A) likes B) matches C) colors
    D) resembles E) fits

27. When I came in, John and Mary _____ about the best way to learn English.
    A) were saying B) were teaching C) were speaking
    D) were telling E) were talking

28. Let's go into the garden and _____ some roses to take to your mother.
    A) dig B) pick C) pull
    D) break E) detach

29. Would you go upstairs and _____ my handbag, please.
    A) take B) bring C) carry
    D) fetch E) obtain

30. The houses with even numbers are on the left side of the street and those with _____ numbers are on the right.
    A) odd B) unequal C) irregular
    D) level E) divided

31. Every morning I do the crossword _____ in the newspaper.
    A) problem B) puzzle C) question
    D) test E) theme

32. There is an index _____ of this book.
    A) in the end B) on the end C) from the end
    D) at the end E) with the end

33. It was so cold that the water in the lake _____.
    A) chilled B) iced C) froze
    D) hardened E) boiled

34. John _____ his examination but his brother failed.
    A) succeeded B) made C) resulted
    D) passed E) qualified

35. The Government will have _____ this proposal very carefully.
    A) to go for B) to go after C) to go into
    D) to go round E) to go under

36. The Post Office is only a few yards _____.
    A) in the road B) on the road C) above the road
    D) under the road E) up the road

37. Will you help me _____ this parcel, please?
    A) tie up B) lie down C) tie in
    D) tie for E) tie with

38. If you didn't keep scratching that spot on your face, it would soon _____.
    A) remedy B) cure C) restore
    D) heal E) mend

39. Mary has given me a _____ for chocolate cake.
    A) prescription B) description C) diet
    D) list E) recipe

40. Mrs. Simpson _____ £1000 to the Dogs' Home when she died.
    A) remained B) left C) presented
    D) offered E) permitted

TEST 10

1. My brother _____ his dog not to chase sheep.
   A) has learned B) has trained C) has educated
   D) has instructed E) has informed

2. Is there any _____ of your coming to London again in the Spring?
   A) opportunity B) occasion C) facility
   D) chance E) ability

3. He visited an _____ castle in an old part of the city.
   A) antique B) ancient C) aged
   D) elderly E) olden

4. Peter is going _____ for the Job as Manager of the Sales Department.
   A) to propose B) to present C) to pretend
   D) to submit E) to apply

5. I don't think I know him, although his face seems _____.
   A) friendly B) known C) knowing
   D) familiar E) usual

6. Some people had to escape in boats when the river _____ its banks.
   A) overthrew B) overflowed C) overcame
   D) overpowered E) overhung

7. Is there a telephone _____ anywhere near here, please?
   A) place B) shop C) box
   D) compartment E) room

8. For her wedding the _____ was dressed in white.
   A) bridesmaid B) bride C) bridegroom
   D) best man E) wife

9. Mr. Black _____ to arrive on the 2:30 train.
   A) is anticipated B) is hoped C) is wanted
   D) is expected E) is proposed

10. I always _____ asleep as soon as I get into bed.
    A) fall B) go C) get
    D) turn E) make

11. You will have _____ those potatoes before you cook them.
    A) to open B) to peel C) to shell
    D) to skin E) to pare

12. I don't like these oranges, they have too many _____.
    A) stones B) nuts C) seeds
    D) pips E) buds

13. I tried to telephone him last night but his number _____.
    A) was occupied B) was employed C) was engaged
    D) was taken E) was used

14. Frank got very _____ marks in his history examination.
    A) reduced B) unimportant C) secondary
    D) imperfect E) low

15. You will have to _____, Aunt Mary is rather deaf.
    A) speak up B) call up C) ring up
    D) stand up E) sit up

16. Three people _____ in this lake last June.
    A) were sunk B) were flooded C) were drowned
    D) were downed E) were drained

17. You've been working all day. It's _____ you went home.
    A) good time B) bad time C) long time
    D) short time E) high time

18. The children walked to the _____ of the cliff and looked down at the sea below.
    A) rim B) edge C) limit
    D) brim E) border

19. The water in this stream has dried up because of the _____ of rain this summer.
    A) smallness B) littleness C) loss
    D) lack E) shortness

20. The sun rises in the East and _____ in the West.
    A) disappears B) vanishes C) sets
    D) goes E) appears

21. There were twenty-five _____ waiting in the doctor's surgery.
    A) customers B) visitors C) patients
    D) waiters E) clients

22. Mr. Brown has a very _____ job as Sales Manager.
    A) responsible B) controlled C) ordered
    D) dutiful E) careful

23. There is a _____ of sugar in Europe at the moment.
    A) want B) need C) requirement
    D) omission E) shortage

24. Beethoven is my _____ composer.
    A) best B) nicest C) selected
    D) favorite E) first

25. I am going to watch the tennis _____ on television this afternoon.
    A) contest B) game C) match
    D) sport E) trial

26. The doctor told him to keep the tablets in his mouth and _____ them slowly.
    A) swallow B) suck C) bite
    D) drink E) eat

27. I can't open the drawer in my desk, it's _____.
    A) fixed B) bolted C) set
    D) stuck E) unmoved

28. Old Mr. Pottinger _____ his pension every Friday.
    A) pays B) earns C) draws
    D) acquires E) obtains

29. Mr. Higgins is quite sure he saw a flying _____ when he was walking home from the pub.
    A) plate B) saucer C) dish
    D) cup E) tray

30. Please tell Anne that my private affairs are nothing to _____ her.
    A) do with B) do for C) do over
    D) do down E) do in

31. Mr. Heppel was flown to London on _____.
    A) affairs B) matters C) business
    D) concerns E) interests

32. Peter has entered a newspaper _____ for the best-dressed man in London.
    A) exhibition B) contest C) show
    D) test E) competition

33. Captain Saunders was accused of _____ at cards.
    A) deceiving B) cheating C) tricking
    D) trapping E) catching

34. Sam never told his wife how much he _____ as a window cleaner.
    A) paid B) obtained C) deserved
    D) earned E) profited

35. In spite of the storm, the Captain _____ the ship safely into port.
    A) pushed B) directed C) drove
    D) steered E) managed

36. The teacher _____ out the words she had written on the blackboard.
    A) cleaned B) dusted C) rubbed
    D) washed E) scraped

37. Would you mind _____ your radio a little, please?
    A) turning in B) turning down C) turning out
    D) turning over E) turning to

38. I don't think you can lift that case _____ I help you.
    A) since B) without C) not
    D) unless E) with

39. We are _____ into our new house on Saturday.
    A) moving B) proceeding C) entering
    D) arriving E) transporting

40. Susan was alone in the house when the fire _____.
    A) broke off B) broke out C) broke in
    D) broke up E) broke away

TEST 11

1. The spade is a gardening _____.
   A) instrument   B) machine   C) tool
   D) weapon   E) piece

2. The thieves buried the _____ under an oak-tree.
   A) show   B) store   C) harvest
   D) treasure   E) stock

3. James is very _____ about the cost of his dental treatment.
   A) sorry   B) pained   C) worried
   D) ashamed   E) sorrowful

4. The children had great _____ when they went to the fair.
   A) excitement   B) enjoyment   C) interest
   D) fun   E) joy

5. What _____ of toothpaste do you buy?
   A) class   B) make   C) order
   D) style   E) mark

6. My father began to lose hair when he was thirty and now he is quite _____.
   A) hairless   B) beardless   C) smooth
   D) shiny   E) bald

7. It is not far to the church if you take the short _____ by Friars Lane.
   A) turning   B) corner   C) cut
   D) pass   E) slit

8. His car battery has _____; he'll have to get it recharged.
   A) run off   B) run out   C) run away
   D) run down   E) run in

9. Mary looked as pretty as a _____ in her new dress.
   A) painting   B) picture   C) postcard
   D) flower   E) engraving

10. It will do you _____ to have a holiday.
    A) well   B) better   C) good
    D) fine   E) great

11. My mother says she doesn't like _____ buttons on my shirts.
    A) attaching   B) sewing   C) connecting
    D) fixing   E) joining

12. People of all _____ come to Hutton's Holiday Camp.
    A) years   B) limes   C) dates
    D) ages   E) days

13. Have a _____ of coffee; it will make you feel better.
    A) swallow   B) sip   C) touch
    D) chew   E) bite

14. She is very intelligent. I _____ her to pass the examination easily.
    A) hope   B) expect   C) wish
    D) desire   E) need

15. They wanted to plan their holidays so they collected some _____ from the travel agency.
    A) books   B) volumes   C) sheets
    D) papers   E) brochures

16. We hope to hear from you at your _____.
    A) opportunity   B) convenience   C) expedience
    D) liberty   E) possibility

17. The weather _____ said it would rain again tomorrow.
    A) expectancy   B) prophecy   C) prediction
    D) forecast   E) horoscope

18. I'm very thirsty. I would _____ a cup of tea.
    A) desire   B) fancy   C) wish
    D) long   E) like

19. She couldn't make up her _____ whether to buy the green skirt or the blue one.
    A) brain   B) heart   C) mind
    D) soul   E) head

20. Oh dear, I have a _____ tire. I must put some air in it.
    A) shallow   B) flat   C) low
    D) bent   E) level

21. A good hen _____ six or seven eggs a day.
    A) lies   B) lays   C) puts
    D) places   E) reproduces

22. The rapid rise in the cost of _____ is worrying many people.
    A) existing   B) living   C) surviving
    D) breathing   E) respiring

23. You must look in the _____ section of the newspaper to find out what films are showing.
    A) variety   B) diversion   C) recreation
    D) hospitality   E) entertainment

24. He had a very bad cold and couldn't stop _____.
    A) snoring   B) sneezing   C) sighing
    D) yawning   E) spitting

25. Mr. Smith walked along the corridor and came face to _____ with his boss.
    A) eye   B) figure   C) face
    D) head   E) front

26. She _____ going to the dentist although her teeth needed attention.
    A) put in   B) put out   C) put through
    D) put off   E) put away

27. It's very easy to _____ your temper when someone annoys you.
    A) mislay   B) lose   C) miss
    D) forget   E) damage

28. If the World Population _____ continues, it will be impossible to feed everybody.
    A) outbreak   B) bang   C) blast
    D) explosion   E) contraction

29. The brave man was greatly honored when the general said "You _____ a medal."
    A) earn   B) expect   C) deserve
    D) reserve   E) justify

30. I wish to see the manager to _____ about the terrible food in this restaurant.
    A) inquire   B) complain   C) criticize
    D) revolt   E) disapprove

31. She couldn't quite remember his name although it was on the _____ of her tongue.
    A) tip   B) top   C) back
    D) front   E) end

32. The soldier took careful aim, then _____ several shots.
    A) exploded   B) broke   C) fired
    D) banged   E) bombed

33. It's very hot in this room; that fire _____ a good heat.
    A) gives away   B) gives in   C) gives out
    D) gives up   E) gives round

34. A woman who has never married is called a _____.
    A) widow   B) widower   C) divorcee
    D) housewife   E) spinster

35. The criminal didn't want to be recognized so he _____ himself.
    A) camouflaged   B) covered   C) concealed
    D) disguised   E) dressed

36. It's possible to tell the time in the dark if your watch has a _____ dial.
    A) light   B) bright   C) radiant
    D) luminous   E) shining

37. She wasn't able to buy any of the things she wanted so she returned home _____.
    A) full-handed   B) empty-handed   C) empty-headed
    D) left-handed   E) right-handed

38. He never stops smoking; one cigarette after another. I'm afraid he's become a _____ smoker.
    A) line   B) rope   C) chain
    D) fiber   E) cord

39. When it is raining and the sun is shining at the same time, a _____ can often be seen in the sky.
    A) waterfall   B) rainbow   C) arc
    D) crescent   E) curve

40. The man was very _____ as he had injured his leg badly when he was a boy.
    A) blind   B) deaf   C) dumb
    D) lame   E) limp

TEST 12

1. They managed to _____ all their unwanted things at the jumble sale.
   A) get rid of B) get even with C) get away with
   D) get over to E) set out of

2. There was a terrible storm at sea last night and one of the sailors _____.
   A) floated B) drowned C) dived
   D) sank E) swam

3. Let's continue the meeting by discussing the next _____ on the agenda.
   A) item B) factor C) passage
   D) piece E) bit

4. I'm paying for my car by monthly _____ as I didn't have enough money to pay cash.
   A) deposits B) receipts C) amounts
   D) percentages E) installments

5. Schubert didn't finish one of his symphonies so it will always be _____.
   A) defective B) undeveloped C) incomplete
   D) unready E) deficient

6. Suddenly I understood perfectly and everything _____ place.
   A) fell down B) fell out C) fell in
   D) fell into E) fell for

7. The Director of the Company _____ some figures from the report in front of him.
   A) spoke B) said C) told
   D) quoted E) referred

8. He was one of the _____ people I've ever known; he never stopped eating.
   A) greediest B) laziest C) proudest
   D) angriest E) shyest

9. The men _____ the millionaire's small daughter and demanded a large sum of money for her return.
   A) eloped B) stole C) removed
   D) kidnapped E) hi-jacked

10. You must be careful what you say to Susan; her feelings are easily _____.
    A) damaged B) injured C) broken
    D) hurt E) cracked

11. You keep _____ the same subject, and I've asked you not to mention it again.
    A) bringing forward B) bringing up C) bringing to
    D) bringing about E) bringing together

12. That shop down the road always _____ its goods well in the window.
    A) shows B) reveals C) uncovers
    D) exposes E) displays

13. Please wipe your feet on the door _____ before you come in.
    A) mat B) rug C) carpet
    D) tile E) blanket

14. Although most of the children in the class were rather dull, there were one or two _____ ones.
    A) light B) bright C) skilful
    D) wise E) thoughtful

15. The _____ with Charles is, he doesn't know his own mind.
    A) upset B) trouble C) puzzle
    D) complication E) inconvenience

16. I hate January when all the _____ start coming in. I never seem to have enough money to pay them all.
    A) receipts B) accounts C) estimates
    D) bills E) lists

17. The workers were _____ in their demand for better conditions.
    A) united B) combined C) joined
    D) stuck E) attached

18. The judge _____ the criminal to twenty years in prison.
    A) condemned B) punished C) disciplined
    D) inflicted E) sentenced

19. I want to know the answers to these questions, so I shall have to look at the _____ at the back of the book.
    A) index B) key C) register
    D) record E) table

20. I wouldn't like to spend a night alone in that house. It is said to be _____ by a headless ghost.
    A) obsessed B) tormented C) haunted
    D) infested E) upset

21. The girl in the shop was _____ how to use a new kind of electric cooker.
    A) proving B) establishing C) exposing
    D) demonstrating E) teaching

22. That poor woman's husband died a few weeks after they were married. It was a real _____.
    A) sorrow B) tragedy C) wrong
    D) evil E) sadness

23. He didn't seem to know what was happening at all, he looked completely _____.
    A) doubtful B) bewildered C) undecided
    D) defeated E) doomed

24. The economy of this country is very unstable at the moment. It's balanced on a _____ edge.
    A) knife B) sword C) axe
    D) saber E) dagger

25. The little boy was _____ for breaking the window.
    A) condemned B) sentenced C) penalized
    D) persecuted E) punished

26. There has been a lot of _____ about the housing shortage in big cities.
    A) circulation B) advertising C) publicity
    D) communication E) instruction

27. I _____ my car badly when I hit a tree.
    A) dented B) hollowed C) depressed
    D) impressed E) pitted

28. He is _____ to both those girls over there. One is his sister and the other is his cousin.
    A) allied B) affiliated C) related
    D) identified E) classified

29. When he was left on a desert island, he was able to _____ for a year on fruit and water.
    A) remain B) continue C) stay
    D) persist E) survive

30. If I were you I'd put that meat in the refrigerator or it will _____ in this hot weather.
    A) go off B) go on C) go over
    D) go against E) go by

31. To play golf well you must take lessons from a good _____.
    A) conductor B) guide C) coach
    D) trainer E) leader

32. The Browns had to use all their _____ to buy their new house.
    A) keepsakes B) savings C) reserves
    D) leavings E) remains

33. When I was staying in Germany last year, I _____ quite a lot of German.
    A) picked out B) picked on C) picked up
    D) picked over E) picked upon

34. What are you cooking in that saucepan? It _____ good.
    A) makes B) feels C) sniffs
    D) smells E) flavors

35. I know Mary has two brothers, but I don't know which is the _____.
    A) elder B) more aged C) more ancient
    D) lower E) higher

36. I hope the Government will _____ the rate of income tax.
    A) increase B) decrease C) reduce
    D) deduct E) degrade

37. Jane's school report last term was very _____.
    A) satisfying B) satisfactory C) fulfilling
    D) full E) fortunate

38. Mary has gone to the baker's to buy a _____ of bread.
    A) piece B) packet C) bit
    D) pound E) loaf

39. When I was turning out my cupboard I _____ this photograph of uncle Harry.
    A) came over B) came round C) came across
    D) came to E) came into

40. Lucy says she bought her new trouser suit in _____.
    A) a disposal B) a sale C) a reduction
    D) an offering E) a production

TEST 13

1. When he was questioned by the police, the thief didn't _____ the truth.
   A) say   B) reply   C) answer   D) tell   E) respond

2. When their mother died, the children were _____ by their Aunt Mary.
   A) brought in   B) brought round   C) brought to   D) brought forward   E) brought up

3. Don't touch that wire or you may get an electric _____.
   A) shock   B) current   C) attack   D) feeling   E) surprise

4. Mr. Brown thinks he knows _____ about football, but he doesn't.
   A) anything   B) everybody   C) everything   D) somebody   E) nobody

5. The High Street is so narrow that the Council have decided to _____ it.
   A) increase   B) extend   C) widen   D) lengthen   E) shorten

6. Your brother is very tall. What is his exact _____?
   A) size   B) length   C) breadth   D) measure   E) height

7. If Maria comes to England, it will be a good _____ for her to improve her English.
   A) possibility   B) opportunity   C) advantage   D) probability   E) experience

8. Please _____ your hand if you want to ask the teacher a question.
   A) rise   B) pull   C) push   D) lift   E) raise

9. _____ 100 if you want to speak to the telephone operator.
   A) Ask   B) Hear   C) Dial   D) Describe   E) Turn

10. Our school _____ for the summer holidays on 10th July.
    A) breaks up   B) breaks down   C) breaks in   D) breaks off   E) breaks through

11. If you've got a _____ of cards, I'll show you some tricks.
    A) packet   B) collection   C) pack   D) set   E) parcel

12. This church was _____ by the famous architect Archibald Sparrow.
    A) outlined   B) designed   C) produced   D) composed   E) made

13. It's Grandmother's birthday tomorrow, so don't forget to wish her many happy _____.
    A) returns   B) days   C) anniversaries   D) years   E) congratulations

14. The _____ from the airport was very tiring as we had to drive through the fog.
    A) travel   B) voyage   C) flight   D) journey   E) crossing

15. If I bought a ticket in the lottery, I might _____ £1000.
    A) bet   B) buy   C) sell   D) win   E) let

16. John hopes to _____ his examination in September.
    A) make   B) take   C) do   D) offer   E) present

17. When you come to London, I can _____ for the night.
    A) put you down   B) put you off   C) put you up   D) put you right   E) put you away

18. Your new flat _____ me very much of the one we had in Birmingham.
    A) remembers   B) recalls   C) recollects   D) receives   E) reminds

19. The deer is one of the shyest _____ animals in existence.
    A) savage   B) untamed   C) wild   D) strange   E) free

20. Do open the window; this room seems very _____.
    A) moldy   B) stuffy   C) smoked   D) rancid   E) breathless

21. There is a _____ on the suitcase, but it has no name on it.
    A) paper   B) ticket   C) sign   D) stamp   E) label

22. The air hostess told the passengers to _____ their seat belts.
    A) tie   B) attach   C) fasten   D) fix   E) set

23. My sister works at a home for the deaf and _____.
    A) mute   B) dumb   C) silent   D) speechless   E) voiceless

24. The price of this TV set is not listed in the _____.
    A) catalogue   B) guidebook   C) directory   D) record   E) schedule

25. The police were able to trace the criminal because he left his _____ on the door handle.
    A) fingerprints   B) finger-nails   C) fingertips   D) ringer ends   E) finger-marks

26. Ann refused to take _____ in the preparations for the school concert.
    A) place   B) part   C) notice   D) leave   E) offence

27. Any candidate caught _____ in the examination will be disqualified.
    A) deceiving   B) deluding   C) conjuring   D) swindling   E) cheating

28. The farmer put a _____ in his field to frighten the birds away from his crops.
    A) scarecrow   B) monster   C) demon   D) goblin   E) corpse

29. He has been making money _____ since he started his new business.
    A) head over heels   B) hand over fist   C) head to foot   D) ear to ear   E) top to toe

30. It was so cold my fingers were quite _____.
    A) senseless   B) numb   C) insensible   D) unconscious   E) paralyzed

31. You should take more exercise if you want to keep _____.
    A) fit   B) fat   C) fine   D) fresh   E) flat

32. The twins are so alike that I can never _____ the difference between them.
    A) tell   B) say   C) decide   D) make   E) find

33. I took the doctor's prescription to the chemist's to be ____.
    A) made out   B) made up   C) made over   D) made into   E) made for

34. My boss has _____ playing golf three afternoons a week.
    A) taken over   B) taken to   C) taken for   D) taken out   E) taken in

35. The Prime Minister made an excellent _____ in the House yesterday.
    A) discourse   B) discussion   C) lecture   D) speech   E) talk

36. I have never been on good _____ with my sister-in-law.
    A) responses   B) exchanges   C) terms   D) feelings   E) affections

37. The _____ on this tombstone is dated 1742.
    A) description   B) inscription   C) recording   D) outline   E) engraving

38. Have you had any _____ of John lately?
    A) enquiries   B) news   C) details   D) particulars   E) facts

39. Did you notice the _____ on Walter's face when he heard Hugo had been made Manager?
    A) appearance   B) description   C) expression   D) disposition   E) exposition

40. Children usually _____ after an illness much more quickly than adults.
    A) pick up   B) pick over   C) pick on   D) pick out   E) pick off

# TEST 14

1. I had to sign for this letter because it came in _____ envelope.
   A) a recommended B) a registered C) an endorsed
   D) a receipted E) a sealed

2. When I bought this clock I was given a six months' _____.
   A) reservation B) guarantee C) undertaking
   D) safeguard E) security

3. A _____ for the company said that the question of safety regulations was being looked into.
   A) speaker B) spokesman C) officer
   D) reporter E) interpreter

4. During the war there was so little food that it had to be _____.
   A) preserved B) regulated C) rationed
   D) retained E) re-distributed

5. Mr Jackson is permanently _____ as the result of a car accident.
   A) dislocated B) incapable C) disabled
   D) powerless E) inactive

6. She _____ all her savings form the bank to pay for her flight to Australia.
   A) drew in B) drew up C) drew along
   D) drew out E) drew off

7. Her shopping bag broke, _____ its contents all over the road.
   A) dispersing B) dispensing C) scattering
   D) overflowing E) distributing

8. When you come to the crossroads, you will see the _____ showing the way to Middleton.
   A) advertisement B) signal C) signpost
   D) announcement E) indicator

9. The crops in this field have all been _____ with insecticide.
   A) sprayed B) washed C) rinsed
   D) cleaned E) disinfected

10. I can't use my hair-drier because I forgot to buy a _____ for it.
    A) tap B) switch C) socket
    D) pin E) plug

11. The baby is very fretful; he must be _____ some teeth.
    A) making B) cutting C) incising
    D) producing E) grinding

12. The attic was thick with _____ as no one had cleared it for years.
    A) rust B) powder C) dust
    D) sediment E) soot

13. The artist studied in Paris for _____ of roughly five years.
    A) a decade B) an age C) a time
    D) a period E) an interval

14. The two young people fell in love at _____.
    A) first impression B) first sight C) short notice
    D) long distance E) first appearance

15. When you get to the airport, your luggage will have to be _____.
    A) reckoned B) balanced C) scaled
    D) estimated E) weighed

16. If you are interested in becoming a _____ of the club, telephone the secretary during office hours.
    A) member B) partner C) sharer
    D) player E) student

17. The first English dictionary was _____ by Dr Johnson.
    A) compiled B) co-ordinated C) collected
    D) composed E) constructed

18. When you go out, will you get me _____ of the Farming Gazette?
    A) an edition B) a copy C) a publication
    D) a paper E) a sheet

19. I didn't _____ I was talking to the Manager, until he told me his name.
    A) identify B) distinguish C) recognize
    D) accept E) realize

20. I just cannot work out the answer to this question; I _____.
    A) give off B) give out C) giveaway
    D) give into E) give up

21. At the election you must mark your paper, fold it and drop it into the _____ box.
    A) voting B) ballot C) nomination
    D) selection E) electoral

22. When you return to your country, don't forget to _____ with me.
    A) keep in hand B) keep time C) keep in touch
    D) keep in step E) keep together

23. The corrupt builder wanted to obtain the contract so he offered a _____ to the civil servant.
    A) bribe B) bait C) stimulus
    D) tip E) bonus

24. The tramp was wearing very shabby clothes and looked very _____.
    A) down at heel B) down to earth C) up to date
    D) up and coming E) out of shape

25. It was very _____ in the cottage with the comfortable armchairs by the fire.
    A) snug B) gratifying C) easy
    D) downy E) refreshing

26. There were some black-faced sheep _____ about the hillside.
    A) thrown B) arranged C) scattered
    D) littered E) crumpled

27. The news _____ that prices were going to rise next week.
    A) got ahead B) got on C) got through
    D) got up E) got out

28. The child _____ his breath in wonder when he saw the Christmas tree.
    A) kept B) blew C) sighed
    D) held E) gasped

29. That man's wife is terrible; he _____ him all the time, nagging from morning till night.
    A) keeps in with B) keeps up with C) keeps on at
    D) keeps away E) keeps back from

30. Don't leave your things all over the room, _____ up the place.
    A) mixing B) cluttering C) filling
    D) huddling E) breaking

31. The philosopher was a great thinker and was often _____ by a brilliant idea.
    A) seized B) grabbed C) grasped
    D) held E) clutched

32. The trader asked a high price, but I managed to _____.
    A) beat him off B) beat him up C) beat him down
    D) beat him back E) beat him in

33. The woman _____ for her husband's life when he was found guilty of murder.
    A) bid B) disputed C) pleaded
    D) debated E) sued

34. Don't _____ me or I won't be able to stop laughing.
    A) pat B) massage C) scratch
    D) tickle E) stroke

35. That pop group are going to make _____ recording next week.
    A) alive B) an alive C) an awake
    D) a living E) a life

36. Mary _____ her engagement the week before the wedding because she realized she didn't love her fiance.
    A) broke up B) broke out C) broke down
    D) broke off E) broke away

37. He _____ £5000 in stocks and shares.
    A) inserted B) installed C) invested
    D) inducted E) indented

38. The new magazine about car maintenance _____ tomorrow.
    A) comes down B) comes off C) comes on
    D) comes out E) comes round

39. That couple are well-suited; they live in perfect _____.
    A) order B) control C) harmony
    D) melody E) duet

40. He is so _____, he is never satisfied with anything.
    A) discontented B) disconcerted C) discomforted
    D) disconnected E) discredited

Test 14

TEST 15

1. Johnny _____ very badly at Mary's birthday party.
   A) conducted   B) behaved   C) showed
   D) operated   E) looked

2. Mr. Jones has _____ painting since he retired.
   A) taken up   B) taken off   C) taken over
   D) taken in   E) taken down

3. How many _____ does Peter learn at school?
   A) topics   B) themes   C) ideas
   D) subjects   E) objects

4. It wasn't my _____ that the plate broke.
   A) blame   B) mistake   C) error
   D) fault   E) slip

5. Ask Joan if she would give me _____ with the washing-up.
   A) a leg   B) a hand   C) a help
   D) an assistance   E) an aid

6. The Browns _____ anyone who hasn't much money as they have.
   A) look up to   B) look away from   C) look down on
   D) look out for   E) look round at

7. Part of that electric plug is _____; you ought to tighten it.
   A) safe   B) loose   C) free
   D) disjoined   E) unattached

8. I'm reading a book about _____ of Shakespeare.
   A) the living   B) the existence   C) the way
   D) the life   E) the road

9. Sally _____ a little money every week for her holiday.
   A) puts in   B) puts off   C) puts by
   D) puts over   E) puts upon

10. My brother has curly hair but mine is quite _____.
    A) even   B) regular   C) uneven
    D) level   E) straight

11. John always gets very annoyed if he can't get his own _____.
    A) wish   B) desire   C) will
    D) object   E) way

12. It's no use shouting at grandmother, she's as deaf as a _____.
    A) post   B) pin   C) pole
    D) door   E) wall

13. If you leave that butter in the sun, it will _____.
    A) thaw   B) dissolve   C) set
    D) harden   E) melt

14. When I peel onions, I can't stop my eyes _____.
    A) spilling   B) watering   C) leaking
    D) dripping   E) dropping

15. I'm going home tomorrow so I mustn't forget to buy some _____.
    A) memories   B) reminders   C) recollections
    D) souvenirs   E) remembrances

16. I caught the train by the skin of my _____.
    A) mouth   B) teeth   C) lips
    D) nose   E) cheeks

17. Peter doesn't drink alcohol, he only drinks _____ drinks.
    A) squashed   B) crushed   C) smooth
    D) dry   E) soft

18. Whose _____ was it to go for this long, uninteresting walk?
    A) thought   B) desire   C) dream
    D) purpose   E) idea

19. When he was running across the field, he _____ a log.
    A) fell down   B) fell over   C) fell off
    D) fell into   E) fell upon

20. John put the suitcases in the _____ of the car.
    A) shoe   B) toe   C) boot
    D) slipper   E) foot

21. The doctor gave me _____ for some medicine.
    A) an order   B) a letter   C) an instruction
    D) a recipe   E) a prescription

22. John always _____ the 8:30 train to work.
    A) traps   B) captures   C) catches
    D) holds   E) attaches

23. We couldn't eat the meat because it had _____.
    A) gone on   B) gone out   C) gone off
    D) gone in   E) gone over

24. Susan couldn't remember what she had to buy for the weekend because she had lost her shopping _____.
    A) record   B) list   C) register
    D) form   E) code

25. Grandmother is always _____ her glasses.
    A) misusing   B) misplacing   C) mistaking
    D) mislaying   E) mishandling

26. I hate to hear a clock _____ when I'm trying to go to sleep.
    A) clicking   B) sounding   C) humming
    D) ticking   E) ringing

27. _____ for the job should write to the Personnel Manager.
    A) attendants   B) entrants   C) applicants
    D) contenders   E) competitors

28. I don't think this medicine _____ with me.
    A) goes   B) suits   C) agrees
    D) fits   E) accords

29. All the workers in the firm get a Christmas _____ of £50.
    A) repayment   B) prize   C) reward
    D) bonus   E) refund

30. The notice on the gate said "_____ the dog."
    A) take care of   B) be careful of   C) beware of
    D) take notice of   E) be afraid of

31. You ought to be _____ yourself for being so rude to old Mrs. Green.
    A) sorry for   B) unhappy about   C) ashamed of
    D) repenting for   E) unfriendly to

32. Just as the violinist began to play, one of the _____ on his violin broke.
    A) cords   B) tapes   C) strings
    D) wires   E) chords

33. The little girl woke up screaming because she had had a _____.
    A) daydream   B) nightmare   C) fantasy
    D) vision   E) reverie

34. Have you any _____ where you left your car keys?
    A) knowledge   B) information   C) notion
    D) idea   E) thought

35. The magistrate _____ the parents for not exercising proper control over the delinquent boy.
    A) blamed   B) faulted   C) judged
    D) accused   E) exposed

36. I'd like to _____ the holiday arrangements once more before we leave tomorrow.
    A) go for   B) go over   C) go round
    D) go about   E) go by

37. Mr. Brown always _____ his letters to his secretary as soon as he has opened his post.
    A) answers   B) writes   C) copies
    D) dictates   E) replies

38. He made a note of the appointment in his _____.
    A) journal   B) diary   C) ledger
    D) register   E) directory

39. How _____ is your house from the station?
    A) long   B) distant   C) near
    D) far   E) close

40. I have got to get up early tomorrow so I must remember to _____ my alarm clock.
    A) time   B) set   C) fix
    D) turn   E) point

TEST 16

1. The inspector was a very _____ man and rechecked the evidence several times.
   A) complete   B) wholesome   C) thoughtful
   D) thorough   E) attentive

2. My friend exercises regularly and is in much better _____ than I am.
   A) figure   B) size   C) shape
   D) frame   E) outline

3. Mr. Brown kept the _____ round his garden neatly clipped.
   A) hedge   B) fence   C) railings
   D) plants   E) flowers

4. Tomorrow is a special _____ night for the guitarist who has injured his hand and can't play again.
   A) benefit   B) welfare   C) merit
   D) charity   E) goodwill

5. Mr. Jones was always interfering and poking his nose into everyone's _____.
   A) situation   B) job   C) work
   D) business   E) life

6. I can't _____ the sound of a knife scraping on a plate.
   A) bear   B) support   C) sustain
   D) suffer   E) forbear

7. I'm sure they couldn't have arranged it; they must have met _____.
   A) at random   B) by chance   C) with luck
   D) by fate   E) by design

8. If you want to know how to wash that sweater, look at the _____ inside the collar.
   A) badge   B) ticket   C) notice
   D) sign   E) tab

9. Oh dear. I don't seem to have my bag, I must have _____ it in the Post Office.
   A) missed   B) overlooked   C) forgotten
   D) left   E) misplaced

10. He had injured his arm badly and had to keep it in a _____ for several weeks.
    A) cradle   B) swing   C) sling
    D) litter   E) stretcher

11. Peter's car _____ in the country so he had to walk to the nearest village for help.
    A) broke up   B) broke down   C) broke away
    D) broke off   E) broke open

12. She tied a scarf round her head to _____ her hair from the rain.
    A) cover   B) hide   C) keep
    D) shelter   E) protect

13. The telephone operator said she would put the caller _____ when the line was free.
    A) through   B) up   C) in
    D) forward   E) over

14. When I've passed my driving test I'll be able to get a permanent driving _____.
    A) certificate   B) license   C) permit
    D) voucher   E) warrant

15. The train doesn't leave for an hour yet. What shall we do to _____?
    A) mark time   B) waste time   C) spend time
    D) keep time   E) kill time

16. Most people think they pay too much _____ tax to the Government.
    A) income   B) salary   C) wages
    D) earnings   E) money

17. The post _____ hadn't arrived by ten o'clock.
    A) yet   B) already   C) still
    D) nevertheless   E) even

18. I _____ that you ought to apologize.
    A) desire   B) wish   C) want
    D) hope   E) think

19. I've booked two seats in the front _____ for tomorrow's concert.
    A) line   B) row   C) rank
    D) file   E) strip

20. He doubted if he would pass the examination as it was _____ whether he would even finish the paper.
    A) wait and see   B) hit or miss   C) touch and go
    D) this or that   E) open to error

21. My aunt used to pretend that she could tell fortunes from tea _____.
    A) seeds   B) buds   C) leaves
    D) leavings   E) grounds

22. Mr. Sims has walked with a _____ ever since his car accident six years ago.
    A) limp   B) jog   C) trot
    D) hop   E) jump

23. Oh, dear, my pen has _____; can you lend me yours?
    A) run off   B) run down   C) run out
    D) run in   E) run up

24. Would it be possible to have these photographs _____?
    A) expanded   B) enlarged   C) extended
    D) inflated   E) stretched

25. Don't forget to _____ your luggage clearly in case it gets mislaid in transit.
    A) print   B) name   C) sign
    D) identify   E) label

26. The _____ of living has risen by 10% in the last three months.
    A) price   B) expense   C) cost
    D) rate   E) expenditure

27. Marie often buys clothes at that _____ stall in the market.
    A) second-class   B) second-best   C) second-hand
    D) second string   E) second chance

28. Don't eat those berries in case they are _____.
    A) poisonous   B) venomous   C) infectious
    D) emetic   E) contagious

29. I've got such a _____ throat I'm sure I must be going to have a cold.
    A) hurt   B) sensitive   C) irritable
    D) sour   E) sore

30. You can take a short _____ through the woods to the station.
    A) lane   B) road   C) highway
    D) cut   E) alley

31. I'm afraid it will be a long time before we get to the _____ of this unpleasant affair.
    A) base   B) bottom   C) foundation
    D) foot   E) basis

32. John has just passed his driving test, so now he's on the _____ for a cheap car.
    A) outlook   B) pursuit   C) lookout
    D) discovery   E) track

33. At the beginning of the war every man under thirty was _____ to serve in the armed forces.
    A) called in   B) called up   C) called for
    D) called out   E) called over

34. The sight of so much ice cream made the children's mouths _____.
    A) drip   B) ooze   C) wet
    D) moisten   E) water

35. I'm not _____ but I never walk under a ladder if I can help it.
    A) credulous   B) simple   C) supernatural
    D) superstitious   E) ignorant

36. According to Charles Darwin, man is _____ from the apes.
    A) originated   B) entailed   C) revolved
    D) descended   E) elevated

37. The lighted candles on the altar _____ in the draught from the open window.
    A) fluttered   B) wavered   C) trembled
    D) flickered   E) shivered

38. I am going to celebrate my wedding _____ on the 10th December.
    A) birthday   B) name day   C) anniversary
    D) year   E) occasion

39. When the volcano _____, several villages had to be evacuated.
    A) exploded   B) erupted   C) emitted
    D) overflowed   E) overran

40. All the crops on that farm have been _____ with insecticide.
    A) covered   B) spread   C) dispersed
    D) sprayed   E) overlaid

Test 16

TEST 17

1. When I turned on the switch, the lights _____.
   A) cracked   B) fired   C) expired
   D) fused   E) flared

2. Be careful with that knife because it has a very sharp _____.
   A) side   B) steel   C) rim
   D) cut   E) blade

3. They are _____ all those old houses to make room for a new Town Hall.
   A) putting down   B) doing down   C) taking down
   D) pulling down   E) running down

4. _____ the bottle well before you pour out the medicine.
   A) agitate   B) shake   C) stir
   D) spin   E) tumble

5. I'm afraid I took your umbrella by _____.
   A) fault   B) error   C) misdeed
   D) mistake   E) misjudgment

6. The prisoners had spent almost a year digging a _____ before the guards discovered it.
   A) tube   B) subway   C) tunnel
   D) pipe   E) pass

7. I wish you'd let me speak for myself and not _____ the words out of my mouth.
   A) take   B) remove   C) pull
   D) snatch   E) grab

8. To get your illustrated guide to Great Britain just fill in the _____ and send it with 50p to the Tourist Board.
   A) cheque   B) note   C) coupon
   D) bill   E) warrant

9. There's no _____ in going to the cinema now as the film's already started.
   A) reason   B) cause   C) motive
   D) point   E) ground

10. That's absolute nonsense; you're talking out of the _____.
    A) tip of your tongue   B) back of your head
    C) skin of your teeth   D) depth of your soul
    E) side of your mouth

11. Without exercise many people's bodies become _____.
    A) soggy   B) flabby   C) spongy
    D) doughy   E) squashy

12. "_____ man kills the thing he loves" is a well-known saying.
    A) all   B) none   C) each
    D) any   E) some

13. He fell guilty about breaking off the engagement and often had a _____ of conscience.
    A) spasm   B) twinge   C) sting
    D) pain   E) pinch

14. The members of the team were very _____ and changed their plans at short notice.
    A) flexible   B) supple   C) loose
    D) plastic   E) lenient

15. I visited many historic houses and castles _____ my summer holiday.
    A) within   B) inside   C) during
    D) including   E) wherein

16. She likes classical music and is particularly _____ on Mozart.
    A) overwhelmed   B) hearty   C) eager
    D) keen   E) enthusiastic

17. There's _____ telling what he will do if he's annoyed.
    A) none   B) nobody   C) nothing
    D) no   E) not

18. Tom's very spoilt and always demanding attention; I expect it's because he's _____ child.
    A) an only   B) one   C) a lone
    D) a single   E) an alone

19. Actors have to _____ a play before they give a public performance.
    A) practice   B) repeat   C) rehearse
    D) prepare   E) reproduce

20. There was no _____ of anyone having entered the room.
    A) sight   B) look   C) sign
    D) signal   E) notice

21. If your handbag has been stolen, you must _____ it to the police immediately.
    A) tell   B) report   C) inform
    D) announce   E) record

22. Has John paid you back the £5 you _____ him?
    A) lent   B) borrowed   C) owed
    D) gave   E) charged

23. Who _____ of going for this walk in the rain?
    A) thought   B) decided   C) proposed
    D) insisted   E) wanted

24. When he retired, my father _____ his business to my eldest brother.
    A) made out   B) made away   C) made over
    D) made up   E) made for

25. The _____ at that restaurant is excellent.
    A) attention   B) service   C) serving
    D) care   E) attending

26. I enjoyed that book so much that I read it from _____ to end in one day.
    A) opening   B) beginning   C) start
    D) commencement   E) introduction

27. The kidnappers demanded a _____ of £509.000.
    A) forfeit   B) ransom   C) penalty
    D) fine   E) reward

28. I wish you wouldn't keep _____ my time asking such silly questions.
    A) losing   B) spending   C) wasting
    D) engaging   E) occupying

29. I only received the application _____ for the job yesterday.
    A) paper   B) form   C) order
    D) notice   E) document

30. When he came back from holiday his skin was beautifully _____.
    A) tanned   B) sunburnt   C) toasted
    D) browned   E) burnt

31. Did you have a good _____ when you went to Scotland?
    A) experience   B) stay   C) enjoyment
    D) time   E) amusement

32. Five hundred people were _____ in the earthquake.
    A) sunk   B) buried   C) flooded
    D) overrun   E) overturned

33. When I paid for my groceries in the supermarket, the cashier gave me the wrong _____.
    A) rebate   B) sum   C) exchange
    D) return   E) change

34. He won't be able to drive his car unless he _____ his license.
    A) remits   B) reforms   C) revises
    D) reports   E) renews

35. Yesterday Stephen studied for five hours _____.
    A) on end   B) at length   C) in full
    D) in time   E) at once

36. The _____ for the course are £50 a term.
    A) charges   B) costs   C) payments
    D) fees   E) subscriptions

37. Do you wear your watch on your right _____ because you are left-handed?
    A) hand   B) elbow   C) wrist
    D) palm   E) ankle

38. He arrived at a most _____ moment; I was just getting into the bath.
    A) importunate   B) inopportune   C) uncomfortable
    D) incongruous   E) unfitting

39. This road is _____ to flood in winter.
    A) leading   B) unprotected   C) conducive
    D) liable   E) susceptible

40. Buying in bulk _____ one to make substantial savings.
    A) enables   B) facilitates   C) means
    D) ensures   E) empowers

Test 17

TEST 18

1. This village is only _____ by river.
   A) attainable B) available C) accessible
   D) obtainable E) achievable

2. The man's face was _____ from his infected tooth.
   A) bulging B) swollen C) dilated
   D) expanded E) distended

3. As my exam is next week, I'll take advantage of the day off to _____ on some reading.
   A) catch up B) clear up C) hurry up
   D) makeup E) pick up

4. Many local authorities realize the need to make _____ for elderly people in their housing programs.
   A) assistance B) conditions C) admittance
   D) provision E) rooms

5. The curator of the Museum was most _____ and let me actually examine the ancient manuscript.
   A) favorable B) gratifying C) obliging
   D) pleasing E) promising

6. For parents, one of the problems _____ by rising prices is the continual demand for more pocket money.
   A) given B) posed C) pressing
   D) provided E) forced

7. After speaking for two hours, the lecturer found he could scarcely talk, as he had become _____.
   A) hoarse B) dumb C) inarticulate
   D) speechless E) tongue-tied

8. There is pressure on the British government to _____ the number of immigrants permitted to settle in the U.K.
   A) confine B) depress C) decrease
   D) restrain E) limit

9. In recent years there has been a _____ increase in the cost of living.
   A) powerful B) ponderous C) wide
   D) significant E) violent

10. The drunken couple did nothing to keep the flat clean and tidy and lived in the utmost _____.
    A) pollution B) decay C) corruption
    D) contamination E) squalor

11. She was extremely lucky when her great-uncle died, she _____ a fortune.
    A) came by B) came about C) came into
    D) came through E) came over

12. The accused man was able to prove his innocence at the trial and was _____.
    A) forgiven B) pardoned C) excused
    D) acquitted E) absolved

13. A good boss always _____ responsibility to his assistants.
    A) relegates B) delegates C) removes
    D) consigns E) refers

14. Although nobody _____ his presence, Mr. Smith knew he had been recognized.
    A) acknowledged B) admitted C) assented
    D) attributed E) required

15. He tries to _____ himself with everyone by paying them compliments.
    A) gratify B) please C) ingratiate
    D) commend E) placate

16. He was _____ from the competition because he had not compiled with the rules.
    A) banished B) forbidden C) outlawed
    D) disqualified E) precluded

17. He thanked me _____, too much I thought for the little I had done.
    A) significantly B) profusely C) prolifically
    D) luxuriantly E) sumptuously

18. The police managed to _____ down the owner of the car.
    A) trace B) track C) catch
    D) search E) pursue

19. The party's reduced vote was _____ of lack of support for its policies.
    A) indicative B) confirming C) positive
    D) revealing E) evident

20. Although most of the rooms are small, the hall is _____.
    A) extending B) extended C) spacious
    D) expansive E) abundant

21. Your latest project has little _____ of success.
    A) prediction B) outlook C) preview
    D) prospect E) forecast

22. My enquiries did not _____ any information of value.
    A) extort B) elicit C) arouse
    D) affect E) induce

23. The professor's wife was in the kitchen preparing a salad and _____ cold meal into neat, thin pieces.
    A) sawing B) slitting C) slicing
    D) sandwiching E) slashing

24. The advantage of the new bridge will be the way it _____ the towns on the opposite banks of the river.
    A) attaches B) connects C) communicates
    D) spans E) merges

25. Charles was not sure which profession to enter, but finally _____ for the Law.
    A) chose B) opted C) selected
    D) accepted E) preferred

26. The police _____ their attention to the events that led up to the accident.
    A) confirmed B) contained C) conserved
    D) confined E) completed

27. The large crowds lingering in the streets were quickly _____ by heavy rain.
    A) removed B) dislocated C) deposed
    D) detached E) dispersed

28. We covered a wide _____ of topics in the interview.
    A) fashion B) extent C) collection
    D) number E) range

29. Looked at from your _____, the position is intolerable.
    A) attitude B) state C) standpoint
    D) level E) opinion

30. Although your offer for the house is £200 below the asking _____, they'll probably accept for the sake of a quick sale.
    A) cost B) value C) price
    D) limit E) amount

31. The garden had been badly neglected and was completely _____ with weeds.
    A) overgrown B) suffocated C) enclosed
    D) coated E) overlaid

32. By the end of the day the flood water which had covered most of the town had _____.
    A) receded B) reversed C) replaced
    D) retired E) returned

33. The police arrested the wrong man mainly because they _____ the names they had been given by the witness.
    A) confused B) perplexed C) puzzled
    D) bewildered E) merged

34. Being already a graduate from another university, he was _____ from the entrance examination.
    A) exempted B) excluded C) prohibited
    D) precluded E) deferred

35. Digging the garden is a very _____ task.
    A) industrious B) manual C) laborious
    D) exerting E) conscientious

36. Hopes of finding the missing climbers are now beginning to _____.
    A) reduce B) fade C) dim
    D) faint E) shrink

37. The Minister accused the farmers of _____ the potato shortage in order to force prices up.
    A) depleting B) expecting C) exploiting
    D) misapplying E) misappropriating

38. The stories about his wealth are quite _____; he is not particularly well off.
    A) unprovoked B) incredulous C) unfounded
    D) irrational E) undeserving

39. I don't really know how to _____ the problem.
    A) tackle B) cope C) set in
    D) raw E) efface

40. He had deceived a great many people but she _____ him at once.
    A) saw into B) saw round C) saw through
    D) looked through E) looked into

TEST 19

1. Since 1945 the rivalry in military strength between the world's great powers has produced a _____ balanced peace.
   A) presently   B) precociously   C) previously
   D) deviously   E) precariously

2. The team's coach insisted on a program of _____ training before the big match.
   A) harsh   B) rigorous   C) positive
   D) severe   E) searching

3. I tried to _____ a hint but you didn't notice.
   A) nod   B) drop   C) suggest
   D) let   E) warn

4. What you say is true, but you could have _____ it more tactfully.
   A) talked   B) phrased   C) observed
   D) informed   E) remarked

5. The police are _____ the suburbs for the missing car.
   A) seeking   B) combing   C) looking
   D) socking   E) investigating

6. The climbers _____ their greatest ambition by reaching the summit of the mountain.
   A) obtained   B) sustained   C) maintained
   D) retained   E) realized

7. He was so _____ in the book that he forgot all about his appointment.
   A) distracted   B) attracted   C) gripped
   D) diverted   E) engrossed

8. It is impossible to _____ these points of view: they are too different.
   A) unite   B) reconcile   C) coincide
   D) correspond   E) compromise

9. I am never free on Thursday evenings as I have a _____ arrangement to play chess with a friend.
   A) long-standing   B) long-lived   C) long-range
   D) long-lasting   E) long-service

10. If you are under 18, you are not _____ to join this club.
    A) available   B) legitimate   C) capable
    D) eligible   E) permissible

11. The Chairman is to give a formal _____ at the Annual General Meeting.
    A) discussion   B) address   C) debate
    D) revision   E) dialogue

12. When I arrived in this country I had to start learning the language from _____.
    A) scratch   B) nothing   C) introduction
    D) ignorance   E) blank

13. I spoke to him, but he was too _____ to hear what I said.
    A) preoccupied   B) concentrated   C) absent-minded
    D) cautious   E) thoughtful

14. National emergencies require that the community _____ those of the individual citizen.
    A) overcome   B) overwhelm   C) overpower
    D) override   E) overthrow

15. Because of the strike, British Rail have been forced to _____ all trains to London.
    A) cancel   B) abandon   C) postpone
    D) refer   E) recall

16. The townspeople held a celebration when work on the _____ of the ancient building had been completed.
    A) re-establishment   B) rejuvenation   C) restoration
    D) reproduction   E) reparation

17. All flights in and out of London Airport came to a _____ because of the strike.
    A) terminus   B) closure   C) standstill
    D) stoppage   E) conclusion

18. Dried vegetables are easy to use if you remember to _____ them overnight.
    A) dampen   B) infuse   C) bathe
    D) plunge   E) soak

19. Investors seem to be losing _____ in the car industry.
    A) belief   B) confidence   C) trust
    D) reliability   E) reliance

20. The memorial in the square _____ the soldiers who lost their lives in the war.
    A) celebrates   B) recaptures   C) remembers
    D) commemorates   E) recalls

21. At the end of his trial he was _____ of murder.
    A) convicted   B) convinced   C) penalized
    D) condemned   E) sentenced

22. To _____ greater accuracy, all invoices will be double-checked before leaving the office.
    A) assure   B) ensure   C) insure
    D) ascertain   E) confirm

23. The mountainous areas of the country are _____ populated.
    A) slightly   B) loosely   C) infrequently
    D) sparsely   E) meagerly

24. He is an _____ worker, and rarely does well in examinations.
    A) errant   B) erroneous   C) erotic
    D) erratic   E) exotic

25. He was completely _____ by the thief's disguise.
    A) taken away   B) taken down   C) taken in
    D) taken through   E) taken up

26. His letter was so confused that I could hardly make any _____ of it at all.
    A) interpretation   B) meaning   C) message
    D) sense   E) explanation

27. According to the weather forecast, which is usually _____, it will snow this afternoon.
    A) accurate   B) precise   C) exact
    D) perfect   E) thorough

28. It was nearly Christmas, and the children were in high _____.
    A) mood   B) spirits   C) heart
    D) glee   E) gusto

29. An energetic manager can be a great _____ to his firm.
    A) asset   B) profit   C) influence
    D) surcharge   E) prosperity

30. He was a generous friend but as a businessman he drove a hard _____.
    A) bargain   B) affair   C) arrangement
    D) deal   E) contract

31. This man is so arrogant that he is completely _____ to all criticism.
    A) impervious   B) unaware   C) regardless
    D) unconscious   E) safeguarded

32. I cannot bear the noise of my brother's radio; it _____ me from my work.
    A) disturbs   B) perturbs   C) deranges
    D) interrupts   E) distracts

33. He soon made a _____ for himself on the stage.
    A) popularity   B) fame   C) regard
    D) notoriety   E) famous

34. His aunt died leaving him a small _____.
    A) heritage   B) dowry   C) portion
    D) grant   E) legacy

35. His irresponsible behavior put the whole operation in _____.
    A) risk   B) doubt   C) jeopardy
    D) condemnation   E) alarm

36. When I invited him to dinner he accepted with _____.
    A) consent   B) obligation   C) acknowledgement
    D) alacrity   E) gratification

37. During the fire he _____ the people into groups which carried sand and water to throw on to the flames.
    A) called   B) dispersed   C) organized
    D) made   E) planned

38. Will you _____ Peter to bring his camera tomorrow?
    A) remember   B) remind   C) recall
    D) recollect   E) refer

39. The floor was _____ with blood where the murdered man had fallen.
    A) dyed   B) colored   C) dotted
    D) blotted   E) stained

40. That comedian is very good at _____; she can take off the Prime Minister perfectly.
    A) introductions   B) reproductions   C) presentations
    D) impressions   E) similarities

Test 19

TEST 20

1. If the fire alarm is sounded, all residents are requested to _____ in the courtyard.
   A) combine   B) assemble   C) crowd
   D) mobilize   E) unite

2. The acoustics in the concert hall were very poor, and it would obviously be necessary to _____ my voice.
   A) exaggerate   B) extend   C) amplify
   D) develop   E) increase

3. One rainy night the old bridge _____ into the river without warning.
   A) submerged   B) collapsed   C) degenerated
   D) immersed   E) relapsed

4. The people who objected to the new road were told that since work had already started there was no point in _____.
   A) contradicting   B) protesting   C) provoking
   D) competing   E) refusing

5. When they asked him about it, he said it was no _____ of theirs and wouldn't tell them anything.
   A) connection   B) concern   C) relation
   D) relevance   E) influence

6. Nursery schools can be enormously _____ to socially handicapped children.
   A) admirable   B) beneficial   C) invaluable
   D) meritorious   E) praiseworthy

7. Corruption in the running of the city's largest bank was _____ in the local newspaper.
   A) found   B) discovered   C) detected
   D) exposed   E) commented

8. The lad spent several years as _____ to a master-builder, so that he might learn the trade.
   A) applicant   B) apprentice   C) learner
   D) student   E) pupil

9. He said he couldn't _____ to retire from work and live only on his pension.
   A) accept   B) afford   C) compensate
   D) depend   E) risk

10. After his heavy defeat in the local elections he decided to _____ from the campaign for the Presidency.
    A) abandon   B) renounce   C) retract
    D) withdraw   E) withhold

11. After the outbreak of a mysterious illness, investigation revealed _____ of the town's water supply.
    A) corruption   B) infiltration   C) contagion
    D) pollution   E) eruption

12. She was very interested in the work of certain charities, and made a regular _____ to them.
    A) subscription   B) contribution   C) allowance
    D) subsidy   E) tribute

13. The students visited the museum and spent several hours with the _____, who was very helpful.
    A) commissioner   B) bursar   C) steward
    D) curator   E) agent

14. As soon as the exams were over, the students all went their _____ ways.
    A) homely   B) perspective   C) respective
    D) relative   E) diverted

15. The council members were dissatisfied with the wording of the recommendation, but passed it after _____ had been agreed.
    A) innovations   B) amendments   C) advancements
    D) preferments   E) refinements

16. He _____ his old car for a new model as soon as he had won the money.
    A) interchanged   B) exchanged   C) replaced
    D) converted   E) displaced

17. The brothers showed great _____ to their older sister, who had acted as sole parent to them for many years.
    A) compliance   B) devotion   C) subjection
    D) estimation   E) allegiance

18. His poor standard of play fully justifies his _____ from the team for the match next Saturday.
    A) rejection   B) expulsion   C) exclusion
    D) exception   E) ban

19. Even a small dog in a house can _____ a thief.
    A) deter   B) arrest   C) waylay
    D) counter   E) forestall

20. His carelessness _____ the whole enterprise.
    A) ventured   B) risked   C) jeopardized
    D) chanced   E) hazarded

21. I congratulate you on your _____ in jewelry.
    A) selection   B) choice   C) flavor
    D) taste   E) likes

22. He _____ his rose bushes carefully with insecticide every evening.
    A) distributed   B) spread   C) trickled
    D) strewed   E) sprayed

23. Playing on strong national feelings, they _____ the crowd to burn down the Embassy.
    A) animated   B) inclined   C) incited
    D) instigated   E) impressed

24. Not knowing he had _____ out with his girl friend, I made the mistake of inviting them both to the party.
    A) fallen   B) quarreled   C) parted
    D) put   E) separated

25. All visitors are requested to _____ with the regulations.
    A) agree   B) comply   C) assent
    D) consent   E) concede

26. My father had to take private pupils in order to _____ his salary as a teacher.
    A) expand   B) augment   C) inflate
    D) enlarge   E) complete

27. Even though the football match was not very exciting, the _____ managed to make it sound interesting
    A) commentator   B) newscaster   C) announcer
    D) presenter   E) narrator

28. The rain soon worked its way _____ the roof of the old cottage.
    A) over   B) in   C) by
    D) through   E) round

29. The Managing Director has asked to see the sales _____ resulting from our recent advertising campaign.
    A) numbers   B) calculations   C) amounts
    D) quantities   E) figures

30. TV, if properly used, can _____ a child's imagination.
    A) cause   B) incite   C) arise
    D) invoke   E) stimulate

31. The country's mineral resources have been _____ by foreign powers.
    A) disused   B) deprived   C) worn out
    D) extorted   E) exploited

32. He earns his living by _____ old paintings.
    A) reviving   B) restoring   C) retrieving
    D) recovering   E) renewing

33. Unless stricter hunting laws are introduced, seals will soon be _____.
    A) defunct   B) out-dated   C) archaic
    D) extinct   E) obsolete

34. Inflation is very hard on people of _____ means.
    A) scarce   B) impoverished   C) limited
    D) needy   E) shortened

35. A new system of quality control was _____ to overcome the defects in the firm's products.
    A) installed   B) inaugurated   C) introduced
    D) inserted   E) invested

36. Ask the publishers to send you their latest _____ of English text-books.
    A) catalogue   B) prospectus   C) brochure
    D) pamphlet   E) booklet

37. It is easier to adapt to new situations if one has a _____ attitude.
    A) changeable   B) flexible   C) moveable
    D) malleable   E) pliable

38. He was smoking; I could see the tip of his cigarette _____ in the darkness.
    A) shining   B) sparkling   C) gleaming
    D) glinting   E) glowing

39. Although he was under no _____, the shopkeeper replaced the defective battery free of charge.
    A) urgency   B) guarantee   C) obligation
    D) insistence   E) authority

40. I haven't the _____ idea what you mean.
    A) lightest   B) dimmest   C) faintest
    D) furthest   E) smallest

Test 20

TEST 21

1. She heard a _____ at the door and went to see who was outside.
   A) hit B) knock C) lean D) strike E) touch

2. A young art student acted as our _____ when we visited the National Gallery.
   A) coach B) conductor C) guide D) lead E) trainer

3. Please _____ your bill before you leave the shop and make sure that it is correct.
   A) check B) control C) esteem D) figure E) prove

4. If you hear the baby _____, please tell me.
   A) cry B) say C) shout D) weep E) whisper

5. The bus conductor told him to get off because he couldn't pay the _____.
   A) bill B) fare C) fee D) journey E) travel

6. I felt a sharp _____ when I put my hand in the boiling water.
   A) ache B) harm C) hurt D) pain E) suffer

7. I am very fond of Graham Greene's novels. He is my _____ modern author.
   A) favored B) favorite C) likely D) popular E) preferred

8. She chose some attractive _____ paper for the Christmas present.
   A) covering B) envelope C) involving D) packing E) wrapping

9. It's rude to interrupt when someone else is _____.
   A) discussing B) remarking C) saying D) talking E) telling

10. Look, Mother! Jack has _____ you some flowers.
    A) brought B) carried C) lifted D) present E) taken

11. He _____ out of the window for a moment and then went on working.
    A) glanced B) glimpsed C) regarded D) saw E) viewed

12. The company made a record _____ last year.
    A) benefit B) earn C) profit D) wage E) winning

13. These cars originally had two doors but the latest _____ has four.
    A) brand B) mark C) model D) pattern E) trade

14. He was killed in a car _____.
    A) blow B) crash C) flash D) hit E) shock

15. He's a nice man but he's _____ to drink too much at parties.
    A) adequate B) apt C) common D) probable E) suitable

16. He has a bad cold and won't be _____ to play in the match tomorrow.
    A) adequate B) appropriate C) fit D) proper E) suitable

17. He _____ his wife and children and left them to take care of themselves.
    A) abandoned B) let C) missed D) spoilt E) wasted

18. We want to make our products cheaper than our _____.
    A) colleagues' B) competitors' C) enemies' D) experts' E) partners'

19. It's the _____ in this country for the father of the bride to pay for the wedding.
    A) common B) custom C) habit D) normal E) use

20. He is a very _____ player. He practices for two hours every morning.
    A) amateur B) anxious C) excited D) impatient E) keen

21. The bank will _____ you the money if you are prepared to pay them eight per cent interest on it.
    A) borrow B) lend C) make D) possess E) put

22. I _____ to him for my bad behavior.
    A) apologized B) coped C) excused D) forgave E) pardoned

23. The sky is _____ I don't think it will rain.
    A) clean B) clear C) cloudy D) open E) tidy

24. I want to see all of you here tomorrow morning at nine o'clock without _____.
    A) fail B) fault C) late D) miss E) neglect

25. He _____ the letter carefully and put it in the envelope.
    A) bent B) curved C) folded D) turned E) twisted

26. The price of the meal _____ a service charge.
    A) encloses B) enters C) envelopes D) includes E) inspects

27. He shouldn't be allowed to play tennis in the club. He's not a _____.
    A) belong B) member C) partner D) representative E) social

28. He has always wanted to see his name in _____.
    A) news B) paper C) press D) print E) publication

29. He _____ his head, wondering how he could solve the problem.
    A) scratched B) scraped C) screwed D) shaved E) wound

30. Everyone who applies for a job with the company is given a/an intelligence _____.
    A) experience B) fitting C) proof D) test E) trial

31. Do you _____ to go to the party?
    A) attempt B) attend C) intend D) pretend E) think

32. We locked the animals in the cage to _____ them from getting away.
    A) avoid B) hinder C) object D) prevent E) resist

33. They're old customers of ours. We've been _____ with them for many years.
    A) competing B) dealing C) shopping D) supplying E) treating

34. I don't think I'll beat him. I'm out of _____.
    A) fitness B) game C) play D) practice E) sport

35. If you are _____ to customers, they'll walk out of the shop.
    A) brush B) rough C) rude D) rusty E) tough

36. We must get there _____ or other. If there are no buses, we'll have to take a taxi.
    A) anyhow B) anyway C) anywhere D) somehow E) somewhere

37. I'll _____ the children for you while you are out.
    A) look after B) look for C) look on D) look out E) look over

38. I wish I could _____ smoking.
    A) give away B) give from C) give off D) give out E) give up

39. We'll have to _____ the meeting until next week because no one can come tomorrow.
    A) put down B) put off C) put on D) put round E) put up

40. We went to the railway station to _____ our friends _____.
    A) see \ off B) see \ out C) set \ out D) tell \ goodbye E) wave \ out

TEST 22

1. He was sent to prison for _____ a bank.
   A) borrowing   B) lending   C) robbing
   D) stealing   E) taking

2. She bought a new _____ for the party.
   A) clothes   B) clothing   C) dress
   D) vest   E) wear

3. My favorite _____ is roast beef.
   A) dish   B) eat   C) menu
   D) plate   E) receipt

4. Several of the explorers did not survive the terrible _____ across the desert.
   A) excursion   B) journey   C) step
   D) travel   E) voyage

5. What a beautiful dress! It _____ you perfectly.
   A) goes   B) likes   C) matches
   D) mixes   E) suits

6. As the two teams were _____ at the end of the game, they had to play again to decide the winners of the competition.
   A) correct   B) equal   C) exact
   D) fair   E) just

7. The books I borrowed are overdue. I'll have to take them back to the _____.
   A) bible   B) bookshop   C) library
   D) magazine   E) review

8. Naturally I'm _____ that I didn't pass the examination but I'll do better next time.
   A) deceived   B) despaired   C) disappointed
   D) disillusioned   E) tricked

9. He was the only person to _____ the crash. Everyone else was killed.
   A) alive   B) cure   C) recover
   D) relieve   E) survive

10. I _____ him to go to the Lost Property office to see if his umbrella had been found.
    A) advertised   B) advised   C) announced
    D) noticed   E) remarked

11. I _____ in bed all night thinking about it.
    A) laid   B) lay   C) led
    D) lied   E) stood

12. It was on the top shelf, out of _____.
    A) achievement   B) arrival   C) attempt
    D) reach   E) touch

13. Before you take on the job, will you give me a rough _____ of how much it will cost?
    A) esteem   B) estimate   C) realization
    D) value   E) worth

14. The competitors in the car rally had to follow the _____ laid down by the organizers.
    A) address   B) direct   C) progress
    D) route   E) street

15. When, the clock _____ twelve, we raised our glasses and drank to celebrate the New Year.
    A) beat   B) hit   C) shot
    D) struck   E) turned

16. He had no way of making a fire so he had to eat the fish _____.
    A) crude   B) raw   C) rough
    D) rude   E) wild

17. It was so hot that I had to go indoors. I couldn't _____ it any longer.
    A) carry   B) hold   C) pass
    D) stand   E) support

18. The concert was so _____ that the audience went to sleep.
    A) bored   B) boring   C) exhausted
    D) tired   E) tiring

19. What a beautiful _____! It's a pity we have no flowers to put in it.
    A) crystal   B) cup   C) glass
    D) mug   E) vase

20. Stick this _____ on the parcel that says "Fragile". Then people will see that they must handle it carefully.
    A) advertisement   B) advice   C) label
    D) sign   E) signal

21. I've _____ for a job in Mexico. I hope I get it.
    A) applied   B) appointed   C) implied
    D) presented   E) succeeded

22. Look, Mother; James has brought you a _____ of flowers.
    A) branch   B) bucket   C) bunch
    D) bush   E) growth

23. Although the town had changed in the ten years since he had last visited it, much of it was still _____ to him.
    A) accustomed   B) common   C) familiar
    D) relative   E) used

24. When his aunt died, he _____ a lot of money from her.
    A) earned   B) inherited   C) paid
    D) spent   E) won

25. This year the company made a _____ but next year we hope to make a profit.
    A) loose   B) lose   C) loss
    D) lost   E) lot

26. I'm afraid the lift is out of _____ so we'll have to walk up the stairs.
    A) function   B) movement   C) order
    D) practice   E) running

27. I _____ to inform you that we cannot exchange articles once they have left the shop.
    A) regret   B) resent   C) respect
    D) sense   E) sorry

28. I _____ hands with him when I was introduced to him.
    A) gave   B) greeted   C) nodded
    D) shook   E) waved

29. His shoes were so old that his _____ were sticking out of them.
    A) ankles   B) fingers   C) thumbs
    D) tips   E) toes

30. Would you _____ looking after the baby for me while I'm out?
    A) agree   B) like   C) matter
    D) mind   E) object

31. I _____ you to drive carefully today. The roads are icy.
    A) propose   B) recommend   C) refer
    D) regard   E) suggest

32. Good _____! I hope you win.
    A) chance   B) luck   C) run
    D) sort   E) wish

33. The trade _____ of the company is a flying horse.
    A) brandy   B) class   C) mark
    D) model   E) stain

34. The hotel room was so dirty that I was _____ and complained to the manager.
    A) ashamed   B) disgusted   C) disgusting
    D) embarrassed   E) shameful

35. It's no use waiting for him any longer. We _____ as well go without him.
    A) can   B) just   C) may
    D) must   E) should

36. Her husband treated her badly. I'm surprised she _____ it for so long.
    A) put by   B) put off   C) put through
    D) put up   E) put up with

37. They were such good friends. I was surprised when they _____.
    A) fell down   B) fell off   C) fell out
    D) fell over   E) fell through

38. He could hardly _____ such a generous offer.
    A) turn down   B) turn for   C) turn off
    D) turn round   E) turn up

39. He _____ for his office every morning at eight o'clock.
    A) began out   B) set about   C) set out
    D) set to   E) started up

40. Vitamin C is _____ in lemons; therefore, lemons can help us fight colds.
    A) simple   B) abundant   C) single
    D) unmixed   E) temporary

TEST 23

1. They _____ our team by three goals to one.
   A) beat   B) conquered   C) earned
   D) gained   E) won

2. He works at a big steel _____ outside the town.
   A) fabric   B) factory   C) industry
   D) product   E) society

3. I congratulated him on winning the _____.
   A) match   B) play   C) practice
   D) recital   E) sport

4. A _____ of mine, my cousin John, is coming to stay with us.
   A) familiar   B) known   C) neighbor
   D) parent   E) relative

5. He has been very _____ since his wife died.
   A) lonely   B) only   C) single
   D) sole   E) unique

6. As all the hotels in the town were full up, we tried to find accommodation in a _____ village.
   A) close   B) native   C) near
   D) nearby   E) neighbor

7. The fish sauce was lovely, Janet. Would you mind letting me have the _____ or is it a family secret?
   A) card   B) course   C) prescription
   D) receipt   E) recipe

8. His parents died when he was a baby and he was _____ by his aunt.
   A) brought out B) brought up   C) grown
   D) grown up   E) taken out

9. I _____ on seeing the manager. The service here is terrible.
   A) ask   B) demand   C) insist
   D) repeat   E) underline

10. He _____ me of someone I knew at school.
    A) memories   B) refers   C) regards
    D) remembers E) reminds

11. I _____ £5 from my father because I was short of money.
    A) asked   B) borrowed   C) lent
    D) spent   E) wasted

12. His office is on the sixth _____ of the building.
    A) flat   B) floor   C) ground
    D) level   E) stage

13. The main interest of the Trade Union is to raise its members' _____ of living.
    A) ability   B) capacity   C) condition
    D) degree   E) standard

14. The _____ for the race to begin was the starter firing a pistol.
    A) advice   B) attention   C) dispatch
    D) notice   E) signal

15. If you leave your bicycle out in the rain, it will get _____.
    A) crude   B) rough   C) rude
    D) rusty   E) tough

16. It must have rained _____ the night. The ground's still wet.
    A) ago   B) during   C) for
    D) since   E) while

17. He's so _____ by nature that he never knows what to say to strangers.
    A) disgusted B) embarrassing   C) shameful
    D) shy   E) upset

18. I want to _____ the car to see how it goes before I buy it.
    A) experiment B) prove   C) taste
    D) try on   E) try out

19. A _____ is a person who comes from another country.
    A) foreigner B) host   C) stranger
    D) tramp   E) wanderer

20. When they reached the _____ they had to show their passports before crossing into Germany.
    A) border   B) cliff   C) edge
    D) front   E) shore

21. They _____ a hundred workers because they had no work for them.
    A) disposed   B) resigned   C) sacked
    D) shot   E) threw

22. At _____ we didn't get on very well but later we became friends.
    A) beginning B) first   C) least
    D) once   E) principle

23. Policemen have to wear _____ because so many people ask them the time.
    A) bells   B) clocks   C) hours
    D) watches   E) whistles

24. She's happiest when she has a house _____ of people to entertain.
    A) enough   B) filled   C) full
    D) lot   E) plenty

25. Don't take what he said so seriously. He was only _____.
    A) amusing   B) enjoying   C) funny
    D) joking   E) tricking

26. Don't be afraid of the dog. He won't do you any _____.
    A) bite   B) harm   C) hurt
    D) pain   E) wound

27. I'll pay you back the money I _____ you at the end of the month.
    A) debt   B) doubt   C) lend
    D) owe   E) own

28. His landlady threw him out because he hadn't paid the _____.
    A) due   B) fee   C) hire
    D) let   E) rent

29. She _____ and fell from the top of the stairs to the bottom.
    A) slipped   B) sloped   C) smashed
    D) spilt   E) split

30. The elephant fell into a _____ the villagers had set for him in the long grass.
    A) track   B) damp   C) trap
    D) trick   E) trip

31. I ____ of his course of action and told him to go ahead.
    A) accepted   B) agreed   C) approved
    D) consented E) passed

32. Emotional speeches often _____ strong feelings.
    A) arise   B) arouse   C) get up
    D) give up   E) rise

33. I took _____ of the opportunity to tell him what I thought.
    A) advantage B) benefit   C) gain
    D) occasion   E) profit

34. He suffers from a speech _____ and so he cannot pronounce the letter 'r' properly.
    A) break   B) defect   C) error
    D) fault   E) mistake

35. He's the greatest _____ expert on French art.
    A) alive   B) live   C) lively
    D) living   E) nowadays

36. He never attends _____ at the university so he may not know enough to get his degree.
    A) lectures   B) performances   C) rehearsals
    D) reunions   E) subjects

37. The weather forecast said it would rain but it looks as if it's going to _____ fine.
    A) turn down B) turn into   C) turn out
    D) turn over E) turn up

38. He's fond of _____ his colleagues but he goes on working for the same firm.
    A) running down B) running into   C) running out
    D) running over E) running up against

39. The plane _____ at 7 o'clock.
    A) took away B) took down   C) look off
    D) look out   E) took up

40. My car _____ so I had to walk.
    A) broke down B) broke off   C) broke up
    D) fell down E) fell through

TEST 24

1. We _____ goodbye to them as the train left.
   A) greeted B) saluted C) saw off D) shook E) waved

2. He will be given a pension when he _____ at the age of 65.
   A) disappears B) dismisses C) resigns D) retires E) sacks

3. He took a _____ of cigarettes out of his pocket.
   A) block B) dozen C) packet D) parcel E) piece

4. I'm sure you'll _____ the film. It's very good.
   A) amuse B) delight C) divert D) enjoy E) entertain

5. He fell in love with her at first _____.
   A) scene B) sight C) spectacle D) view E) vision

6. I'm _____ if I hurt your feelings. Please forgive me.
   A) afraid B) pardon C) pitiful D) shameful E) sorry

7. The doctor has told him that he must not go back to work so soon after such a long _____.
   A) disease B) failing C) illness D) pain E) weakness

8. No one imagined that the apparently _____ business man was really a criminal.
   A) honor B) respectable C) respectful D) respective E) responsive

9. Where do you _____ the writing paper? In this desk?
   A) drawer B) guard C) hold D) keep E) maintain

10. Please _____ your hand if you want to ask a question.
    A) arouse B) get up C) put out D) raise E) rise

11. As you are only 16, you must have your parents' _____ before you can get married.
    A) allowance B) consent C) let D) permit E) subscription

12. The bank are offering £500 ____ to anyone who can give them useful information about the robbery.
    A) cost B) price C) prize D) reward E) salary

13. How long do you intend to _____ in this country?
    A) permanent B) remind C) rest D) stay E) vacate

14. She put a _____ of chocolate on the cake.
    A) color B) cover C) layer D) level E) plain

15. I'll have to take the toy back to the shop to exchange it because the mechanism is _____.
    A) blame B) defect C) false D) faulty E) few

16. Dinner will be served _____ but we have time for a drink before then.
    A) actually B) currently C) lately D) presently E) suddenly

17. He _____ at me to show he appreciated the joke.
    A) glimpsed B) grinned C) sneered D) stared E) watched

18. They're _____ to build a new factory here.
    A) planning B) pretending C) projecting D) suggesting E) thinking

19. There's a great _____ of pollution on the beaches this summer.
    A) deal B) lot C) many D) number E) quality

20. It was not an accident. He did it on _____.
    A) decision B) determination C) intention D) purpose E) security

21. I've bought some attractive _____ and I'm going to make a dress out of it.
    A) clothing B) costume C) material D) matter E) pattern

22. Don't touch things that don't _____ to you!
    A) belong B) involve C) own D) possess E) retain

23. There are so many _____ in the road that you have to drive very carefully.
    A) bends B) crosses C) curls D) currents E) folds

24. I like the hat but it doesn't _____ me. Have you got the same thing in a larger size?
    A) dress B) fit C) go well D) match E) suit

25. I'm very _____ to you for all your help.
    A) agreed B) graceful C) grateful D) reliable E) thanks

26. The school claim to _____ students all the English they need in three months.
    A) explain B) instruct C) learn D) teach E) understand

27. One of the water _____ burst during the recent cold weather and the kitchen was flooded.
    A) channels B) conductors C) pipes D) tubes E) ways

28. I only ____ a straw hat to protect my head when the sun is very hot.
    A) bear B) carry C) dress D) put E) wear

29. I'm afraid we haven't got what you want in _____ at the moment. We can order it for you.
    A) reserve B) sale C) shop D) stock E) work

30. I wasn't able to _____ the meeting because I was too busy.
    A) assist B) attempt C) attend D) present E) take place

31. He _____ to hit me if I didn't do as he said.
    A) pretended B) said C) thought D) threatened E) warned

32. He said he was not guilty but the police proved he had _____.
    A) denied B) laid C) lay D) lied E) meant

33. I don't feel like swimming. I'd rather sun-bathe on the _____.
    A) beach B) coast C) dust D) harbor E) shore

34. He bought his house on the _____ plan, paying a certain amount of money back to the bank every month.
    A) hire B) installment C) part D) piece E) share

35. He was the _____ child in the family so he had no brothers or sisters to play with.
    A) alone B) individual C) lonely D) only E) unique

36. I haven't seen him _____ he came to dinner with us last week.
    A) for B) meanwhile C) since D) when E) while

37. He'll _____ his shyness when he's older.
    A) get away B) get down C) get off D) get over E) get up

38. Throw some water on her face and then perhaps she'll _____.
    A) come back B) come down C) come on D) come out E) come round

39. We've ____ bread. I'll have to go to the baker's to buy some more.
    A) run away with B) run down C) run off D) run out of E) run over

40. The good service at the restaurant ____ the poor meal to some extent.
    A) made for B) made out C) made over D) made up E) made up for

TEST 25

1. The _____ outside the house said: 'Private'.
   A) advice B) label C) notice
   D) signal E) threat

2. Are you going to _____ your house in London while you are abroad?
   A) dispose B) hire C) let
   D) remove E) sale

3. How unkind of him to _____ to help you!
   A) agree B) admit C) deny
   D) ignore E) refuse

4. Close the door, please: I don't like sitting in a _____.
   A) blow B) current C) draught
   D) vent E) wind

5. I had to stand in a _____ for hours to get the tickets for the performance.
   A) file B) procession C) queue
   D) tail E) turn

6. When he was a boy his hobby was stamp _____.
   A) assembly B) collecting C) finding
   D) gathering E) picking

7. He lost his _____ and threw a book at me.
   A) feeling B) mood C) sense
   D) spirit E) temper

8. I learnt to _____ a bicycle when I was six years old.
   A) conduct B) drive C) guide
   D) ride E) run

9. Do as you think best. It doesn't _____ whether he agrees or not.
   A) care B) decide C) import
   D) matter E) mind

10. I don't think you've _____ Mrs. Walker before I'll introduce you to her.
    A) discovered B) found C) known
    D) met E) presented

11. If the boss sees you doing that, you'll get into _____.
    A) mess B) nuisance C) problem
    D) struggle E) trouble

12. My husband's at _____. He'll speak to you when he comes home.
    A) busy B) employ C) job
    D) work E) works

13. It's no good asking me to calculate the cost. I'm hopeless at _____.
    A) characters B) counters C) figures
    D) prizes E) shapes

14. The road was so _____ that the car bounced up and down.
    A) rare B) sharp C) steep
    D) sudden E) uneven

15. You should be _____ of yourself for behaving so badly.
    A) ashamed B) confused C) disgusted
    D) embarrassed E) shameful

16. I _____ an answer to my letter in the next few days.
    A) expect B) hope C) promise
    D) suppose E) wait

17. The car broke down but the _____ in the garage soon fixed it.
    A) driver B) machinist C) manufacturer
    D) mechanic E) motorist

18. Why are you arresting me? I haven't done anything _____.
    A) crime B) error C) faulty
    D) mistaken E) wrong

19. Roses are quite _____ flowers in English gardens.
    A) accustomed B) annual C) common
    D) used E) vulgar

20. Benjamin Franklin _____ the lightning conductor.
    A) discovered B) found C) invented
    D) resulted E) solved

21. I didn't know his _____ so I couldn't write to him.
    A) address B) direction C) letter
    D) route E) way

22. The only problem about sitting outside here in the evening is that you are likely to be _____ by mosquitoes.
    A) bitten B) grasped C) ground
    D) murdered E) picked

23. You must _____ facts and not try to run away from the unpleasant truth.
    A) eye B) face C) front
    D) look E) sight

24. There was a sudden _____ of lightning, which lit up the whole street.
    A) bum B) fire C) flash
    D) splash E) split

25. When he _____ he wants to be an engine driver.
    A) ages B) becomes C) grows
    D) grows up E) increases

26. I just _____ to stop the child from running into the road.
    A) achieved B) controlled C) could
    D) managed E) succeeded

27. As soon as his party came into _____ he raised the salaries of Member of Parliament.
    A) force B) position C) power
    D) right E) strength

28. There was an interesting _____ of the film in The Sunday Times last weekend.
    A) comment B) remark C) resume
    D) review E) revision

29. I didn't realize you wanted to keep the letter. I've _____ it up.
    A) broken B) pulled C) smashed
    D) torn E) wrapped

30. We're sorry you're ill and send you our best wishes for a speedy _____.
    A) recovery B) relief C) repair
    D) repose E) survival

31. When he was young, all he _____ at the factory was £1 a week.
    A) earned B) gained C) inherited
    D) sacked E) won

32. She _____ at me for a long time without saying anything.
    A) glimpsed B) saw C) stared
    D) viewed E) watched

33. He threw the box out of the window and saw it fall to the _____ outside.
    A) flat B) floor C) ground
    D) plain E) soil

34. You've made a very _____ decision. Any reasonable person would have done the same thing.
    A) sensational B) sensed C) sensible
    D) sensitive E) sentimental

35. The water here is very _____. You can get across the stream on foot.
    A) broad B) flat C) narrow
    D) pure E) shallow

36. I am staying in a youth _____ in the center of the town.
    A) home B) hostel C) inn
    D) lodge E) pub

37. The little boy had blue eyes and fair hair so he _____ his mother.
    A) took after B) took down C) took from
    D) took off E) took over

38. There's no food left and the shops are shut so you'll have to _____.
    A) go for B) go off C) go on
    D) go through E) go without

39. You sometimes _____ quite valuable things in antique shop.
    A) come across B) come back C) come into
    D) come off E) come round

40. I'll _____ you at 8:30 and give you a lift to the office.
    A) call at B) call for C) call in
    D) call round E) call to

Test 25

Answers

BOOK 2 - PART A

Elementary vocabulary Test 1 (Page 220)

1-B	2-D	3-A	4-C	5-C	6-D	7-A	8-A
9-B	10-C	11-A	12-B	13-B	14-C	15-D	16-B
17-C	18-D	19-B	20-A	21-B	22-C	23-B	24-B
25-C	26-D	27-A	28-C	29-A	30-D	31-C	32-A
33-C	34-B	35-C	36-C	37-A	38-C	39-D	40-B
41-D	42-A	43-B	44-A	45-A	46-D	47-B	48-C
49-C	50-A	51-B	52-A	53-D	54-C	55-B	56-A
57-D	58-C	59-D	60-D	61-A	62-D	63-B	64-A
65-C	66-A	67-B	68-A	69-C	70-B	71-C	72-D
73-B	74-B	75-D	76-B	77-C	78-D	79-C	80-A
81-C	82-D	83-B	84-B	85-A	86-C	87-D	88-D
89-C	90-B	91-A	92-D	93-B	94-D	95-A	96-D
97-C	98-B	99-A	100-C				

Elementary vocabulary Test 2 (Page 222)

1-C	2-D	3-A	4-A	5-D	6-A	7-D	8-D
9-C	10-A	11-A	12-C	13-B	14-C	15-D	16-A
17-A	18-B	19-C	20-D	21-B	22-D	23-D	24-C
25-A	26-B	27-D	28-A	29-C	30-A	31-D	32-B
33-C	34-B	35-D	36-A	37-C	38-C	39-A	40-B
41-D	42-C	43-A	44-D	45-A	46-C	47-A	48-B
49-A	50-D	51-A	52-D	53-C	54-B	55-D	56-C
57-C	58-A	59-B	60-B	61-A	62-D	63-B	64-A
65-C	66-D	67-C	68-B	69-D	70-D	71-D	72-B
73-A	74-C	75-C	76-C	77-B	78-D	79-A	80-D
81-B	82-D	83-A	84-B	85-C	86-A	87-D	88-C
89-B	90-A	91-C	92-C	93-C	94-B	95-A	96-B
97-D	98-C	99-D	100-B				

Elementary vocabulary Test 3 (Page 224)

1-A	2-B	3-B	4-A	5-B	6-D	7-B	8-A
9-D	10-A	11-D	12-A	13-C	14-B	15-C	16-D
17-A	18-C	19-B	20-D	21-C	22-A	23-B	24-A
25-A	26-C	27-D	28-A	29-B	30-C	31-D	32-B
33-D	34-A	35-A	36-C	37-B	38-B	39-D	40-D
41-D	42-A	43-C	44-D	45-C	46-D	47-B	48-B
49-A	50-D	51-A	52-D	53-D	54-C	55-B	56-A
57-D	58-A	59-D	60-C	61-B	62-C	63-D	64-A
65-B	66-C	67-C	68-A	69-B	70-A	71-C	72-B
73-D	74-C	75-B	76-A	77-B	78-A	79-B	80-A
81-D	82-C	83-D	84-D	85-C	86-B	87-D	88-C
89-B	90-B	91-B	92-D	93-B	94-A	95-C	96-B
97-D	98-D	99-C	100-B				

Elementary vocabulary Test 4 (Page 226)

1-D	2-D	3-A	4-C	5-D	6-C	7-C	8-B
9-D	10-D	11-C	12-C	13-A	14-C	15-C	16-D
17-D	18-D	19-D	20-A	21-C	22-D	23-D	24-A
25-C	26-D	27-B	28-C	29-D	30-C	31-A	32-D
33-D	34-C	35-B	36-D	37-D	38-D	39-B	40-C
41-C	42-B	43-B	44-B	45-A	46-A	47-B	48-C
49-B	50-B	51-B	52-D	53-B	54-C	55-D	56-B
57-D	58-B	59-D	60-B	61-D	62-C	63-A	64-A
65-B	66-D	67-A	68-D	69-C	70-C	71-C	72-C
73-B	74-C	75-B	76-A	77-D	78-C	79-A	80-A
81-A	82-D	83-B	84-D	85-D	86-B	87-D	88-C
89-B	90-A	91-C	92-C	93-D	94-C	95-B	96-B
97-A	98-D	99-A	100-B				

Classified topics (Page 228)

ANIMALS

1-A	2-B	3-C	4-D	5-A	6-B	7-B	8-C
9-D	10-A	11-C	12-D	13-D	14-B	15-A	

BATHROOM

1-D	2-C	3-B	4-A	5-A	6-B	7-C	8-D
9-A	10-A	11-B	12-B	13-C	14-C	15-D	

CLOTHES

1-A	2-A	3-D	4-D	5-C	6-B	7-A	8-C
9-C	10-B	11-D	12-A	13-A	14-B	15-A	

DINING ROOM

1-B	2-B	3-A	4-C	5-A	6-D	7-D	8-A
9-B	10-A	11-C	12-C	13-C	14-A	15-A	

ENVIRONMENT

1-A	2-A	3-C	4-B	5-D	6-A	7-C	8-D
9-A	10-C	11-C	12-B	13-B	14-A	15-A	

FAMILY RELATIONSHIPS

1-C	2-D	3-D	4-A	5-A	6-B	7-A	8-A
9-A	10-C	11-D	12-D	13-B	14-A	15-A	

FOOD

1-D	2-C	3-B	4-A	5-A	6-B	7-B	8-D
9-A	10-A	11-C	12-C	13-C	14-A	15-A	

HEALTH

1-C	2-A	3-A	4-D	5-B	6-C	7-C	8-A
9-A	10-B	11-B	12-D	13-A	14-A	15-A	

JOBS

1-A	2-A	3-B	4-D	5-C	6-B	7-C	8-D
9-A	10-A	11-B	12-B	13-C	14-A	15-A	

LIVING ROOM

1-A	2-B	3-C	4-D	5-A	6-B	7-C	8-D
9-D	10-C	11-B	12-B	13-A	14-A	15-A	

MUSIC AND THEATER

1-C	2-C	3-B	4-B	5-A	6-A	7-A	8-A
9-A	10-C	11-B	12-B	13-B	14-A	15-A	

SPORTS

1-B	2-B	3-C	4-A	5-A	6-D	7-D	8-D
9-A	10-A	11-B	12-A	13-A	14-C	15-D	

TRANSPORT

1-A	2-A	3-C	4-C	5-C	6-D	7-B	8-B
9-A	10-A	11-A	12-D	13-C	14-D	15-A	

WEATHER

1-B	2-B	3-A	4-B	5-A	6-C	7-C	8-D
9-D	10-B	11-B	12-A	13-C	14-C	15-B	

Synonyms (Page 233)

1-D	2-A	3-A	4-C	5-C	6-B	7-C	8-A
9-A	10-C	11-C	12-B	13-A	14-C	15-B	16-D
17-E	18-C	19-D	20-B	21-B	22-D	23-D	24-D
25-A	26-B	27-D	28-C	29-C	30-B	31-A	32-B
33-E	34-A	35-C	36-B	37-E	38-C	39-A	40-D
41-A	42-A	43-C	44-C	45-C	46-A	47-A	48-B
49-D	50-C	51-E	52-E	53-C	54-D	55-A	56-C
57-C	58-D	59-B	60-B	61-B	62-B	63-D	64-D
65-D	66-D	67-A	68-B	69-B	70-A	71-A	72-D
73-A	74-D	75-B	76-C	77-D	78-D	79-B	80-A
81-D	82-A	83-D	84-A	85-C	86-D	87-B	88-B
89-C	90-A	91-D	92-A	93-B	94-D	95-C	96-D
97-C	98-C	99-A	100-C				

Antonyms (Page 236)

1-A	2-D	3-D	4-D	5-D	6-D	7-C	8-A
9-A	10-D	11-D	12-B	13-C	14-B	15-B	16-C
17-D	18-A	19-A	20-C	21-B	22-A	23-B	24-D
25-C	26-A	27-D	28-B	29-C	30-D	31-C	32-C
33-D	34-D	35-D	36-C	37-C	38-B	39-C	40-D
41-D	42-B	43-C	44-E	45-A	46-D	47-D	48-B
49-A	50-B	51-B	52-E	53-C	54-D	55-C	56-E
57-D	58-B	59-C	60-C	61-C	62-B	63-E	64-E
65-B	66-C	67-B	68-B	69-D	70-B	71-A	72-A
73-A	74-A	75-A	76-A	77-C	78-D	79-A	80-A
81-A	82-A	83-A	84-D	85-C	86-D	87-C	88-A
89-B	90-A	91-D	92-C	93-C	94-C	95-B	96-B
97-B	98-D	99-B	100-A	101-C	102-C	103-D	104-C
105-C	106-C	107-D	108-D	109-A	110-C	111-C	112-A
113-D	114-A	115-A	116-A	117-C	118-D	119-A	120-D
121-D	122-A	123-C	124-C				

The logic List (Page 239)

1-D	2-C	3-A	4-B	5-A	6-D	7-C	8-D
9-D	10-B	11-A	12-B	13-A	14-B	15-A	16-C
17-C	18-D	19-D	20-D	21-A	22-D	23-B	24-B
25-D	26-A	27-C	28-A	29-D	30-C	31-D	32-B
33-B	34-A	35-C	36-B	37-A	38-C	39-D	40-B
41-A	42-D	43-B	44-B	45-B	46-C	47-B	48-A
49-C	50-B	51-C	52-C	53-C	54-D	55-B	56-E
57-E	58-C	59-A	60-C	61-B	62-B	63-D	64-C
65-A	66-C	67-E	68-B	69-C	70-B	71-B	72-E
73-B	74-D	75-E	76-D	77-B	78-C	79-E	80-A
81-D	82-E	83-C	84-A	85-A	86-C	87-E	88-D
89-B	90-C	91-C	92-D	93-E	94-C	95-D	96-D

Vocabulary A-Z (Page 241)

A A A A A
1- airplane
2- actors
3- an adult
4- Australia
5- an air conditioner
6- an alarm clock
7- alive
8- an ashtray
9- attractive
10- an astronaut

B B B B B
1- bachelor
2- baggage
3- barber
4- barefoot
5- blood
6- British
7- burglar
8- bullet
9- by
10- button

C C C C C
1- cocoa
2- China
3- cup
4- castle
5- captain
6- cab
7- cage
8- Cairo
9- chair
10- cheap

D D D D D
1- dog
2- a diamond
3- dozen
4- drunk
5- deaf
6- dentist
7- dictionary
8- desserts
9- diet
10- decade

E E E E E
1- elbow
2- empty
3- enlargement
4- exit
5- expensive
6- engine
7- everywhere
8- equator
9- earthquakes
10- end

F F F F F
1- farmer
2- favorite
3- form
4- fog
5- fool
6- fortnight
7- fragile
8- freckles
9- free
10- frying

G G G G G
1- garden
2- Germany
3- glove
4- golf
5- glue
6- grandparents
7- gray/grey
8- grapes
9- guitar
10- gum

H H H H H
1- hammer
2- handsome
3- hat
4- hate
5- hips
6- honeymoon
7- a hospital
8- a hundred
9- hurricane
10- hell

I I I I I
1- ice
2- illegal
3- in
4- ink
5- insect
6- instrument
7- international
8- Irish
9- island
10- inside

J J J J J
1- jacket
2- jade
3- jam
4- jigsaw puzzle
5- job
6- judge
7- joke
8- Jupiter
9- journey
10- jingle

K K K K K
1- kangaroo
2- kettle
3- key
4- kilo
5- kiss
6- kitchen
7- knee
8- knife
9- kid
10- knock

L L L L L
1- lunch
2- library
3- leather
4- lost
5- leaves
6- loan
7- lift
8- living
9- lemon
10- license

Answers

M M M M M
1- mad
2- medium
3- metal
4- mustache
5- motels
6- musician
7- moist
8- melts
9- mirror
10- medicine

N N N N N
1- narrow
2- neck
3- needle
4- noon
5- nuts
6- neighbor
7- negative
8- neutral
9- nap
10- nylon

O O O O O
1- Oyster
2- oil
3- oral
4- odd
5- octopus
6- onion
7- opportunity
8- operate
9- once
10- owner

P P P P P
1- Parent
2- Poor
3- Power
4- Precious
5- Pun
6- Punctual
7- Please
8- Pins
9- Product
10- Pair

Q Q Q Q Q
1- quake
2- quantity
3- queen
4- quarter
5- queue
6- quick
7- quite
8- quiz
9- quote
10- quit
11- quarrel

R R R R R
1- raisin
2- raw
3- real
4- rear
5- receive
6- rave
7- razor
8- rude
9- rubber
10- rural

S S S S S
1- sad
2- saddle
3- salary
4- search
5- selfish
6- similar
7- smile
8- spider
9- spot
10- sofa

T T T T T
1- tires
2- twins
3- toothpaste
4- target
5- thunder
6- turkey
7- tailor
8- thermometer
9- transportation
10- typhoon

U U U U U
1- uncle
2- unique
3- unclean
4- usual
5- upside-down
6- used
7- underground
8- upper
9- urban
10- urgent

V V V V V
1- vacation
2- vacuum
3- vegetarian
4- vertical
5- volleyball
6- velvet
7- vanished
8- valley
9- village
10- volunteer

W W W W W
1- wrist
2- whale
3- watch
4- wink
5- weight
6- weapons
7- wave
8- warehouse
9- well
10- wax

X X X X X
1- Xerox
2- xylophone
3- X-mas
4- x-ray
5- xenophobic

Y Y Y Y Y
1- yo-yo
2- yolk
3- yoghurt
4- young
5- yes
6- yell
7- year
8- yard
9- yen
10- yesterday

Z Z Z Z Z
1- zigzag
2- zipper
3- zebra
4- zero
5- zoom
6- zone
7- zucchini
8- Zen
9- zoo
10- Z

Miscellaneous *(Page 245)*

A "Pair of" Quiz

1- a pair of gloves
2- a pair of glasses
3- a pair of socks
4- a pair of earrings
5- a pair of sunglasses
6- a pair of pants
7- a pair of shoes
8- a pair of pajamas
9- a pair of slippers
10- a pair of scissors

Automobile Vocabulary

1-A 2-D 3-B 4-D 5-A 6-C 7-C 8-B
9-B 10-D

Body

1- eyes
2- ears
3- teeth
4- hands
5- nose
6- mouth
7- legs
8- feet
9- knees
10- back

Clothes 1

1- gloves
2- hat
3- scarf
4- jeans
5- tie/necktie
6- socks
7- coat
8- shirt
9- skirt
10- suit

Clothes 2

1- scarf
2- pants
3- gloves
4- socks
5- shirt
6- jacket
7- gown
8- trousers

Colors 1

1- red
2- blue
3- white
4- green
5- yellow
6- purple
7- orange
8- pink
9- brown
10- black

Answers

Colors 2

1- navy	2- green	3- red
4- yellow	5- white	6- seven
7- blue	8- five	
9- red, yellow, green		

Colors 3

1- blue	2- yellow	3- red
4- green	5- white	6- brown
7- brown	8- black	9- white
10- purple		

Colors 4

1- green	2- red	3- yellow
4- blue	5- black	6- pink
7- brown	8- white	9- purple
10- oranges		

Country - Nationality - Language

1-B 2-A 3-C 4-B 5-B 6-B 7-A 8-C
9-B 10-C

Days

1- Friday	2- Thursday	3- Monday
4- Monday	5- Saturday	6- Sunday
7- Tuesday	8- Wednesday	9- Wednesday
10- Monday		

Educational Subjects

1- Art	2- Math	3- Geography
4- Chemistry	5- Physics	6- Music
7- History	8- Economics	9- Biology
10- Physical education		

Place Names

1- zoo	2- art museum
3- movie theatre or cinema	4- aquarium
5- sports stadium	6- bar or pub
7- concert hall	8- amusement park
9- bank	10- post office
11- travel agency	12- funeral parlor or undertaker
13- dry cleaners	14- plumber
15- employment agency	16- law firm
17- realtor or estate agents	18- Laundromat

Family

1- aunt	2- brother in law	3- grandmother
4- niece	5- grandson	6- brother
7- uncle	8- cousin	9- nephew
10- grandfather		

Food

1- sour	2- full	3- dry
4- rich	5- thirsty	6- moist
7- starve	8- succulent	9- bitter
10- sweet		

Group Nouns

1- transportation	2- fruit	3- furniture
4- drinks	5- luggage	6- dogs
7- holidays	8- food	9- vegetables
10- money		

House Words

1- In the kitchen	2- In the laundry
3- In the closet	4- In the bathroom
5- In the yard/in the garden	6- In the dining room
7- In the living room	8- In the garage
9- In the pantry	10- In the bedroom

Household Appliances

1- washing machine	2- vacuum cleaner	3- microwave
4- iron	5- TV	6- telephone
7- dishwasher	8- kettle	9- toaster
10- freezer	11- refrigerator	

Jobs

1-C 2-B 3-A 4-C 5-B 6-C 7-A 8-B
9-B 10-C

Months

1- December	2- July	3- June
4- January	5- April	6- August
7- November	8- May	9- January
10- June		

Nationalities

1-B 2-C 3-B 4-A 5-B 6-C 7-C 8-B
9-C 10-B

Nationalities & Languages

1-B 2-C 3-A 4-B 5-A 6-B 7-C 8-B
9-C 10-A

Occupations: What is my job?

1- secretary	2- lawyer
3- doctor or nurse	4- teacher
5- clerk or salesperson	6- veterinarian
7- firefighter	8- police officer
9- dentist	10- mailman

Opposites - Nouns

1-h 2-c 3-e 4-b 5-g 6-f 7-d 8-j
9-a 10-i

Opposites - Adjectives 1

1-f 2-e 3-b 4-h 5-g 6-i 7-d 8-j
9-a 10-c

Opposites - Adjectives 2

1-f 2-b 3-h 4-c 5-e 6-j 7-a 8-g
9-d 10-i

Answers

Opposites - Adjectives 3

| 1-d | 2-e | 3-g | 4-c | 5-j | 6-a | 7-i | 8-h |
| 9-f | 10-b | | | | | | |

Opposites - Verbs 1

| 1-g | 2-f | 3-d | 4-a | 5-c | 6-h | 7-b | 8-e |

Opposites 1

1- tall
2- heavy
3- big
4- handsome
5- long
6- expensive
7- far
8- rich
9- polite
10- happy

Opposites 2

1- clean
2- tight
3- sharp
4- loud
5- deep
6- straight
7- dark
8- thick
9- high
10- wide

Opposites 3

1- short
2- tall
3- small
4- cheap
5- thin
6- old
7- slow
8- ugly
9- down
10- wide

People Who Wear Uniforms

1- firefighters
2- police
3- nurses
4- mail carriers
5- pilots
6- chefs
7- sailors
8- flight attendant
9- teller
10- waiter
11- waitress

Soccer Vocabulary

| 1-A | 2-C | 3-A | 4-C | 5-B | 6-B | 7-C | 8-A |
| 9-B | 10-C | | | | | | |

Things We Carry

1- raincoat / umbrella
2- camera
3- book bag/satchel
4- briefcase
5- wallet
6- purse
7- handkerchief
8- newspaper
9- key
10- shopping bag/carrier bag

Time Words

1- minute
2- hour
3- half an hour
4- day
5- week
6- fortnight
7- month
8- season
9- year
10- decade
11- century
12- millennium

Transportation Verbs

1- arrive
2- depart
3- disembark
4- drive / ride
5- take-off
6- land
7- sail
8- tow
9- fly
10- ride

What Vegetable?

1- Tomatoes
2- Corn
3- Pumpkins
4- Spinach
5- Carrots
6- Beet roots
7- Potatoes
8- Beans
9- Garlic
10- Peppers

What's the Category?

1- clothing
2- birds
3- occupations
4- insects
5- transportation
6- flowers
7- fish
8- mammals
9- seasons
10- shoes
11- vegetables
12- trees
13- food
14- fruit
15- liquids
16- cereals
17- relatives
18- number
19- sports
20- weather
21- cities
22- countries

Which Word is Different?

1- snake
2- peach
3- wrestling
4- man
5- Rome
6- pineapple
7- Tom
8- bread
9- cat
10- bag

Word Groups 1

1- odd numbers
2- writers, novelists
3- composers
4- shapes
5- first names of girls
6- vegetables
7- baseball positions
8- cities in England
9- American Presidents
10- Greek alphabet

Word Groups 2

1- even numbers
2- American states
3- forms of transport
4- nationalities
5- types of fast food
6- first names of boys
7- jewelry
8- car makers
9- songs by the Beatles
10- organs of the body

Word Groups 3

1- jobs
2- mountains
3- African countries
4- footwear
5- cosmetics
6- types of currencies
7- cartoon characters
8- James Bond movies
9- Australian cities
10- ice cream flavors

Word Groups 4

1- Roman numerals, Consonants
2- fashion houses
3- continents
4- birds
5- school subjects
6- breeds of dogs
7- capital cities
8- baby animals
9- Olympic venues

Word Groups 5

1- types of flowers
2- all in Egypt
3- all played James Bond
4- precious stones or gems
5- all are red
6- all are types of weather
7- baseball teams
8- athletes
9- emotions

Word Relationships

1- foot
2- youth
3- walking
4- racket or racquet
5- women
6- Japanese
7- girl
8- your
9- dentist
10- ate
11- uncle
12- shoot
13- more important
14- second
15- the month before last

Answers

BOOK 2 - PART B

Snonyms (Page 251)

1-B	2-C	3-B	4-B	5-B	6-C	7-C	8-B
9-A	10-B	11-B	12-A	13-B	14-E	15-C	16-B
17-B	18-B	19-C	20-C	21-D	22-D	23-C	24-A
25-A	26-A	27-C	28-C	29-A	30-C	31-E	32-D
33-C	34-A	35-A	36-B	37-D	38-C	39-E	40-B
41-C	42-E	43-A	44-C	45-E	46-A	47-A	48-D
49-A	50-B	51-C	52-B	53-A	54-B	55-A	56-A
57-C	58-A	59-A	60-E	61-D	62-A	63-B	64-D
65-A	66-C	67-C	68-C	69-D	70-C	71-D	72-E
73-E	74-E	75-B	76-A	77-A	78-C	79-D	80-B
81-D	82-C	83-D	84-B	85-A	86-A	87-B	88-D
89-A	90-B	91-A	92-D	93-C	94-A	95-D	96-B
97-A	98-C	99-D	100-D	101-D	102-B	103-B	104-B
105-D	106-D	107-A	108-B	109-D	110-B	111-B	112-B
113-A	114-A	115-D	116-B	117-D	118-C	119-D	120-A
121-C	122-D	123-D	124-D	125-D	126-B	127-A	128-A
129-B	130-B	131-B	132-D	133-D	134-D	135-C	136-C
137-C	138-B	139-B	140-C	141-A	142-A	143-D	144-D
145-B	146-D	147-C	148-C	149-A	150-B	151-D	152-B
153-D	154-C	155-B	156-C	157-C	158-C	159-A	160-A
161-B	162-C						

Antonyms (Page 255)

1-A	2-C	3-D	4-E	5-B	6-A	7-D	8-D
9-E	10-B	11-B	12-C	13-A	14-B	15-A	16-C
17-D	18-C	19-C	20-C	21-E	22-D	23-E	24-C
25-A	26-E	27-C	28-D	29-A	30-C	31-D	32-A
33-C	34-E	35-B	36-D	37-B	38-D	39-A	40-E
41-B	42-D	43-B	44-D	45-B	46-B	47-D	48-D
49-C	50-D	51-B	52-D	53-B	54-C	55-B	56-B
57-A	58-A	59-E	60-C	61-B	62-D	63-E	64-A
65-D	66-E	67-C	68-B	69-D	70-A	71-A	72-B
73-B	74-E	75-E	76-C	77-D	78-B	79-D	80-B
81-B	82-A	83-B	84-A	85-D	86-B	87-C	88-A
89-B	90-B	91-B	92-A	93-C	94-D	95-A	96-D
97-B	98-D	99-C	100-C	101-B	102-C	103-D	104-A
105-B	106-C	107-C	108-D	109-B	110-A	111-A	112-A
113-B	114-D	115-A	116-D	117-D	118-A	119-A	120-B
121-A	122-B	123-B	124-B	125-D	126-A	127-B	128-A
129-C	130-D	131-C	132-C	133-B	134-B	135-D	136-A
137-C							

The logic List (Page 258)

1-A	2-D	3-A	4-A	5-A	6-A	7-B	8-A
9-B	10-A	11-C	12-B	13-A	14-C	15-A	16-A
17-B	18-C	19-D	20-A	21-C	22-B	23-C	24-A
25-C	26-D	27-B	28-A	29-D	30-A	31-A	32-C
33-B	34-C	35-B	36-A	37-A	38-B	39-B	40-C
41-B	42-C	43-B	44-B	45-D	46-C	47-D	48-D
49-C	50-D	51-B	52-A	53-A	54-A	55-C	56-B
57-B	58-C	59-B	60-B	61-C	62-A	63-B	64-C
65-D	66-A	67-B	68-A	69-A	70-D	71-C	72-D
73-B	74-B	75-A	76-C	77-C	78-A	79-C	80-C
81-C	82-A	83-C	84-C	85-D	86-A	87-D	88-C
89-B	90-B	91-A	92-B	93-A	94-A	95-A	96-B
97-A	98-B	99-B	100-B				

Miscellaneous (Page 259)

Analogies 1 - Find the Appropriate Match

1- Barber
2- Shorten
3- Shuttlecock
4- Shallow
5- Roughness
6- Worse
7- Irresponsible
8- Court
9- Sailor
10- Swollen
11- Widow
12- Stings
13- Gloves
14- Moo
15- Students
16- Wolves
17- Fast
18- Triangular
19- Piglet
20- Reptile

Analogies II - Find the Appropriate Match

1- Pork
2- Kitten
3- Christmas
4- Carbohydrate
5- A brood of
6- Sweet
7- To
8- Milk
9- Living room
10- Leg
11- Soften
12- Departure
13- Phenomena
14- Little
15- Five cents
16- Minus
17- Hard
18- Fill up
19- Leap year
20- Pack/Packet of

Beverages

1- cocoa
2- a soda
3- wine
4- brandy
5- whisky
6- tea
7- beer
8- liquor
9- coffee
10- ayran

Business Expressions 1

1-C	2-E	3-D	4-C	5-E	6-A	7-A	8-E
9-E	10-A						

Business Expressions 2

1-B	2-B	3-E	4-C	5-E	6-A	7-A	8-E
9-A	10-A						

Business Expressions 3

1-E	2-A	3-B	4-A	5-E	6-B	7-D	8-C
9-E	10-B						

Change the Words

1- Instead
2- continue
3- used
4- snowdrift
5- bucket
6- outdoors
7- outfought
8- overlook
9- excuse

Count/Non-Count Food Partitives

1-B	2-C	3-A	4-D	5-B	6-C	7-B	8-A
9-B	10-D	11-C	12-D	13-A	14-B	15-D	16-B
17-A	18-C	19-B	20-A				

Gender-Free Language

1- flight attendant
2- police officer
3- letter carrier
4- chairperson
5- spokesperson
6- anchor
7- poet
8- actor
9- homemaker
10- workforce, personnel
11- spouse
12- parenting
13- supervisor
14- selling ability
15- people, humankind

Answers

Finish the Sentence

1-A	2-C	3-C	4-A	5-B	6-B	7-A	8-A
9-C	10-B						

Food and Nutrition Quiz

1-B	2-C	3-E	4-B	5-A	6-C	7-D	8-B
9-D	10-E	11-C	12-A	13-D			

What Fruit...?

1- apple 2- grapes 3- pineapple
4- banana 5- orange 6- cherries
7- melon 8- pear 9- plum
10- strawberry

House Words

1- in the kitchen 2- in the bedroom
3- in the bathroom 4- in the living room
5- in the closet 6- in the garage
7- in the shed 8- in the nursery
9- in the laundry 10- in the toilet

Interjections

1-A	2-C	3-A	4-B	5-B	6-C	7-B	8-A
9-A	10-A						

Meat

1- beef 2- bacon 3- pork
4- lamb 5- mutton 6- venison
7- game 8- fish 9- poultry
10- offal

The logic list

1-D	2-B	3-D	4-A	5-B	6-B	7-D	8-C
9-C	10-B	11-A	12-B	13-D	14-E		

The most general meaning

1-E	2-D	3-B	4-D	5-E	6-E	7-C	8-B
9-D	10-C						

Types of Hats

1- hats 2- cap 3- helmets
4- beret 5- veil 6- headscarf
7- turban 8- crown 9- hood
10- bonnet

Word definition

1-B	2-D	3-B	4-D	5-A	6-D	7-E	8-D
9-D	10-C	11-C	12-E	13-D			

Use of English (Page 264)

TEST A

1-B	2-A	3-A	4-A	5-D	6-C	7-D	8-A
9-A	10-B	11-D	12-B	13-A	14-C	15-C	

TEST B

1-A	2-C	3-A	4-D	5-A	6-B	7-D	8-B
9-C	10-A	11-B	12-A	13-D	14-B	15-C	

TEST C

1-B	2-C	3-A	4-D	5-B	6-D	7-B	8-D
9-B	10-C	11-A	12-A	13-A	14-D	15-C	

TEST D

1-A	2-B	3-A	4-D	5-C	6-C	7-A	8-A
9-C	10-B	11-A	12-D	13-A	14-C	15-B	

TEST E

1-D	2-B	3-A	4-C	5-B	6-C	7-C	8-A
9-B	10-C	11-A	12-D	13-A	14-D	15-C	

TEST F

1-A	2-C	3-D	4-C	5-A	6-D	7-C	8-B
9-C	10-C	11-B	12-A	13-D	14-C	15-D	

TEST G

1-C	2-A	3-B	4-D	5-C	6-B	7-D	8-B
9-A	10-A	11-D	12-B	13-C	14-C	15-D	

TEST H

1-B	2-A	3-C	4-B	5-A	6-B	7-C	8-D
9-B	10-A	11-D	12-B	13-C	14-A	15-D	

TEST I

1-C	2-B	3-A	4-C	5-D	6-C	7-B	8-D
9-A	10-C	11-B	12-B	13-D	14-A	15-D	

TEST J

1-D	2-C	3-B	4-C	5-D	6-B	7-C	8-A
9-B	10-D	11-B	12-C	13-A	14-D	15-A	

TEST K

1-C	2-B	3-C	4-A	5-D	6-B	7-A	8-D
9-A	10-B	11-C	12-A	13-C	14-B	15-D	

TEST L

1-C	2-A	3-B	4-D	5-C	6-C	7-A	8-C
9-C	10-A	11-C	12-D	13-A	14-D	15-B	

TEST M

1-B	2-C	3-A	4-D	5-D	6-B	7-C	8-B
9-D	10-B	11-D	12-C	13-C	14-A	15-C	

TEST N

1-B	2-C	3-D	4-D	5-B	6-A	7-B	8-C
9-A	10-D	11-D	12-D	13-C	14-C	15-D	

TEST O

1-D	2-C	3-D	4-A	5-A	6-D	7-C	8-A
9-D	10-C	11-C	12-D	13-C	14-D	15-C	

TEST P

1-C	2-A	3-C	4-D	5-A	6-D	7-D	8-B
9-D	10-B	11-C	12-B	13-D	14-A	15-A	

TEST R

1-B	2-C	3-B	4-D	5-D	6-A	7-B	8-A
9-B	10-D	11-D	12-B	13-A	14-C	15-C	

Everyday Vocabulary *(Page 270)*

At the airport

1-B	2-C	3-A	4-B	5-D	6-A	7-B	8-D
9-A	10-C	11-C	12-B	13-A	14-D	15-A	16-C
17-B	18-A	19-B	20-C	21-B			

In the air

1-A	2-C	3-B	4-C	5-A	6-B	7-D

Bank Account

1-C	2-A	3-C	4-B	5-D	6-B	7-A

Current and deposit accounts

1-B	2-A	3-C	4-B	5-D	6-A

Using your account

1-D	2-B	3-A	4-A	5-C

Spending

1-A	2-B	3-C	4-B	5-A	6-D	7-C

Books and Reading 1

1-d	2-f	3-b	4-h	5-e	6-c	7-a	8-g

Books and Reading 2

1-D	2-B	3-B	4-C	5-B	6-D	7-A	8-A
9-A	10-D						

Cars and driving

1-A	2-C	3-B	4-C	5-C	6-A	7-B	8-D
9-D	10-D	11-B					

A visit to the cinema

1-A	2-D	3-C	4-D	5-A	6-B	7-C	8-B
9-A	10-C	11-B	12-A	13-D			

A film review

1-A	2-B	3-D	4-D	5-C	6-A	7-B	8-C
9-D	10-C						

Medical staff and patients

1-k	2-h	3-b	4-a	5-c	6-f	7-g	8-e
9-i	10-j	11-d					

Doctors' surgeries and hospitals

1-A	2-C	3-D	4-C	5-D	6-D	7-B	8-B
9-C	10-A	11-B	12-A	13-B	14-A		

Education

1-B	2-A	3-A	4-D	5-B	6-C	7-D	8-C
9-C	10-B	11-C	12-C	13-B	14-D	15-A	16-B
17-A							

Elections

1-C	2-A	3-A	4-D	5-A	6-D	7-D	8-B
9-C							

Government

1-D	2-A	3-D	4-C	5-A	6-C	7-B	8-A
9-D	10-C						

Renting a flat

1-C	2-A	3-B	4-A	5-D	6-B	7-C	8-A
9-D	10-B						

Buying a house

1-D	2-C	3-C	4-B	5-B	6-B	7-A	8-D
9-C	10-A	11-D					

Eating out

1-A	2-D	3-C	4-D	5-C	6-A	7-B	8-B
9-A	10-C	11-D	12-B				

Entertaining at home

1-B	2-C	3-D	4-C	5-C	6-A	7-A	8-D
9-B	10-A	11-D	12-B				

Gambling

1-D	2-B	3-D	4-C	5-A	6-B	7-B	8-A
9-A	10-C						

Smoking

1-A	2-B	3-A	4-B	5-D	6-C	7-C	8-A
9-B	10-D						

Drinking

1-D	2-B	3-C	4-B	5-D	6-C	7-C	8-D
9-A	10-A						

Industry

1-C	2-B	3-D	4-A	5-B	6-C	7-B	8-D
9-A	10-D	11-A					

Agriculture

1-C	2-A	3-C	4-A	5-A	6-D	7-C	8-D
9-D	10-B						

A summit meeting

1-B	2-D	3-A	4-B	5-C	6-C	7-D	8-A
9-B	10-A						

Diplomatic relations
1-D 2-B 3-A 4-D 5-C 6-B 7-A 8-C

An arrest
1-C 2-A 3-C 4-D 5-C 6-A 7-C 8-D
9-D 10-B 11-B 12-B 13-A 14-D 15-A 16-A
17-B

Law and punishment
1-C 2-A 3-D 4-D 5-C 6-A 7-B 8-C
9-B 10-D

Classical music
1-D 2-C 3-B 4-A 5-A 6-B 7-D 8-C
9-A 10-D 11-C

Popular music
1-A 2-D 3-C 4-B 5-A 6-B 7-A 8-C
9-D 10-B

Famine and flood
1-C 2-A 3-B 4-A 5-D 6-B 7-D 8-C
9-B

Earthquake and epidemic
1-C 2-A 3-D 4-C 5-D 6-A 7-B 8-A
9-B 10-B

Fire
1-C 2-B 3-A 4-D 5-C 6-A 7-D 8-B

Public Transport
1-D 2-B 3-A 4-D 5-C 6-B 7-C 8-A
9-A 10-B 11-C 12-B 13-B 14-C 15-B 16-B
17-C 18-A 19-D 20-D 21-A 22-C 23-D 24-A
25-A

Romance
1-B 2-C 3-A 4-D 5-B 6-A 7-C 8-B
9-D 10-A

Marriage
1-D 2-B 3-D 4-A 5-C 6-A 7-C 8-B
9-B 10-C

Going shopping
1-A 2-D 3-C 4-D 5-C 6-B 7-B 8-A
9-A 10-A 11-C 12-B 13-B 14-D 15-C

Sports facilities and athletics
1-C 2-B 3-A 4-B 5-D 6-C 7-B 8-C
9-D 10-A 11-D 12-A

Football
1-B 2-C 3-D 4-A 5-B 6-D 7-A 8-C
9-B 10-C 11-D 12-A

Television
1-C 2-B 3-A 4-A 5-B 6-B 7-C 8-D
9-D 10-A

Newspapers
1-B 2-C 3-C 4-B 5-A 6-D 7-C 8-B
9-D 10-D 11-D 12-A 13-A

Journeys
1-B 2-C 3-B 4-D 5-C 6-A 7-D 8-C
9-B 10-A

Argument
1-D 2-B 3-D 4-B 5-A 6-C 7-A 8-C

Sadness
1-C 2-A 3-B 4-B 5-A 6-D 7-B 8-A
9-C 10-D

Birth
1-C 2-A 3-B 4-A 5-C 6-A 7-D 8-B
9-B 10-C 11-D

Death
1-B 2-A 3-D 4-C 5-A 6-A 7-B 8-D
9-C 10-C 11-D

Advertising
1-C 2-B 3-A 4-B 5-D 6-D 7-C 8-A

Art
1-B 2-D 3-D 4-B 5-A 6-C 7-A 8-C
9-A 10-B

Photography
1-D 2-A 3-A 4-C 5-B 6-D 7-B 8-C

Military Service
1-B 2-A 3-C 4-A 5-C 6-D 7-D 8-B

Police
1-B 2-D 3-B 4-C 5-D 6-A 7-C 8-A

Security Work
1-B 2-C 3-A 4-C 5-D 6-D 7-C 8-B
9-A

The Seaside
1-B 2-C 3-A 4-D 5-B 6-C 7-A 8-D
9-B 10-A

Mountains
1-D 2-B 3-C 4-A 5-B 6-A 7-A 8-B
9-C 10-D

Answers

Electrical Appliances
1-A 2-C 3-B 4-B 5-A 6-D 7-C 8-D
9-B 10-A

The Telephone
1-D 2-C 3-B 4-A 5-A 6-D 7-C 8-B

Computers
1-B 2-C 3-A 4-A 5-B 6-C 7-D 8-D

Sounds
1-A 2-C 3-C 4-B 5-D 6-D 7-B 8-C
9-B 10-A 11-A 12-C 13-B 14-C 15-B 16-A
17-D 18-D

Animal Sounds
1-d 2-a 3-f 4-c 5-h 6-b 7-e 8-i
9-g 10-j 11-m 12-n 13-k 14-r 15-l 16-q
17-p 18-o

Human Sounds
1-A 2-C 3-D 4-B 5-C 6-B 7-D 8-A
9-D 10-A 11-C 12-B

Ways of Looking
1-C 2-D 3-B 4-B 5-D 6-B 7-A 8-A
9-A 10-C

Walking
1-D 2-C 3-A 4-D 5-C 6-C 7-D 8-B
9-A 10-B 11-B 12-A

Body Movements 1
1-d 2-a 3-b 4-c 5-l 6-g 7-e 8-j
9-k 10-h 11-f 12-i

Body Movements 2
1-c 2-e 3-a 4-b 5-d 6-g 7-h 8-f

Body Movements 3
1-c 2-e 3-d 4-a 5-g 6-b 7-h 8-f

Connectors
1-D 2-B 3-D 4-A 5-C 6-B 7-A 8-A
9-B 10-C 11-D 12-D 13-C 14-D

Tools
1-C 2-C 3-B 4-A 5-C 6-D 7-D 8-B
9-D 10-A 11-C 12-D 13-B 14-A

Collective Nouns
1-B 2-C 3-B 4-A 5-C 6-B 7-A 8-D
9-D 10-B 11-A 12-C 13-A 14-B 15-A 16-B
17-B 18-C 19-A 20-D 21-D 22-C 23-A 24-C
25-A 26-D

Law Breakers 1
1-b 2-e 3-a 4-c 5-g 6-d 7-f 8-k
9-h 10-l 11-j 12-i 13-m

Law Breakers 2
1-d 2-a 3-b 4-e 5-c 6-f 7-h 8-k
9-l 10-g 11-j 12-i

Occupations 1
1-d 2-e 3-a 4-g 5-k 6-j 7-b 8-c
9-f 10-h 11-i

Occupations 2
1-e 2-c 3-h 4-j 5-i 6-g 7-f 8-b
9-a 10-d

Occupations 3
1-e 2-d 3-a 4-c 5-j 6-b 7-k 8-i
9-f 10-h 11-g

People
1-b 2-e 3-a 4-c 5-g 6-i 7-h 8-d
9-f 10-l 11-m 12-j 13-k

Quantities
1-b 2-e 3-a 4-c 5-h 6-g 7-d 8-f
9-k 10-l 11-n 12-i 13-m 14-j 15-p 16-o

Slang
1-e 2-c 3-a 4-b 5-k 6-d 7-j 8-h
9-f 10-i 11-g

American Words 1
1-j 2-a 3-c 4-f 5-i 6-e 7-h 8-d
9-g 10-n 11-p 12-m 13-l 14-o 15-k 16-b
17-q

American Words 2
1-b 2-l 3-g 4-d 5-p 6-q 7-s 8-r
9-a 10-m 11-o 12-j 13-k 14-i 15-n 16-e
17-f 18-h 19-c

Answers

BOOK 2 - PART C

Classified Phrasal Verbs (Page 287)

1-C	2-B	3-C	4-A	5-B	6-C	7-B	8-A
9-C	10-B	11-A	12-B	13-C	14-A	15-C	16-C
17-A	18-B	19-B	20-A	21-C	22-A	23-C	24-A
25-C	26-A	27-C	28-A	29-B	30-B	31-C	32-A
33-A	34-B	35-A	36-C	37-B	38-A	39-A	40-C
41-A	42-A	43-C	44-B	45-A	46-B	47-A	48-B
49-C	50-B	51-C	52-B	53-A	54-C	55-B	56-B
57-B	58-A	59-B	60-B	61-B	62-A	63-A	64-C
65-B	66-C	67-A	68-C	69-B	70-A	71-A	72-C
73-C	74-B	75-B	76-B	77-A	78-A	79-B	80-A
81-C	82-B	83-A	84-C	85-A	86-A	87-C	88-C
89-B	90-A	91-C	92-C	93-A	94-A	95-C	96-C
97-B	98-A	99-B	100-C	101-B	102-C	103-A	104-C
105-B	106-C	107-A	108-B	109-C	110-C	111-B	112-A
113-C	114-A	115-A	116-B	117-B	118-A	119-C	120-C
121-C	122-B	123-A	124-A	125-C	126-B	127-C	128-B
129-B	130-C	131-A	132-A	133-C	134-B	135-B	136-C
137-B	138-A	139-C	140-A	141-B	142-A	143-B	144-A
145-C	146-A	147-B	148-C	149-A	150-C	151-B	152-B
153-C	154-A	155-A	156-A	157-B	158-B	159-C	160-B
161-A	162-A	163-B	164-A	165-C	166-B	167-B	168-A
169-C	170-C	171-A	172-B	173-B	174-C	175-B	176-C
177-A	178-C	179-C	180-A	181-A	182-B	183-C	184-C
185-B	186-A	187-C	188-B	189-C	190-B	191-A	192-C
193-C	194-A	195-A	196-C	197-A	198-C	199-B	200-A
201-C	202-C	203-B	204-B	205-A	206-B	207-A	208-C
209-B	210-C	211-B	212-C	213-C	214-A	215-B	216-C
217-B	218-B	219-A	220-B	221-A	222-C	223-B	224-A
225-C	226-A	227-B	228-A	229-C	230-A	231-B	232-C
233-B	234-A	235-C	236-C	237-A	238-A	239-B	240-B
241-C	242-C	243-B	244-A	245-A	246-C	247-A	248-B
249-B	250-B	251-A	252-B	253-B	254-C	255-A	256-A
257-B	258-C	259-C	260-A	261-C	262-B	263-A	264-B

Test 1 (Page 292)

1-B	2-D	3-B	4-B	5-B	6-A	7-B	8-C
9-A	10-B	11-B	12-C	13-B	14-B	15-C	16-B
17-B	18-D	19-C	20-C	21-D	22-C	23-A	24-B
25-C	26-A	27-C	28-B	29-B	30-A	31-A	32-C
33-C	34-C	35-C	36-A	37-D	38-D	39-A	40-A
41-D	42-B	43-C	44-C	45-B	46-D	47-B	48-A
49-B	50-C	51-D	52-B	53-A	54-D	55-A	56-D
57-C	58-A	59-A	60-C	61-A	62-D	63-C	64-B
65-C	66-A	67-C	68-D	69-B	70-B	71-C	72-D
73-B	74-B	75-B	76-A	77-C	78-B	79-C	80-C
81-D	82-C	83-D	84-A	85-C	86-C	87-B	88-B
89-A	90-C	91-D	92-C	93-D	94-D	95-D	96-A
97-D	98-B	99-D	100-B				

Test 2 (Page 294)

1-D	2-C	3-D	4-A	5-D	6-D	7-D	8-A
9-B	10-A	11-A	12-D	13-D	14-B	15-C	16-B
17-A	18-B	19-B	20-B	21-C	22-A	23-A	24-C
25-C	26-A	27-B	28-C	29-D	30-D	31-B	32-B
33-C	34-C	35-D	36-D	37-B	38-D	39-B	40-D
41-C	42-A	43-C	44-C	45-B	46-D	47-A	48-C
49-C	50-D	51-A	52-A	53-C	54-D	55-C	56-D
57-D	58-B	59-C	60-C	61-C	62-A	63-B	64-C
65-A	66-D	67-D	68-A	69-C	70-C	71-B	72-C
73-D	74-B	75-B	76-A	77-D	78-D	79-D	80-C
81-A	82-D	83--B	84-D	85-D	86-D	87-D	88-B
89-D	90-B	91-B	92-B	93-A	94-D	95-A	96-B
97-A	98-A	99-A	100-A				

Test 3 (Page 297)

1-C	2-B	3-D	4-C	5-D	6-C	7-A	8-A
9-D	10-C	11-D1	2-C	13-B	14-D	15-D	16-B
17-D	18-A	19-B	20-B	21-C	22--D	23-D	24-B
25-A	26-B	27-A	28-D	29-C	30-C	31-B	32-B
33-C	34-C	35-C	36-A	37-B	38-D	39-A	40-A
41-D	42-B	43-A	44-A	45-D	46-C	47-B	48-B
49-A	50-A	51-C	52-A	53-D	54-D	55-C	56-D
57-A	58-D	59-D	60-B	61-A	62-C	63-D	64-C
65-B	66-C	67-B	68-D	69-B	70-A	71-C	72-C
73-D	74-C	75-D	76-C	77-D	78-D	79-D	80-C
81-B	82-C	83-C	84-C	85-D	86-D	87-B	88-C
89-D	90-D	91-C	92-D	93-B	94-C	95-A	96-A
97-A	98-A	99-A	100-C				

Test 4 (Page 299)

1A	2-C	3-C	4-A	5-C	6-C	7-B	8-D
9-D	10-B	11-A	12-C	13-A	14-B	15-A	16-A
17-C	18-C	19-A	20-C	21-B	22-A	23-C	24-A
25-B	26-A	27-C	28-A	29-C	30-A	31-D	32-B
33-D	34-C	35-A	36-B	37-D	38-D	39-C	40-D
41-B	42-C	43-C	44-B	45-D	46-A	47-B	48-D
49-C	50-D	51-D	52-A	53-C	54-A	55-D	56-B
57-B	58-A	59-D	60-C	61-C	62-B	63-D	64-A
65-D	66-C	67-C	68-A	69-D	70-B	71-A	72-C
73-A	74-A	75-C	76-D	77-B	78-A	79-D	80-B
81-D	82-D	83-A	84-D	85-D	86-C	87-B	88-C
89-C	90-D	91-A	92-B	93-D	94-A	95-C	96-C
97-D	98-B	99-A	100-C	101-C	102-A	103-D	104-B
105-A	106-A	107-B	108-D	109-C	110-A	111-B	112-D
113-C	114-D	115-B	116-A	117-D	118-D	119-A	120-A
121-D	122-A	123-A	124-B	125-B	126-D	127-D	128-A
129-B	130-C	131-A	132-D	133-D	134-A	135-B	136-D
137-A	138-A	139-D	140-B	141-C	142-A	143-D	144-D
145-A	146-A	147-A	148-B	149-D	150-D		

BOOK 2 - PART D

TEST 1 (Page 303)

1-D	2-B	3-A	4-E	5-C	6-C	7-B	8-D
9-C	10-B	11-D	12-E	13-B	14-C	15-A	16-E
17-C	18-D	19-D	20-A	21-A	22-B	23-A	24-C
25-B	26-B	27-B	28-A	29-C	30-C	31-B	32-B
33-A	34-B	35-B	36-C	37-A	38-B	39-E	40-B

TEST 2 (Page 304)

1-A	2-B	3-C	4-A	5-A	6-D	7-B	8-A
9-A	10-E	11-C	12-C	13-C	14-E	15-B	16-D
17-D	18-B	19-C	20-C	21-A	22-D	23-C	24-D
25-E	26-E	27-C	28-C	29-A	30-A	31-B	32-B
33-B	34-B	35-A	36-B	37-C	38-B	39-A	40-B

TEST 3 (Page 305)

1-C	2-A	3-B	4-D	5-C	6-A	7-C	8-C
9-B	10-C	11-B	12-E	13-C	14-D	15-D	16-C
17-E	18-A	19-C	20-E	21-E	22-B	23-D	24-E
25-E	26-C	27-A	28-B	29-B	30-A	31-C	32-C
33-A	34-B	35-A	36-B	37-C	38-C	39-A	40-A

TEST 4 (Page 306)

1-D	2-B	3-E	4-C	5-E	6-D	7-D	8-E
9-B	10-E	11-E	12-B	13-A	14-C	15-A	16-C
17-B	18-D	19-E	20-E	21-C	22-C	23-D	24-D
25-B	26-C	27-C	28-E	29-C	30-A	31-B	32-C
33-A	34-B	35-D	36-C	37-E	38-E	39-C	40-B

TEST 5 (Page 307)

1-C	2-E	3-B	4-D	5-E	6-A	7-A	8-D
9-B	10-A	11-C	12-C	13-E	14-B	15-C	16-E
17-D	18-A	19-E	20-C	21-B	22-D	23-A	24-E
25-B	26-A	27-B	28-B	29-C	30-D	31-D	32-C
33-B	34-B	35-B	36-A	37-E	38-B	39-D	40-E

TEST 6 (Page 308)

1-E	2-D	3-E	4-C	5-D	6-C	7-B	8-D
9-C	10-D	11-B	12-D	13-E	14-C	15-E	16-B
17-A	18-C	19-C	20-C	21-D	22-C	23-A	24-B
25-D	26-D	27-A	28-A	29-B	30-D	31-B	32-C
33-C	34-D	35-D	36-B	37-C	38-C	39-B	40-E

TEST 7 (Page 309)

1-E	2-B	3-E	4-E	5-D	6-B	7-A	8-D
9-B	10-D	11-C	12-A	13-B	14-B	15-D	16-C
17-C	18-B	19-E	20-B	21-B	22-E	23-E	24-A
25-C	26-E	27-C	28-A	29-A	30-D	31-D	32-B
33-B	34-E	35-D	36-A	37-D	38-C	39-C	40-B

TEST 8 (Page 310)

1-C	2-A	3-A	4-A	5-E	6-C	7-C	8-B
9-C	10-D	11-D	12-E	13-C	14-C	15-C	16-E
17-C	18-B	19-B	20-C	21-A	22-D	23-A	24-D
25-D	26-B	27-C	28-E	29-C	30-E	31-B	32-E
33-C	34-A	35-B	36-A	37-C	38-D	39-D	40-D

TEST 9 (Page 311)

1-E	2-D	3-A	4-D	5-B	6-D	7-C	8-D
9-C	10-B	11-A	12-A	13-C	14-D	15-B	16-E
17-B	18-D	19-C	20-E	21-B	22-E	23-C	24-B
25-D	26-B	27-E	28-B	29-D	30-A	31-B	32-D
33-C	34-D	35-C	36-D	37-A	38-D	39-E	40-B

TEST 10 (Page 312)

1-B	2-D	3-B	4-E	5-D	6-B	7-C	8-B
9-D	10-A	11-B	12-D	13-C	14-E	15-A	16-C
17-E	18-B	19-D	20-C	21-C	22-A	23-E	24-D
25-C	26-B	27-D	28-C	29-B	30-A	31-C	32-B
33-B	34-D	35-D	36-C	37-B	38-D	39-A	40-B

TEST 11 (Page 313)

1-C	2-D	3-C	4-D	5-B	6-E	7-C	8-B
9-B	10-C	11-C	12-B	13-B	14-B	15-E	16-B
17-D	18-E	19-C	20-B	21-B	22-B	23-E	24-B
25-C	26-B	27-D	28-B	29-C	30-B	31-A	32-C
33-C	34-C	35-E	36-D	37-B	38-C	39-B	40-D

TEST 12 (Page 314)

1-A	2-B	3-A	4-E	5-C	6-D	7-D	8-A
9-D	10-D	11-B	12-E	13-A	14-B	15-B	16-D
17-A	18-E	19-B	20-C	21-D	22-B	23-B	24-B
25-E	26-C	27-A	28-C	29-E	30-A	31-D	32-B
33-C	34-D	35-A	36-C	37-B	38-E	39-C	40-B

TEST 13 (Page 315)

1-D	2-E	3-A	4-C	5-C	6-E	7-B	8-E
9-C	10-A	11-C	12-B	13-A	14-D	15-D	16-B
17-C	18-E	19-C	20-B	21-E	22-C	23-A	24-A
25-A	26-B	27-E	28-A	29-B	30-B	31-A	32-A
33-B	34-B	35-D	36-C	37-B	38-B	39-C	40-A

TEST 14 (Page 316)

1-B	2-B	3-B	4-C	5-C	6-D	7-C	8-C
9-E	10-E	11-C	12-C	13-D	14-B	15-E	16-A
17-A	18-B	19-E	20-E	21-B	22-C	23-A	24-A
25-A	26-C	27-E	28-C	29-C	30-B	31-A	32-B
33-C	34-D	35-A	36-D	37-C	38-D	39-C	40-A

TEST 15 (Page 317)

1-B	2-A	3-D	4-D	5-B	6-C	7-B	8-D
9-C	10-E	11-E	12-A	13-E	14-B	15-D	16-B
17-E	18-E	19-B	20-C	21-E	22-C	23-C	24-B
25-B	26-D	27-C	28-E	29-D	30-C	31-C	32-C
33-B	34-C	35-A	36-C	37-D	38-B	39-D	40-B

TEST 16 (Page 318)

1-E	2-C	3-A	4-A	5-D	6-A	7-B	8-E
9-D	10-C	11-B	12-E	13-A	14-B	15-E	16-A
17-C	18-E	19-B	20-A	21-C	22-A	23-C	24-B
25-E	26-C	27-C	28-A	29-E	30-D	31-B	32-C
33-B	34-E	35-D	36-D	37-D	38-C	39-B	40-D

Answers

TEST 17 (Page 319)

1-D	2-E	3-D	4-B	5-D	6-C	7-A	8-C
9-D	10-C	11-B	12-C	13-E	14-A	15-C	16-D
17-D	18-A	19-C	20-D	21-B	22-A	23-A	24-C
25-B	26-B	27-B	28-C	29-B	30-A	31-D	32-B
33-E	34-E	35-A	36-D	37-C	38-B	39-D	40-A

TEST 18 (Page 320)

1-C	2-B	3-A	4-D	5-A	6-B	7-A	8-E
9-D	10-E	11-C	12-D	13-B	14-A	15-C	16-D
17-B	18-B	19-A	20-C	21-D	22-B	23-C	24-B
25-B	26-D	27-D	28-E	29-C	30-C	31-A	32-A
33-A	34-A	35-C	36-B	37-C	38-C	39-A	40-C

TEST 19 (Page 321)

1-E	2-B	3-B	4-B	5-A	6-E	7-E	8-B
9-A	10-D	11-B	12-A	13-A	14-D	15-A	16-C
17-A	18-B	19-B	20-D	21-A	22-B	23-D	24-A
25-C	26-D	27-A	28-B	29-A	30-A	31-A	32-E
33-A	34-A	35-C	36-E	37-C	38-B	39-E	40-B

TEST 20 (Page 322)

1-B	2-C	3-B	4-B	5-B	6-B	7-D	8-B
9-B	10-D	11-D	12-B	13-D	14-C	15-B	16-B
17-B	18-C	19-A	20-C	21-D	22-C	23-C	24-A
25-B	26-B	27-A	28-D	29-E	30-E	31-E	32-B
33-D	34-C	35-C	36-A	37-B	38-E	39-C	40-C

TEST 21 (Page 323)

1-B	2-C	3-A	4-A	5-B	6-D	7-B	8-E
9-D	10-A	11-A	12-C	13-C	14-B	15-B	16-C
17-A	18-B	19-B	20-E	21-B	22-A	23-B	24-A
25-C	26-D	27-B	28-D	29-A	30-D	31-C	32-D
33-B	34-D	35-C	36-D	37-A	38-E	39-B	40-A

TEST 22 (Page 324)

1-C	2-C	3-A	4-A	5-E	6-B	7-C	8-C
9-E	10-B	11-B	12-D	13-B	14-D	15-D	16-B
17-D	18-B	19-E	20-C	21-A	22-C	23-C	24-B
25-C	26-C	27-A	28-D	29-C	30-D	31-B	32-B
33-C	34-B	35-C	36-E	37-C	38-A	39-C	40-B

TEST 23 (Page 325)

1-A	2-B	3-A	4-E	5-A	6-D	7-E	8-B
9-C	10-E	11-B	12-B	13-E	14-E	15-D	16-B
17-D	18-E	19-A	20-A	21-C	22-B	23-D	24-C
25-D	26-B	27-D	28-E	29-A	30-C	31-C	32-B
33-A	34-B	35-D	36-A	37-C	38-B	39-C	40-A

TEST 24 (Page 326)

1-E	2-D	3-C	4-D	5-B	6-E	7-C	8-B
9-D	10-D	11-B	12-D	13-D	14-C	15-D	16-D
17-B	18-A	19-A	20-D	21-C	22-A	23-A	24-B
25-C	26-D	27-C	28-E	29-D	30-C	31-D	32-D
33-A	34-B	35-D	36-C	37-D	38-E	39-D	40-E

TEST 25 (Page 327)

1-C	2-B	3-E	4-C	5-C	6-B	7-E	8-D
9-D	10-D	11-E	12-D	13-C	14-E	15-A	16-A
17-D	18-E	19-C	20-C	21-A	22-A	23-B	24-C
25-D	26-D	27-C	28-D	29-D	30-A	31-A	32-C
33-C	34-C	35-E	36-B	37-A	38-E	39-A	40-A

www.ingramcontent.com/pod-product-compliance
Lightning Source LLC
Chambersburg PA
CBHW081115080526
44587CB00021B/3607